A Sierra Club Totebook®

Hiking the Southwest
Arizona, New Mexico, and West Texas

Dave Ganci

Sierra Club Books   San Francisco

The Sierra Club, founded in 1892 by John Muir, has devoted itself to the study and protection of the earth's scenic and ecological resources—mountains, wetlands, woodlands, wild shores and rivers, deserts and plains. The publishing program of the Sierra Club offers books to the public as a nonprofit educational service in the hope that they may enlarge the public's understanding of the Club's basic concerns. The point of view expressed in each book, however, does not necessarily represent that of the Club. The Sierra Club has some fifty chapters coast to coast, in Canada, Hawaii, and Alaska. For information about how you may participate in its programs to preserve wilderness and the quality of life, please address inquiries to Sierra Club, 530 Bush Street, San Francisco, CA 94108.

Library of Congress Cataloging in Publication Data

Ganci, David, 1937–
   Hiking the Southwest.

   Bibliography: p. 401
   Includes index.
   1. Hiking—Southwestern States—Guide-books.
   2. Parks—Southwestern States—Guide-books.
   3. Southwestern States—Description and travel—Guide-books.
I. Title.
GV199.42.S68G36   1983   917.8   82–19418
ISBN 0–87156–338–X

Illustrations by Nancy Warner
Printed in the United States of America
10 9 8 7 6 5 4 3 2 1

Contents

To all National Forest Service
personnel, from trail maintenance
volunteer to wilderness ranger; from
receptionist to supervisor.

With special thanks to my mother,
Gwen Ganci, who typed most of the
manuscript, and to my collaborator,
John Annerino.

Acknowledgments

The unsung heroes of this trail guide are the many hard-working land use agency employees who helped and advised me. Information on national parks and monuments, state parks, county parks, city parks, Bureau of Land Management areas, and national forest lands was gathered over a period of two-and-a-half years, involving many hours of correspondence and many more hours on the trails. In every instance, I found land use administrators and field personnel helpful and encouraging.

I am especially grateful to the national forest personnel, because so much of this guide concerns the National Forest Systems of trails and wilderness. These people bear many responsibilities in carrying out their mandate of multiple use, yet they are too often considered dispensable when the need for budget-cutting arises in any new political administration. This leads to the cutting back of part-time, and in some cases, full-time help, and lower priority given to trail maintenance. Even with this handicap, the Forest Service is continuing with its overall plan to gather and make available to the public trail information in their respective areas of responsibility.

My hat is off to these folks and their never-ending battle against political maneuvering, vandalism, carelessness, forest fires, and budget-cutting.

A second acknowledgment goes to my friend and partner, John Annerino. John was my collaborator on the Arizona chapter, hiking and describing the majority of trails in the national park, national forest, and Bureau of Land Management sections. John's experience in the Arizona wilderness is surpassed by no one of my acquaintance. His personal specialty is long-distance wilderness running, and he has taken on the task of running many of the wilderness and roadless areas in the Southwest, as well as ancient Indian trails and trade routes, and the length of the Grand Canyon by both the South and North rims. In the process, he has built up a storehouse of wilderness running and bivouacking tactics, and thin-edge survival techniques. John makes his living writing about and photographing the Southwest. His work has appeared in many publications, including *Rocky Mountain, Runner's World, Arizona Highways, Navajo Times,* and *Arizona Magazine.*

An Introduction to the Southwest

Arizona, New Mexico, and West Texas (the trans-Pecos region) are part of a geographic region known as the Southwest. The boundaries of the Southwest are defined differently by different geographers. Some would include parts of Colorado, Utah, Nevada, Oklahoma, and California. However, no single book could cover the hiking opportunities in this larger region with any degree of detail, so extensive are the lands open to recreational use. So the scope of this guide reflects a narrower definition of the Southwest: encompassing all of Arizona and New Mexico, and an adjacent portion of West Texas between the Rio Grande and the Pecos River. As we will see, even this more limited region is a vast recreational resource with thousands of miles of hiking trails and many national parks and monuments, so our coverage will necessarily be selective.

A physical description of the boundaries of this area includes zones of thinly populated, difficult-to-navigate country: the immense Mohave Desert on the west; the Colorado River canyonlands on the north; the southern Rocky Mountains and Llano Estacado on the east; and, for our discussion, the Mexican boundary on the south.

Overall, the region is characterized by a generally dry climate with little surface water; hot, desert areas; mountain "islands" rising up from the desert floor; cattle-country grasslands; irrigated farm country; hot summers and generally mild winters. Overall, it is a land of wide-open, good-for-the-soul expanses. This openness has traditionally been reflected in the character of its human inhabitants and their attitude toward strangers. Of late, however, there is growing suspicion that the strangers want to change the landscape for profit and degrade the scenic and spirtual values of this open land.

Geologists have apportioned all of North America into physiographic provinces according to the origins, age, landforms, and bedrock of various segments. The Southwest extends over five such provinces: the Basin and Range, Colorado Plateau, Mountain and Transition, Rocky Mountain, and Great Plains. The provinces are discussed state by state in the "Landscape" section of each chapter.

Within each province, the landscape may be divided into life zones according to climate and elevation. The life zones

Shaded portion depicts the area covered by this book.

are much the same for each state discussed and may be visualized as horizontal habitats in the Southwest's many-layered geography.

LIFE ZONES

In the 1890s the eminent American botanist Clinton Hart Merriam observed and described the fact that plant and animal habitats are limited according to elevation and climate. Using the Southwestern landscape as a field laboratory, Merriam defined seven North American life zones: Tropical, Lower Sonoran, Upper Sonoran, Transition, Canadian, Hudsonian, and Arctic-Alpine. All but the Tropical Zone are found in the Southwest.

The boundaries between life zones are not rigid; zones overlap and blend into each other. However, each zone generally contains a distinctive association of animals and plants according to climate. Since plant-eating animals are restricted by their dietary habits, the range of the plant life determines the range of the animals. The carnivores in turn are limited to the range within which their prey lives. A classic exception is the coyote, a ubiquitous Southwestern resident that has adapted to many life zones and conditions—including the dwelling places of that other highly adaptable creature, man.

Life zone locations depend on both latitude and altitude. Since a gain in altitude of 1,000 feet is about equivalent to moving 200 latitudinal miles north, conditions on top of the highest peaks in the Southwest in certain ways resemble those in the Arctic at sea level.

The reason that the plant and animal populations change with altitude is climate. Air temperature decreases one degree with every 300 to 400 feet gained. As moisture-laden air rises, it cools and condenses, then falls as rain or snow, creating gradations of moisture and temperature. Consequently, mountain slopes are occupied by life forms better adapted to cold but less tolerant of drought than lower-elevation species are.

A good way to observe the progression of life zones is to ascend one of those mountain "islands" that jump up from the desert floor in many areas of the Southwest, forming horizontal strata of natural history from creosote bush to Alpine lichens.

Within a given life zone, smaller areas occur, each with its distinctive plant and animal life. The general grouping (or groupings) of plants common to a particular zone is called a biotic community and is identified by the name of one or more dominant plant species: for example, the sagebrush or oak woodland community. Within these communities are smaller microhabitats such as lakes, rivers, swamps, sand dunes, springs, and caves, which produce microclimates and specialized life forms.

Lower Sonoran Zone

The Lower Sonoran Zone includes the valleys and plains of southern Arizona and western New Mexico, extending from sea level (near the Colorado River) to about 5,000 feet. Most of the human population of these states lives in this life zone, using irrigation and ground water to develop cropland, cities, and industry. The most common native plant life includes mesquite, creosote, cactus, and sagebrush. The desert shrub, sagebrush, and chaparral biotic communities thrive at these elevations.

Upper Sonoran Zone

The Upper Sonoran Zone ranges from 5,000 feet to 7,000 feet and is characterized by a generally dry and mild climate. Plains and foothills that support the chaparral, oak woodland, desert grassland, and pinyon-juniper communities make up most of this zone.

Transition Zone

A gradual transition from the pinyon-juniper to the ponderosa pine and fir communities is evident in this 7,000-foot to 9,500-foot life zone. Colder, wetter weather enables many shrubs, vines, berry plants, ferns, and grasses to grow here.

Canadian Zone

This zone lies at altitudes of 8,500 feet to 11,500 feet. Maples, ashes, spruces, firs, and 16 varieties of grasses grow here. The land is high enough to collect snow from winter storms and contribute to the spring runoff. Mountain slopes, high plains, and high valleys characterize the topography.

Hudsonian Zone

From 11,500 feet to 12,500 feet, this elevated zone is covered with snow from six to nine months of the year. It is the most important zone for watershed runoff. Dwarfed trees are found in this zone; growing close to the earth protects them from winds. Only hardy, well-adapted species can survive.

Arctic-Alpine Zone

The highest of all zones in the Southwest is found on the summits of the San Francisco Peaks and White Mountains in Arizona and on Mt. Wheeler and Mt. Truchas in the Sangre de Cristo Mountains in New Mexico. Few trees grow in this zone, and only the hardiest of alpine plants can survive.

Table 1. Life Zones of the Southwest

Life Zones	Moisture	Plant Life	Animal Life

Lower Sonoran
 	
Sea level to 5,000 feet; warm climate; population centers and agriculture
	Less than 10 inches annual rain; irrigation and wells	Mesquite
		Ironwood
		Paloverde
		Catclaw
		Bursage
		Creosote
		Yucca
		Jojoba
		Ocotillo
		Saguaro cactus
		Barrel cactus
		Prickly pear
		Cholla cactus
			Many types of
			  insects
			Squirrels
			Woodrat
			Kangaroo rat
			Gopher
			Cottontail rabbit
			Jackrabbit
			Desert mule deer
			Whitetail deer
			Javalina
			Desert bighorn
			  sheep
			Skunks
			Badgers
			Bobcats
			Reptiles
			Great bird variety

Zone	Elevation / Terrain	Climate	Plants	Animals
Upper Sonoran	5,000 feet to 7,000 feet; plains and foothills; mild climate; rich soil	Dry	Lower Sonoran plants Grasses Juniper Pinyon Oak Sagebrush Willows	Antelope Wild turkey Quail Mountain lion Black bear Eagles Reptiles
Transition	7,000 feet to 9,500 feet; mountain slopes, broad mesas	Some rain and snow	Pinyon Juniper Grasses Oak Ponderosa pine Douglas fir Maples Manzanita White fir Poison ivy	Foxes Porcupine Elk Deer Black bear Wild turkey

Table 1. Life Zones of the Southwest (continued)

Life Zones	Moisture	Plant Life	Animal Life
Canadian			
8,500 feet to 11,500 feet; dense forests; higher mountain slopes	Heavy rain and snow	Aspen Blue spruce Willow Ponderosa pine Many grasses	Elk Deer Snowshoe rabbit Many squirrels Bighorn sheep
Hudsonian			
11,500 feet to 12,500 feet; high mountain slopes; timberline	Deep snow, some year-round	Spruce Firs Limber pine	Pika Rocky Mountain bighorn sheep Mountain jay Marmot
Arctic-Alpine			
12,500 feet to 13,160 feet; treeless; frost year-round; mountain peaks	Deep snow, some year-round	Hardy alpine plants Forget-me-nots Lichens Mosses	Pikas Chipmunks

HOW TO USE THIS GUIDE

Hiking Trails

Whether their objective was to reach the next settlement, deliver a message, run down a deer, or simply "to go," people have long used trails to get from one point to another. The earliest human residents of the Southwest followed game trails through the underbrush of the widely scattered but lush riparian communities, across deserts, and up mountains to windy plateaus. They sometimes traveled thousands of miles in a lifetime—first on foot and later on horseback, after the Spaniards reintroduced the horse to North America.

The Pagago Indians of southwestern Arizona ran marathons to the Gulf of California to gather salt. The white treasure seekers tried to reach the gold fields of California by crossing endless stretches of desert on foot and horse trails. Fast-riding Pony Express riders used trails, as did homesteaders by the thousands, rustlers, miners, and cattlemen.

It has been only during the last several decades that people have built trails for recreational use. Many were constructed by the Civilian Conservation Corps during the depression years. Since that time, reasons for using hiking trails—and thousands of miles of previously existing trails— have become as diverse as the topography they penetrate and traverse. On any weekend or holiday one can see a wide spectrum of recreational visitors pursuing their specialized activities in the Southwest's wildlands: the endurance rider conditioning her Appaloosa; the birdwatcher tiptoeing up on a coppery-tailed trogon; the rockclimber marching to the base of a climb; the modern prospector stealing into his favorite panning area; the day-hiker striding to an isolated viewpoint; the wilderness runner whisking through incomparable running country; the avid backpacker on a week-long trek; and—in season—the ski-tourer sliding through the snow-covered woods, following summertime trail routes.

When trying to condense a large area into a hiking guide, one must establish priorities. Volumes could be written about this region and its hiking, camping, and backpacking potential. My strategy is to concentrate on the national forests, wilderness areas, and other areas of particular scenic attraction. One or more trails in a particular area are described in detail to give the flavor to be expected from the experience. Other trails are highlighted, and information on where to obtain further details is provided. The trails in this guide range over every physiographic region and life zone in the Southwest, permitting a great variety of hiking experiences.

Trail conditions, as described in this guide, may vary from good to rocky to washed-out to overgrown with brush; in some places trails may even be imperceptible. All trails are subject to erosion, and unless they are so heavily traveled as to become ruts, a season of heavy rain or snow runoff can change their characteristics for the rest of the season. Merely to follow a signed trail is not sound hiking practice. It is essential to study your planned route in advance on topographic maps, and to learn to navigate by terrain features, compass, time, and distance.

Everything changes, and trails in the Southwest are no exception. The information in this guide is the latest available at the time of writing, but do not assume that every detail will be the same when you trek into one of the areas described. Trail signs may disappear, be turned around, burned as firewood, or stolen. (Black bears have been known to eat trail signs, with a preference for pine according to the Arizona Game and Fish Department.) Remember, too, that lines on a map are a depiction, not a guarantee. Land use agencies can reroute a trail, rendering the guidebook obsolete in that particular area. Don't rely on old hiking guides for the reasons stated above.

Check with the local land use agency or district office by mail before your trip, and again when you reach your destination, to obtain up-to-date information on trail conditions. Make an appointment with the field ranger or naturalist, if possible; more than just helping you find your way, their detailed knowledge of their territory can help you get the most from your experience.

A guidebook is not a road map, nor should it be. This one does not mention every curve and junction, but leaves some thinking and planning to the reader. What challenge is there in following a step-by-step procedure through the wilderness? Do use this guide as a reference along with the proper topo maps and local information. Do learn to read terrain features on a map and in the field. Always know where you are on the topo map, and you will rarely be even temporarily disoriented.

Official U.S. Forest Service trails are designated by numbers, though most also bear names. Both are given in this book, the number in parentheses.

Supplementary Information

In addition to describing the route of each trail and the terrain through which it passes, many of the detailed trail descriptions in this book include information in the following categories:

Time and Distance: The time needed to complete any hike will vary from individual to individual, depending on the physical condition and goals of the hiker. The naturalist who pauses frequently to observe plants or wildlife may take twice as long as the hiker trying to make time. The size of one's pack also will affect one's rate of travel. Trail conditions can make a big difference in both time and fatigue, as can elevation gain and loss, and inclement weather. Using topo maps to measure your pace on the first couple of hikes will give you an average to go by in your subsequent planning.

The mileages given here are taken from topo and Forest Service maps. While accurate for the most part, these sources have been known to be wrong or out of date. Many of the trails were hiked by the author, but some of the written descriptions rely on information supplied by Forest Service and other land use agency personnel. Use the published time and distance as a guideline and always rely on terrain features and compass.

Natural History: The life zones traversed in each area or in the course of a particular hike may be noted, as well as characteristic plant communities and fauna.

Activities: Mention is made of recreational activities available in the specific areas discussed. These include: cross-country skiing, caving, fishing, horseback riding, mountaineering, rock climbing, and swimming. Local history and cultural information are highlighted.

Seasons: The "best" hiking season for a given area is a subjective matter, of course. This guide assumes that most people want to hike in clear, relatively warm (but not hot) weather; therefore seasons most likely to provide such weather may be indicated. This does not mean that "off-season" hiking can't be just as rewarding; sometimes more so due to the chance for solitude and the discovery of experiencing a new season. Southwestern weather can be unpredictable, so be prepared to back off and retrace your steps if that early October or late May storm drops down on you unexpectedly.

Maps: The maps referred to in trail descriptions include U.S. Geological Survey topographic maps, as well as national forest maps and national park recreation maps. Sources of these maps are listed in the next section. Backpacking stores are good local sources. Get all the available maps of an area you can find. At most Forest Service offices you can purchase NFS maps and special Wilderness Series maps. Most important, know how to read them. If you don't, you are not prepared.

Water: Like gold on the desert, water is where you find it. Most of the trail descriptions in this guide indicate where water is likely to be found, and your topo maps also can provide clues—but don't bet your life on the existence of any source of water that you are not personally sure will be in the area when you are. Wells get capped, springs dry up or are diverted, streams disappear in the dry season, cattle tanks may be defunct or relocated. It is safest to assume that water sources are dry until you have gained experience; maps are not reliable guides here. See Chapter 1 for more on this crucial subject.

Elevations: Approximate high and low points are given for each area or trail.

Nearest Supply Points: These are included for your convenience.

Managing Agencies: These are included for reference, with addresses listed for local offices of each major land use agency. For example, forest districts are listed at the end of each national forest section.

Further Information: Listed here are other publications, both private and official, where you can find more information concerning a particular area. For example, there are no fewer than three guidebooks to trails in Arizona's Superstition Wilderness.

Maps

There are basically two kinds of information on maps: the kind that doesn't change and the kind that does. Topographic features seldom change. Mountains, hills, canyons, stream beds, plains, ridges, and valleys don't move. Everything else depicted on a map is *subject to change;* this includes water sources, roads, trails, bridges, and other manmade features. Even campgrounds change; the Forest Service may decide to close, add, or move one. The date of publication of any map or guide is important. If you have a map dated 1974, many changes may have taken place in the landscape—new roads, new trails, new signs, changed routes, and so on. To reiterate: always use a map as a guide, not as the last word. And check at the local ranger district office for the latest information.

Know how to read terrain features! Take a map-reading course if you don't know how. Or educate yourself with a how-to guide, such as the 1983 Sierra Club book *Land Navigation Handbook,* by W. S. Kals. Familiarity with interpreting terrain features is more valuable than just knowing how to read a compass, but do learn how to use a compass also. With both arts mastered, you will have little reason to fear any terrain or route in any Southwestern wilderness.

The Forest Service maps show trails as dashed lines. Most trails are designated by a number enclosed in a trapezoid. (Do not confuse this with the rectangle containing the Forest Road number.) Special Wilderness Area maps are available in some cases; these may employ a different scale and give more detailed information for the particular area.

Most Forest Service maps do not depict elevation with contour lines; instead, they note elevations on mountaintops. Therefore, it is imperative to obtain the U.S.G.S. topographic maps of an area in order to do thorough route-planning and to estimate time and distance. The topo maps give a clear picture of the ups and downs of the terrain, a most important consideration in mountainous country. It has been my experience that the use of *both* Forest Service and U.S.G.S. maps makes planning and visualizing a hike much easier and therefore more enjoyable along the way. Again, bear in mind that in a region as large as this book encompasses, elevations, distances, and locations of manmade features may vary among different maps covering the same area.

The maps listed below correspond with the text descriptions of trails in national forests and other wilderness areas in Arizona and New Mexico. The chapter on West Texas contains its own map references.

NATIONAL FOREST SERVICE MAPS

Forest Service visitor maps of the national forests in the Southwest show all roads and trails in the Forest Service system and use a scale of one-half inch to the mile. They cost $1.00; advance payment is required. Mail to:

USDA, Forest Service
Office of Information
517 Gold Ave. SW
Albuquerque, NM 87102

The following maps are available:

Arizona

1. Apache-Sitgreaves NF (1977)
2. Coconino NF (1975)
3. North Coronado NF (1975)
4. South Coronado NF (1976)
5. Douglas Ranger District, Coronado NF (1975)
6. South Kaibab NF (1976)
7. North Kaibab NF (1975)
8. Prescott NF (1977)
9. Tonto NF (1975)

New Mexico

1. Carson NF (1975)
2. Santa Fe NF (1975)
3. Sandia-Mountainair Ranger District, Cibola NF (1975)
4. Mt. Taylor Ranger District, Cibola NF (1975)
5. Magdalena Ranger District, Cibola NF (1977)
6. Gila NF (1974)
7. Lincoln NF (1974)
8. Guadalupe Ranger District, Lincoln NF (1979)

WILDERNESS AREA GUIDES AND MAPS

Visitor guides are available for the Pecos (1976), San Pedro Parks (1976), Wheeler Peak (1980), and Mt. Baldy (1978) wildernesses. Each costs $1.00. A two-part visitor's guide to the Gila Wilderness (1980) costs $2.00. All the above are in New Mexico. These guides feature a detailed topographic map with clearly marked trails, entry points, trail lengths, permit requirements, and areas under special restrictions.

One-inch-to-the-mile maps are available for the Superstition (1978), Sierra Ancha (1978), and Mazatzal (1978) wildernesses, all in Arizona. Each map costs $1.00. These maps show trails, major springs, and landmarks, but not topography.

TOPOGRAPHIC MAPS

The Forest Service usually does not sell topographic maps in district offices. These maps can be ordered from the U.S. Geological Survey, Denver Federal Center, Building 41, Denver, Colorado 80225. They can also be found in engineering and survey stores, camping and backpacking stores, map shops, and blueprint shops.

WILDERNESS ISSUES

The Southwest's topography, geologic diversity, and climatic patterns have produced a land for all seasons—a laboratory of interdependent life forms. Life zones crisscross and intermingle. Exotic water communities traverse barren deserts. Within the greatest geologic exposure in the world — the Grand Canyon — are foot trails that trace the earth's history. It is possible to sit on the rim of the Canyon in May and experience rain, snow, sleet, hail, and sunshine in one afternoon. Cacti and pine trees may grow next to each other. Countless examples of interaction and symbiosis are available to both the scientific observer and the casual viewer. Patterns of endless variety are displayed for the artist and photographer. Fascinating evolutionary and adaptive changes can be observed in the plant and animal life that resides in the land of little water.

The pyramid of life—from sun to soil to water to plants to insects to herbivores to carnivores to man—is still forming in the Southwest, as it is everywhere. The key question is: Where do we humans fit into this pyramid, and for how long? We are the only species able to greatly modify the environment. We alone can change millions of years of evolutionary adaptation with the cut of a bulldozer blade, a stick of dynamite, or a dam. And we seem prone to do this without considering the long-range effects of our actions on the landscape.

The Southwest is the fastest growing region in the nation. People who come from other areas often want to transplant their physical surroundings as well, not realizing what kind of environment they are moving into. They see pictures of golfers on vast stretches of green grass growing in the Sonoran Desert, of fountains spouting a never-ending supply of precious water. Some among them are prone to scrape a chunk out of a desert mountain and build homes in the resulting scars. And some leave their calling cards in once-pristine landscapes in the form of spray-paint initials, beer cans, pop tops, cigarette butts, and toilet paper fluttering in the desert breeze.

The responsibility for stewardship of the Southwest's lands is everyone's. We, who would perhaps rather sit in front of our television sets than get involved in local politics, or devote time to learning about land use issues—we are the folks who can change the course of events by establishing zoning regulations, trail access, mountain preserves, green belts, parks. More than the power brokers who seem to control the system, the problem is apathy. People elect politicians, and people can fire them. People must take the trouble to become informed on land use issues in order to protect their freedom of access to the wild lands. A good case in point is the Sagebrush Rebellion.

The Sagebrush Rebellion—What Is It?

In the words of Arizona Governor Bruce Babbitt, quoted from an open letter to Arizona citizens:

> The Sagebrush Rebellion is a simple proposition: Title to our National Forests and the public domain in the 11 western states would be deeded over to the states.
>
> A lot of us in the west oppose the Sagebrush Rebellion because we know who the rebels are and what they really want. Masquerading as impassioned advocates of States' rights, the Sagebrush crowd is nothing but a special interest group whose real goal is to get public lands into private ownership. Many of the sponsors candidly admit that their ultimate objective is to terminate public land ownership in the American west.
>
> For this reason many citizens who enjoy the outdoors have joined in vocal opposition to a federal give-away of the public domain. They know that their historic rights of access for hunting, fishing, backpacking or just plain looking and enjoying

could be replaced overnight by locked gates and barricaded roads. We in Arizona who appreciate and use Arizona's vast and exceptional natural resources must get involved in this initiative effort now. . . .

Quoting again, this time from an article by Stephen Whitney, editor of *Backpacker* magazine's information bulletin, "Footnotes":

Sagebrush Cynicism: Judging solely from news reports, an Easterner unfamiliar with the West might be led to believe that the "Sagebrush Rebellion" is a populist movement. What the media, to their discredit, do not mention is that this attempt to transfer federal lands to the states is a well-financed, highly organized, public relations campaign backed almost entirely by oil, mining, and timber interests, big ranchers, utilities, and their minions in state and local governments and chambers of commerce. If they succeed, according to Wilderness Society public land specialist Terry Sopher, "All these lands could wind up in the hands of private developers. The private gain at public expense would make the 19th-century robber barons look like dedicated public servants by comparison."

Despite the rhetoric, the purpose of the Sagebrush Rebellion is not to get government off the back of the little guy—the hallmark of true populism—but to get it off the backs of the sagebrush rebels. The average man or woman on the street has nothing to gain and everything to lose in the bargain. The politicians and profiteers behind the Sagebrush Rebellion want to be able to drill for oil, mine for coal and other minerals, clear-cut timber, overgraze the range, foul the air, use up scarce water resources, build power plants, and do whatever else might turn a quick buck without some federal agency requiring them to adhere to regulations designed to safeguard the environment and conserve precious resources for future generations. . . .

You, the reader of this book, would do well to get involved in local, state, and federal land use issues before those who already are heavily involved make the decisions pertaining to public lands. Public lands belong to all citizens. We all own a share of every BLM area, national forest, wilderness area, national park, or state park. And by owning a small share, we get access to all of it. That's the greatest real estate bargain in the world. For the small amount in taxes that goes toward managing these lands, we as individuals have access to all of them for a nominal fee. The Sagebrush Rebellion would end all that, and future generations would subsidize the takeover by private interests of land that *belongs to us*. Think about it and get involved, now.

RARE II

A few years ago, the Forest Service and other federal land-managing agencies made an inventory of lands eligible for inclusion in the Wilderness System. Under this Roadless Area Re-Evaluation program, better known as RARE II, public hearings were held in communities near the lands in question to determine whether the public interest would be better served by designating an area as wilderness or opening it to resource development. The government agencies used the testimony given at these hearings to make recommendations to Congress.

Several pieces of Forest Service and BLM land in the Southwest are now in limbo. Their inclusion in the Wilderness System has been recommended to Congress, but Congress has yet to act.

Forest Service and BLM offices can provide current information on the status of RARE II lands, including maps and schedules for public participation.

Environmental Education

It is obvious, to quote Pogo, that we have met the enemy and he is us: our ignorance and apathy. Both require effort to overcome, but the means are available, in the form of environmental education. What is environmental education, and why has it taken so long to become part of the standard school curriculum?

Basically, learning about the environment is an ongoing process that must be pursued over a lifetime, because knowledge changes and increases continually. Over the past 100 years, science has gradually pieced together the concept (and the facts to substantiate it) that we live on a fragile planet amidst fragile life-support systems. These systems took billions of years to develop, and it is apparent that twentieth-century man is capable of radically impinging on them. We do not know the long-term effects of our actions on life on the planet; we guess and hope for the best, often ignoring long-term consequences in the interests of short-term goals.

Environmental education is the process of learning about

natural systems and how they affect humans and other life forms. One of its goals is to evaluate human *impact* upon the landscape. And those of us who frequent the wild areas for recreation have an impact as surely as do those with tractor and bulldozer. We have an obligation to the land and its future inhabitants to learn about how it works and how to keep it working.

Fortunately, an increasing number of public and private schools now teach environmental education, though it is usually low on the priority list. It is up to each community to decide where that priority lies and make those who determine curricula aware of it. It is also up to the individuals in the community to educate themselves about land use problems and solutions, thereby setting an example for the younger generation.

Outdoor and environmental education also is getting a foothold in university systems. Arizona State University, for example, has started a program in its Department of Leisure Studies that concerns itself with land use management and outdoor recreation.

This guidebook is in one sense a personal statement about the wildlands of the Southwest and their immense value as places of beauty and places of challenge and education. It is to the education of both young and old that I hope to contribute in this book. It is not too late to get involved in the future of the Southwest's wildlands and their outdoor recreation potential. It just takes a dedication of time—before it runs out.

CARING FOR THE COUNTRY

A trail guide is a two-edged sword. Do we want to encourage more folks to get out into the backcountry and thus contribute to already overcrowded conditions in some wilderness areas? Or do we want to keep quiet about our favorite remote spots and scenic vistas, to reserve them for those who can "appreciate" them? I once espoused the latter point of view, but no longer. An elitist view of the wildlands is no longer tolerable. Every tax-paying American owns government land and is entitled to enjoy it. Every American should become involved with land use problems. And the only way he or she is going to become concerned about these problems is through firsthand experience. We must build a constituency of educated and enthusiastic wildland users.

A two-edged sword indeed, but not unmanageable. With proper outdoor education programs, oriented towards the "no-trace" ethic, the numbers of wilderness users can be increased and standards maintained at the same time. This means that every hiker who has acquired the "no-trace" ethic must pass it on to fellow hikers and would-be hikers, showing by example how to travel through an area with minimum evidence of his passing. It means approaching people who haven't learned wilderness manners and pointing out—diplomatically, if possible—the collective impact of their actions. It means taking *personal* responsibility for helping land use agencies maintain wild places for the enjoyment and appreciation of future generations.

Backcountry Ethics

"Leave No Trace." It has been said often, but it is important to repeat because it is the only solution to the impact caused by humanity, which is frequenting the wild areas at an average increase of 10 percent annually. The inevitable alternative is regulation, quotas, restrictions. It is a matter of numbers. We should pass through an area as if we were being followed by an enemy and wished to avoid any sign of our presence. This will not eliminate, but will at least minimize, human impact.

Here are the Forest Service's recommendations for implementing the "no-trace ethic."

Plan ahead to avoid impact:

Avoid holidays and weekends if possible.
Travel and camp in small, family-size groups.
Carry horse feed, picket ropes, and hobbles for pack animals.
Buy gear in subdued forest colors.
Repackage foods to reduce the use of containers.
Take a litterbag to carry out all refuse.
Carry a stove and foods requiring little cooking.
Check at Ranger Stations for information about low-use areas.

Travel to avoid impact:

Walk single-file in center of trail.

Stay on main trail even if it is wet or snow-covered.
Never shortcut switchbacks.
Travel cross-country only in rocky or timbered areas.
Look and photograph, never pick or collect.
Avoid popular areas.
Never discard butts, candy, or gum wrappers.

Make no-trace camps:

Seek ridgetop or timbered campsites.
Choose well-drained, rocky, or sandy sites.
Never cut standing trees.
Avoid leveling or digging hip holes and trenches.
Make only small campfires in safe areas.
Carry small firewood from timbered areas outside camp.
Make camp 200 feet away from shorelines of lakes or streams.
Use lightweight, soft shoes; avoid trampling vegetation.
Wash 100 feet away from water sources.
Use biodegradable soaps.
Bury human waste or fish entrails at least six inches deep.
Picket and hobble horses 200 feet from camp or water.
Rotate horses through grazing areas.
Avoid even temporary tying of horses to small trees.
Stay as quiet as possible and enjoy the solitude.
Leave radios and tape players at home.
Leave the dog at home.

Leave a no-trace campsite:

Pick up every trace of litter.
Erase all signs of a fire.
Scatter horse manure, fill in pawed holes.
Replace rocks and logs where they were.
Report significant information to Ranger Stations.
Look for signs of disturbance. Did you leave any traces?

To these I will add a few more guidelines. A lightweight camping stove is preferable to wood fires just about everywhere, but especially at higher elevations or wherever downed wood is scarce. Many excellent models are available.

Toilet paper should be burned, where there is no danger of fire, or well buried. All other garbage, without exception, should be packed out.

It may sound like a lot to remember, but the "freedom of the hills" now requires it. Freedom demands responsibility, and the responsibility grows as the number of people in the backcountry increases.

Forest Service Programs

Two excellent volunteer programs have been initiated by the U.S. Forest Service in recent years: the Adopt-a-Trail program and the Wilderness Information Specialist (W.I.S.) program. Both arose from the agency's need to provide adequate trail management and visitor information within severe budgetary limits.

The Adopt-a-Trail program started as a response to the

enormous effort required to maintain the Appalachian Trail. For many years, hiking organizations and individuals have assumed total responsibility for the maintenance of segments of the trail. In the current program, now operating in many parts of the country, organizations or individuals are signed up under the Volunteers in the National Forest Act; the workers are protected against tort claims and are covered under workman's compensation if they are injured on the job. Training, supervision, tools, transportation, meals, and other out-of-pocket expenses may or may not be furnished, depending on the terms negotiated in the Volunteer Agreement. Usually signs are placed on the trails acknowledging the organization or person responsible for the maintenance.

The Wilderness Information Specialist concept had its beginnings a few years ago in Superstition Wilderness of Arizona. Forest Ranger Jim Bradley, the originator of the idea, was assigned temporarily to Tonto National Forest and trained personnel there to help set up the program.

The original Wilderness Information Specialists were volunteers stationed in camps at wilderness trailheads; their job was to contact visitors entering an area, give them a pep talk on wilderness ethics, and answer questions. The program appealed to many college students with outgoing personalities and was an overwhelming success. It has since been expanded to include such other wilderness management tasks as campsite rehabilitation, contact with visitors inside the areas, litter cleanup, and office work. These jobs are usually rotated so that W.I.S.'s are well informed on all aspects of wilderness use.

The demand for wilderness education has taken the Wilderness Information Specialists to elementary schools, universities, service clubs, youth groups, outing clubs, and senior citizen meetings, where they present the wilderness ethic and good land use management principles.

Information about both programs can be obtained from a local ranger district office or by writing:

National Forest Service Regional Office
517 Gold Avenue, SW
Albuquerque, NM 87102

Staying Safe in the Southwest

Travel by Vehicle

Your adventure into the wildlands of the Southwest begins when the tires of your vehicle leave the highway and start rolling down a dirt road toward a trailhead. And your adventure can come to an abrupt end if that vehicle breaks down or gets stuck.

PLANNING AHEAD

Planning too long a trip in too short a time is a common error leading to vehicle breakdown. Without enough time, people rush and do foolish or chancy things.

Driving alone or with only one vehicle increases the disaster potential in remote country. A second machine can pull another that is stuck, provide battery power, towing service, and, if all else fails, a ride to the nearest tow truck.

You should be just as thorough in vehicle route planning and traveling as in backpacking planning. This means knowing your exact location on a map at all times. If a map is consulted during back-road travel, a route can be back-tracked at night in an emergency, without having to guess about turnoffs or why the highway isn't where you thought it was. Bear in mind that while topographic features usually change little and are represented accurately even on old maps, roads, being manmade, are often re-routed, replaced, or overgrown from disuse. When orienting yourself, rely on topography more than on the location of a road on a map.

Always leave a written plan of your proposed route with

a close friend or relative, in case an emergency arises or a search-and-rescue attempt is needed. Be sure to include your planned date of return, or make arrangements to phone in your whereabouts from some point on your way out.

Equipment

The hiker or backpacker must be equipped with specialized gear to travel safely in the wilderness. You should also equip your vehicle for safe travel. The following items should be considered:

extra water hose
2 mounted spare tires filled to correct pressure
1 large heavy-duty bumper jack and 1 hydraulic axle jack
jumper cables
extra fan belt
tool box
extra battery fully charged
at least 5 gallons of extra gasoline
4-lug crossbar tire iron
1 week's supply of survival rations
1 sparkplug-type tire pump
2 plywood jack pads about 1 foot square
4 pieces of old carpet at least 1 foot by 4 feet
assortment of nuts and bolts
1 long-handled shovel
electric repair tape
2 tarps for laying on ground
extra wire

hose clamps
gasket material
extra oil and transmission fluid
heavy duty flashlight
AT LEAST 10 GALLONS OF WATER

The time and money required to procure all this gear is much less than the time and money required to get a tow truck to come haul the vehicle back to civilization.

COMMON PROBLEMS

Electrical-system problems.   Statistics show that about half of all highway tow-truck assists are caused by battery failure and other electrical problems. An extra charged battery and fan belt may save a long walk or wait.

Cooling-system problems are common in desert terrain and in mountains in summer. The system should be cleaned and flushed before each summer. Hoses should be checked. The thermostat should be working. Wash out spaces in the radiator with a car-wash power sprayer. Carry extra hoses and clamps. Needle-nose pliers can be used to pinch off small radiator leaks.

If the engine overheats, keep it running, open the hood, and pour water over the outside of the radiator. If the temperature drops, try taking off the radiator cap. If it doesn't, shut the engine off and wait till it does cool. You may then have to drive very slowly or wait for nightfall to continue.

Flat tires are common, due to rocky road surfaces, and

two good spares are recommended. A sparkplug-type tire pump is handy if you develop a slow leak or need to reinflate tires after deflating them to get out of soft sand.

What about *soft sand,* a frequent problem in desert driving? If you start spinning your wheels, stop and assess the situation. If stuck, you must jack up the vehicle, making sure to block the other tires. Fill in the hole left by the stuck tire with rocks, limbs, or anything firm. Place sand mats or carpet scraps in the direction of firm ground. Lower the vehicle, let enough air out of *all* the tires so that they bulge out, then slowly drive the vehicle out using second or third gear. Keep the tires underinflated if driving in a sandy area. Reinflate them for driving on a firm surface.

Bent tie-rods occur when the vehicle clearance is too low or the driver is driving too fast on rough roads. Sometimes they can be bent back with a hydraulic jack or by hammering, but the vehicle should be turned around and taken to a garage.

Punctured fuel tanks or oil pans can sometimes be temporarily repaired using metal screws with rubber washers, or with soap, gum, or wooden plugs wrapped with cloth. Extra oil, fuel, and transmission fluid should always be taken into the boondocks.

Vapor lock occurs when the engine is so hot that the fuel in the lines vaporizes and prevents the vehicle from starting. If the engine turns over but won't start, this may be the problem. Wrap the fuel lines and fuel pump with damp cloths.

Broken brake lines can happen to vehicles without enough

clearance. Metal breaks or holes can sometimes be pinched off with pliers (vise-grip models are useful). Fabric or rubber lines can be temporarily patched with marine tape.

DRIVING TECHNIQUES

Staying on established roads is the first rule of desert driving. Short-cutting can lead to disaster, or at least great inconvenience. Moreover, it scars the desert floor and may lead another party into the same situation. Unseen washes, dips, soft spots, holes, and rocks can break you down where you least want to be.

Keep track of features as you travel. Mark intersections on the map and note landmarks like cattle tanks, windmills, creek beds, and corrals for your return trip or for the next journey into the area. If you note features and junctions, it is also much easier to decide whether to walk for help if your vehicle breaks down or to stay with the vehicle.

It is easy to misjudge time and distance during desert travel. The dry, clear air can make distances appear deceptively short, for instance between prominent landmarks in otherwise featureless terrain. While the lack of clutter in the landscape makes determining location easier, far-away high points seem closer than they are. Rely on distances noted on the topographic map and count the contour lines to ascertain elevation differences between landmarks. Keep track of odometer readings and mark them on the map. A desert landmark may look surprisingly different in the afternoon than it did the same morning.

Flash floods in desert areas are another consideration. Flash floods occur when violent thunderstorms drop huge amounts of water over a small area of desert in a short period of time. Tons of water cascade from slopes into canyons in a matter of minutes, sweeping everything in the way. Walls of water up to 10 feet high can crash down a previously dry arroyo and carry vehicles, tents, trailers, and people with them. These storms can occur miles away and catch you in a wash unprepared, so it is dangerous to drive in washes when local thunderstorms are brewing. It is also foolish to try to cross a wash being swept by a flash flood. Every year, someone gets carried away attempting to cross a flooded wash in the desert backcountry.

Thunderstorms usually occur from late June to mid-September. Tropical storms from the Gulf of Mexico and the Gulf of California occur from August to October. If you see a wash running in a normally dry place across the road in front of you, get out and take a closer look. If you have doubts, wait a half hour and the arroyo will likely have dried up. Flash floods are violent when happening but usually don't last long.

OFF-ROAD VEHICLES

Recent research by the U.S. Fish and Wildlife Service on the Mohave Desert in California shows that off-road vehicles (ORVs) destroy ground-dwelling animals by crushing nests and burrows. They disrupt bird life, destroy vegetation and soil that supports root structures, restrict wildflower growth, and alter the habitats of various insect species. A report from the Bureau of Interior Wildlife Research states:

> The present study provides evidence that ORVs detrimentally affect desert wildlife and creosote shrub habitat. The ORVs have been extensively used for less than a decade in the Mojave Desert, but already there has been widespread negative impact on desert communities. The available data indicates that continued intensive ORV activities will be increasingly detrimental to the wildlife resources of the California Desert. The impact of these ORV activities must be recognized in present and future management programs so as to minimize or curtail losses of irreplaceable habitat and associated wildlife living on Natural Resources land, state, military, and private holdings.

The report does not condemn all ORV use, but it does call attention to the problems and the need for regulation to minimize destruction by these vehicles. Furthermore, it should be taken by ORV operators as a request for environmental sensitivity.

GETTING HELP

What happens if a vehicle does break down six miles from any paved road? Fifteen miles? Should you stay with the vehicle in an isolated spot, or try to walk back to the highway? Most survival manuals recommend—demand—that you stay with the vehicle. But I maintain that if you kept track of where you were on the map and if you think it less risky than staying with the machine, you should be able to backtrack. Tell your companions where you are going and when you should be back; if alone, leave a note. The situation will dictate the decision, but here are a few considerations: It will probably be 24 hours after your estimated time of return home before someone will look for you. How long is that from when you broke down? How far are you from any ranch or highway? How much water do you have? Enough to last until you are rescued? Should you travel at night to conserve water? The strengths and weaknesses of your party must be considered. Should some go for help while others stay with the vehicle? If you stay with the vehicle, do you have a device for signaling?

If you decide to stay with the vehicle, use everything available to make a comfortable camp. Use the vehicle's seats for sitting off the hot or cold ground. Set up a shade canopy with tarps or even seat covers in hot, dry, desert country. Open all doors, the trunk, and the hood. Set out signal panels or build fires. Be ready to signal with a mirror. Search-and-rescue efforts usually begin with an air search, and they will look for your *vehicle*, so make it as visible as possible. Surround it with three fires, and, if possible, lay out a big "X" with 40-ft. ground panels nearby.

After you have prepared, sit back and relax, and stay in the shade.

Travel on Foot

The key to hiking safely in the Southwest is an understanding of its diverse geography. The Oriental saying, "Expect nothing but be prepared for everything" is pertinent in this landscape of contrasts. Climate, elevation, and terrain are always considerations. Within a two-hour drive, one can go from weather fit for wearing shorts and shirt sleeves to cold, down-jacket weather, all under clear skies. Let low pressure or a cold front move into the desert, and the shorts and shirt sleeves can give way to the down jacket in 20 minutes, though the hiker may cover little distance. Months of drought can be succeeded by a week of steady winter rain that turns a normally dry desert mountain range into what seems like the Scottish Highlands, with fog, hail, and temporary waterfalls. A pleasant autumn climb of the San Francisco Peaks can turn to an epic in blinding blizzard within an hour when a Pacific Northwest front moves unexpectedly into Arizona. A May wildflower hunt in the Mazatzals can become a trail-breaking snow stomp when a late winter storm moves into the central Arizona mountains. Temperatures can drop from 80 degrees in the Lower Colorado River desert during the day to freezing at night when heat loss by radiation is augmented by cold air moving into the area.

The frequency of such unpleasant surprises can be minimized by obtaining a weather forecast before beginning a hike. Such innovations as satellite photography enable professionals to forecast regional weather more accurately than in the past, but rangers and others intimate with the locale you plan to visit can give further information. These outdoor people know how to apply regional forecasts to local topography and from experience can interpret wind, clouds, and aching knees. Get a regional forecast, then call a land use agency near the area of your proposed hike for local details.

PLANNING AHEAD

Improper preparation compounds all problems that occur on a trip. The main reason for improper planning is lack of time. Too often planning is done in a hurry with little allowance made for unforeseen circumstances. Hikers frequently plan to cover too much territory in too little time. Wishful thinking causes us to want to see more and travel farther than time will allow and to not budget extra time for the unanticipated. City life tends to be hurried and goal-oriented, but wilderness is a good place for a more natural pace. Rushing along a trail to accomplish a list of goals deprives a hiker of the pleasures of seeing, hearing, smelling, and feeling. And it discourages one from taking the time required for minimum-impact camping.

Another aspect of planning is learning about the particular area to be visited. A trip can be enriched by spending time beforehand becoming familiar with the natural history. Visit the botanical gardens, zoos, museums, and libraries that provide information and insight into a geographic region. Information about public gardens, zoos, and museums in each state is supplied in the respective chapters.

In the Desert

Most desert hiking is done from October to May during sunny weather. A selection of clothing should include long pants as well as shorts, a shirt, an extra wool sweater for the possible night temperature drop, a wide-brim hat and sunglasses for protection from the sun, a lightweight sleeping bag, a tube tent for protection from the occasional shower, extra socks, first-aid items including a comb and tweezers for cactus-spine removal, a lightweight stove, food, and lots of water. Lightweight boots are preferred footwear.

Desert foot travel is discussed in detail in *A Sierra Club Naturalist's Guide to the Deserts of the Southwest,* by Peggy Larson; John Hart's *Hiking the Great Basin;* and my own *Hiking the Desert.*

In the Mountains

Most mountain hiking is done between April and October. But those who like winter camping, snowshoeing, ski touring, and melting snow for water can find high, windy places up to 12-13,000 feet in Arizona and New Mexico. Winter mountaineering is a specialized pastime, so this guidebook will be limited to the spring, fall, and summer seasons in the high country.

Remember the changing life zones as you ascend those "islands" that rise from the desert floor. You need clothing and overnight gear suitable for all conditions you may encounter. Many hikers, including the author, have had to retreat from desert mountains when an early or late storm moved in. It is usually simply a matter of more clothing, a warmer sleeping bag, a tent, and rain gear—and perhaps warmer boots if you start out with lightweight boots or running shoes. Excellent discussions of cold weather hiking and mountaineering techniques are found in John Hart's *Walking Softly in the Wilderness* and in Paul Petzoldt's *The Wilderness Handbook*.

WILDLIFE

Typically, newcomers to the Southwest worry about poisonous animals. They have heard or read about tarantulas, rattlesnakes, and scorpions waiting for the novice hiker, especially in the desert. This needless fear is in part encouraged by the ominous, often grotesque shapes characteristic of desert plants and animals and the harshness of the landscape.

Let's start with the worst myth. Sixteen species of rattlesnakes inhabit Arizona, but you will be lucky to see one. They do everything possible to stay out of man's way and expect reciprocal courtesy from the hiker. They will coil and rattle if cornered or provoked and strike only if further harassed. Arizona Game and Fish Department statistics show that 90 percent of all snake bites occur to people who harrass the animal—either trying to catch it, kill it, play with it, or make it coil.

If you happen to see a rattlesnake (identified by the rattles and diamond-shaped head), you should be content to look and marvel at its adaptability. There is no reason to kill the animal to "make the desert safe for others." All manner of snakes and other creatures are around the backcountry traveler all the time, though they may not be seen. They are underground, in trees, cacti, and shrubs, and under rocks. If an animal is killed, another of the same species takes over the territory.

The tarantula, scorpion, black widow spider, centipede, and Gila monster are also part of the landscape and should be enjoyed as such. More people suffer from bee stings than from all other poisonous animals combined. Poisonous animals are covered in greater detail in *A Sierra Club Naturalist's Guide to the Deserts of the Southwest*.

WATER PURIFICATION

Backcountry sources cannot be counted on to provide safe drinking water. Streams, lakes, and ponds, no matter how clear, may be contaminated with parasitic viral or bacterial organisms that can cause human illness. At present, the giardia cyst is especially notorious. Three accepted methods may be used for water disinfection: boiling, chlorination, and iodination. Whichever method is used, first strain the water through a cloth to filter out debris or organic matter, if the water is visibly dirty or cloudy.

Method 1.   Boil the water for about 20 minutes.

Method 2.   Chlorination can be used when boiling is impossible. Use either Halazone tablets or common bleach. Use an unopened bottle of Halazone for each trip. To be effective, Halazone must be protected from heat and from exposure to air. Common bleach is a useful alternative. Read the label to determine the percentage of chlorine in the bleach and mix according to the chart below. Liquid laundry bleach usually has four percent to six percent available chlorine.

| Available Chlorine | Drops to Be Added to Quart or Liter | |
	Clear water	Cloudy water
1%	10	20
4–6%	2	4
7–10%	1	2
Unknown	10	20

Mix thoroughly by stirring or shaking and let the water stand for 30 minutes. A slight chlorine odor should be detectable; if not, repeat the dosage and wait an additional 15 minutes before using the water, which should then be safe. Very dirty or cold water requires prolonged waiting, perhaps overnight, for the disinfectants to work.

Method 3. Iodination involves the use of Globaline tablets, tincture of iodine, or iodine crystals. Use an unopened bottle of Globaline for each trip, as it must be protected from heat and air. If tincture of iodine is used, at 2% strength, 5 drops should be added per quart of clear water, 10 drops per quart of cloudy water. Mix thoroughly and let stand 30 minutes, longer for cold water.

The Landscape

Arizona is nicknamed the "Grand Canyon State" after its unique geologic wonder. But Arizona is more than canyon country. It has plateaus, mesas, high and low deserts, grass-lands, mountain chains covered with winter snows, jagged desert peaks, and, flowing through all this diversity, ribbons of perennial riverine habitat. Two thirds of the state can be classified as desert—the deserts of the Colorado Plateau in the north, the Mohave in the west, and the Sonoran in the south. About one third is characterized by mountains and stream habitat. The geographic diversity of Arizona is exem-plified by a hike from the depths of the Grand Canyon at 2,500 feet elevation, to the summit of 12,600-foot Mt. Hum-phreys in the San Francisco Peaks, 50 air miles to the south. In such a hike the traveler would pass through all six life zones.

The hiker could also trek out from the desert near Tucson and climb to the top of Mt. Lemmon in the nearby Santa Catalina range, crossing through four life zones. In terms of biological diversity, these hikes would be the equivalent of a walk from Mexico to Canada.

Geographers divide the state into three physiographic provinces, the Basin and Range (lowland desert), the Col-orado Plateau province (high desert), and the Mountain and Transition province (central mountain chains). The location of these provinces is shown on the accompanying map.

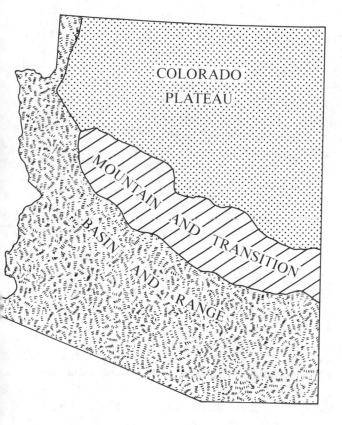

The physiographic provinces of Arizona.

Basin and Range Province

The Basin and Range Province includes southern and western Arizona—the "lower deserts." The landscape is characterized by broad basins separated by sharp-edged mountain ranges. Most of these 150 desert ranges are the exposed edges of fault blocks that extend miles below the surface. A great variety of geologic formations are exposed, some highly mineralized. Igneous and metamorphic formations dominate, composed of granite, basalt, rhyolite, andesite, gneiss, schists, and many volcanics. The Basin and Range Province was once covered by extensive sedimentary formations laid down by ancient seas that once covered the area, but these layers were later washed away, leaving remnants in the form of weathered buttes and small mountain masses.

The basins consist of weathered material eroded from the fault blocks over millions of years and deposited in the broad valleys and sloping *bajadas* between them. These valleys became the water courses and hence the population centers of the region.

One other characteristic of the Basin and Range Province makes it an even more fascinating area for the hiker. Huge mountain masses in southern and southeastern Arizona rise up to 9,000 and 10,000 feet, like "islands" in the desert. Ranges such as the Santa Catalinas bordering Tucson, the Pinalenos near Safford, the Chiricahuas north of Douglas in the extreme southeast corner of the state, and the Baboquivaris close to the Mexican border seem to shoot up from the desert floor, offering a colorful variety of geologic features and vegetation and often are capped with snow in winter. (Some geographers include these ranges in the Mountain and Transition Province.)

Two rainy seasons, occurring in winter and summer, bring climatic variation to the Basin and Range Province. Winter rains are brought to the deserts by cyclonic storms from the Pacific Northwest, which cross the continent from west to east. Long, slow, soaking rains from December to March provide the stream runoff and soil moisture that are so vital to cattlemen, lumbermen, farmers, and wildlife. These winter storms turn the top of Mt. Lemmon into our country's southernmost ski area.

Summer rains are the result of convection currents of hot air that rise from the desert floor, push through the cool air masses above, cool to the point of condensation, and then deluge the hot deserts with violent though brief thunderstorms. The gigantic thunderheads move at great speed but may in a matter of minutes drop a half inch of rain on a locality, causing flash floods and instant erosion of the desert landscape. Sometimes summer "monsoon" storms from the Gulf of Mexico or the Gulf of California move into the lower deserts of Arizona, dropping additional moisture.

The driest months in the deserts are May and June, followed by October and November. The best hiking months are October through May. The months of June through September are too hot for hiking except in the higher mountain "islands." With temperatures that can and do reach 120 degrees in the sun and dry, parched air inducing continual thirst, the summer deserts are best left to the reptiles.

In addition to the hot air temperatures and low humidity, the deserts are characterized by even hotter ground temperatures, high evaporation rates, lack of surface water, sparse vegetation, wide temperature *ranges* from day to night, and rainfall of ten inches or less per year. The scarcity of surface water will be mentioned repeatedly in discussions of each section of the Basin and Range Province. The Sierra cup hanging from the belt, waiting to be filled with cool, crisp stream water, can remain at home during treks in the Sonoran Desert.

Vegetation in the southern deserts is of the type known as Desert Shrub, characterized by the creosote bush–bursage and the palo verde tree–saguaro cactus communities. Plants living under conditions of less than ten inches of annual rainfall have adapted by such methods as reduced leaf area (mesquite and palo verde), specialized leaves (creosote bush and ocotillo), replaced leaves (spiny cactus), and shortened life cycles (ephemeral desert wildflowers, whose life cycle may require but a few weeks). The dependence of plant life on moisture is displayed in subtle gradations of plant communities across the Sonoran Desert. In southeastern Arizona, the area around Tucson, the vegetation is lush and is the most varied in the North American deserts, because this area receives more moisture from both winter and summer rains than other regions. Westward, toward the Colorado River, average precipitation diminishes, and the landscape becomes progressively bleaker, culminating in the barren sparseness of the hottest and driest of our lands, the Colorado River Desert.

The Basin and Range deserts support a variety of animal life, but the hiker must be a patient observer to see much of it. Only a few species have adapted physiologically to the heat and lack of water; most, including man, have adapted by creating their own microhabitats—escaping the summer heat in burrows, caves, and trees, under rocks, inside cactus, and in air-conditioned buildings.

Most orders of insect are represented in the Basin and Range deserts. Grasshoppers, crickets, termites, water bugs, butterflies, moths, flies, beetles, ants, bees, and wasps all find places in the desert ecosystems. They fill a most important niche in the food chain, the link between plant and animal life that allows other desert fauna to survive. They also pollinate the flowers of many plants, including cacti, and hasten the decay of organic matter—another essential role in the food chains. However, the insect is a minimal pest in most areas of the Basin and Range Province, where water and moist habitats are in short supply.

The mammal population includes rodents, which are mainly vegetarians. Ground squirrels, rock squirrels, woodrats, kangaroo rats, gophers, and several kinds of mice burrow into the earth during the day and emerge at night to eat and be eaten. Other mammals occasionally spotted by the quiet hiker are the cottontail rabbit, jackrabbit, desert mule deer, white-tail deer, javelina, bighorn sheep, and coyote. Desert predators include skunks, coatimundi, ringtail cats, badgers, foxes, bobcats, mountain lions, and, again, the omniverous coyotes.

Man might be added as a newcomer to the list of predators, though his influence on the other desert populations is less as a hunter than as a destroyer of habitat. Destruction of natural habitat lowers animal populations and forces species into other territories, where they come in conflict with existing wildlife communities. One winter storm can kill as many deer as hunters do, but the storm passes by, allowing the remaining wildlife populations to recover. Once habitat is destroyed, though, the disappearance of wildlife is more permanent.

Common insect- and seed-eating birds include quail, Gila woodpeckers, doves, flycatchers, thrashers, kingbirds, mockingbirds, and swallows. The most common predatory birds are owls, eagles, hawks, roadrunners, vultures, and ravens.

Reptiles, symbols of the desert, include many lizard species, tortoises, and the snakes, both poisonous and nonpoisonous. The rattlesnake was discussed in Chapter 1.

Mountain and Transition Province

Sweeping from northwest to southeast through Central Arizona, separating the Basin and Range Province to the south from the Colorado Plateau Province to the north is terrain characterized by rugged topography. Large mountain masses are separated by canyons, valleys, streams, and rivers. Elevations vary from 2,000 feet to the 10,713-foot summit of Mt. Graham. Geologically, the topography was formed by granitic and basaltic intrusions below the crust that pushed up through older sedimentary layers. Subsequent erosion removed most of those overlying layers of sandstone and limestone and created this jumbled landscape. The Mogollon Rim, running northwest by southeast above Payson, is commonly considered the boundary between the Mountain and Transition Province and the Colorado Plateau Province. The rim, which is the edge of the layered sedimentary formations of the Plateau Province, continues to the western end of the Grand Canyon.

Five of the six life zones in Arizona are found in the Mountain and Transition Province. (The only missing zone is the Arctic-Alpine.) Various plant communities characterize the foothills and some valleys: chaparral, pinyon–juniper, ponderosa pine, pine–fir, desert grassland, and oak woodland. For its size, this province offers the greatest variety of natural history in the Southwest and is a summer vacation destination for many Arizonans.

With higher elevations, greater relief, and latitude sufficiently north to catch winter storms, this province gets the most rainfall of any region of the state. Rainfall equals plant diversity and more standing and running water. Hikers may want to take their Sierra cups into the Mountain and Transition Province, though there is no guarantee they will get to use them.

Because of the diversity of plant life and more abundant water, there is a more varied animal population, notably grazing and browsing animals such as antelope and deer, than in drier habitats. The black bear inhabits this region, as well as bobcats, turkeys, tree squirrels, and mountain lions. Such permanent water sources as lakes, streams, tanks, and rivers support aquatic life including such game fish as largemouth bass, crappie, catfish, striped bass, pike, and bluegill.

The hiker and backpacker can spend a lifetime exploring this region and see new things on every trip. But it is vital to be prepared for a greater variety of weather than in the deserts, and to be aware of how suddenly storms can move into this area.

Colorado Plateau Province

Northern Arizona is a vast plateau ranging in elevation from 4,000 to 9,000 feet, with occasional mountain massifs ranging to 12,500 feet. The plateau is formed of upthrust sedimentary rocks. From below the Mogollon Rim, the plateau's southern edge, a resemblance between the sedimentary beds and a layer cake may be seen. To continue the analogy, volcanic rocks covering much of the surface may be likened to frosting on the cake. In the Grand Canyon, which cuts a mile into the plateau, the layers display a billion years of the earth's history.

The Colorado Plateau Province is high desert. It is colder than the lower Basin and Range deserts in winter, though only slightly cooler in summer. August temperatures can exceed 100 degrees.

The Colorado Plateau Province may be divided into three districts.

The Grand Canyon District includes the province's outstanding feature, the Grand Canyon, and the plateau north of the river, which is known as the "Arizona Strip." The Strip is geographically isolated from the rest of the state and is culturally tied to Utah. Great north-to-south trending faults, intersecting the Colorado River, characterize the Strip. The North Rim of the Canyon with its high plateaus, which are snow-covered throughout winter, is a paradise for the back-country traveler who wants to experience the isolation of little frequented country.

The Black Mesa District is Indian country; Hopi and Navajo reservations occupy most of the area. It is flat, open desert with little vegetation and dramatic sedimentary formations, highlighted by Monument Valley. Buttes, mesas, and pinnacles abound, erosional remnants of once extensive sandstone and limestone formations. The Little Colorado River and the Painted Desert form the southern boundary of this district. The Black Mesa District is extremely dry and barren; travel with full water bottles.

The Volcanic Plateau District lies south of the Colorado and Little Colorado rivers and north of the Mogollon Rim. Three periods of volcanic eruption produced the lava that covers much of this district. The San Francisco Peaks, rising to Arizona's highest point, is the largest volcanic mass. Climate in this district varies with elevation, but it is mainly hot and dry. The San Francisco Peaks and the White Mountains are exceptions because of their elevation and mass. Both of these volcanic massifs have winter ski areas.

The Plateau Province contains Arizona's only occurrence of arctic–alpine plant communities, atop the San Francisco Peaks and White Mountains. The ponderosa pine biotic community extends across the southern part of the Plateau along the Mogollon Rim and westward onto both rims of the Grand Canyon. The spruce–fir–aspen community, lying above the ponderosa pine community, is found on the Kaibab Plateau north of the Canyon, in the Flagstaff area around the San Francisco Peaks, and in the higher elevations of the White Mountains. In the deep canyons that cut through this province are displayed lower-elevation plant communities.

A variety of animal life frequents the Plateau Province, including the elk, which makes its summer home in the high forests.

Riparian Habitat

Arizona's richest, most diverse habitat borders the life-giving watercourses throughout the state. The biotic communities characteristic of riparian habitat cut across all of the state's other communities with the exception of the spruce–fir–aspen community and the arctic–alpine community, which are found at higher elevations. The riparian habitat supports such hardwoods as sycamore, walnut, and alder, as well as a variety of vines, shrubs, flowering plants, grasses, and aquatic plants, and intense concentrations of wildlife.

These exotic ribbons of blue and green are extremely fragile but important to the ecological balance of the entire natural world. In Arizona, stream flows have been drastically reduced by channeling and damming. Only 10% of the original riparian habitat remains along the lower Colorado River and about 5% along the lower Gila River. Only about

15% of Arizona's total original riparian acreage remains in its natural form.

Arizona's first white settlers sought rivers and streams, not only for the water itself, but for fish and transportation and because stream borders provided wood for fuel and shelter and soil for crops. As the settlements multiplied in size, greatly increasing the need for irrigated agriculture, the waterways remained a finite resource, and the needs of the present population are not compatible with riparian ecology.

Riparian habitats, though the most important type of landscape to man, have received little attention in discussions of the natural environment. Much of Arizona's riparian habitat is publicly owned, and we may hope that increased research, planning, and education of water users will limit man's long-range impact on these precious strips of land.

Many trails follow stream and river courses, a human use little discussed in riparian conflicts. This is a nonexploitative use that should be considered by land use planners, along with the more publicized river running on the larger waterways. Hikers and backpackers, naturally attracted to waterways when planning outings in dehydrating desert areas, will do well to learn about riparian habitats and how to minimize hiker impact there.

Natural Areas

The Arizona State Parks' Natural Area Program is a government plan to protect riparian and other wild habitats. The program started with a grant to the Natural Area Committee of Arizona in 1971. A study identified 75 sites within the state that contained significant examples of rare plant life and recommended the protection of such sites for future scientific study before they were destroyed by private development or government projects. These areas, many including watercourses, have been set aside from any use except for research, education, and such nondestructive recreation as bird watching. No hiking or camping sites are established in these areas. Many include private property, with the consent of the owners. Some are purchases by organizations such as the Nature Conservancy, to be held in perpetuity for the education and enjoyment of future generations.

The Natural Area Program is combined at the state level with the Hiking and Riding Trails Program in order to coordinate the efforts of various state and private committees involved in long-range planning. The coordinator sits on the Natural Area Advisory Council, which is composed of geologists, hydrologists, ecologists, archaeologists, land use experts, and environmental educators drawn from various institutions and regions of the state. The Council makes recommendations regarding proposed natural areas and coordinates the management of these areas. The coordinator also gathers diverse individuals interested in the planning and implementing of rights-of-way for proposed equestrian and hiking trails throughout the state. He or she sits on the Arizona Hiking and Equestrian Trails Committee, consisting of representatives chosen by the Board of Supervisors of each of the 14 Arizona counties. Representatives also come from federal land use agencies such as the Forest Service

and the State Land Department. Industry is represented by
the Arizona Cattle Growers' Association, Arizona Wool
Growers, Arizona Forest Industries, Arizona Horse Breed-
ers' Association, and Arizona Mining Association. Recre-
ational trail users include the Arizona State Horsemen's
Association, the Arizona State Hiking Association, the Sierra
Club, the Boy Scouts of America, and the Southern Arizona
Hiking Club.

Behind the efforts of the state coordinator and the committee members is the interest of volunteers in various communities. They have to be interested enough in the Trails
Program to get involved in establishing routes and developing community support for these routes.

For further information contact:

State Hiking and Riding Trails Coordinator
1688 W. Adams
Phoenix, AZ 85007

Arizona Nature Conservancy
30 N. Tucson Blvd.
Tucson, AZ 85716

The National Forests

KAIBAB NATIONAL FOREST

The Paiute word for the extensive forested plateau that makes up most of the North Rim of the Grand Canyon is *Kaibab,* meaning "mountain lying down." That is one way to look at the plateau that now constitutes the northern part of Kaibab National Forest, once the Paiutes' ancestral lands. Totaling some 1.6 million acres, the Kaibab National Forest includes the forested lands on both the North and South rims of the Grand Canyon, as well as a substantial portion of the forested southern half of the Coconino Plateau. Ranging in height from 3,000 feet to 10,418 feet (on Kendrick Peak), the Kaibab National Forest is characterized by broad sweeps of ponderosa and mixtures of pinyon and juniper with an average elevation of 7,000 feet. The most dramatic physical relief occurs near national forest boundaries above the North and South rims and on the northern escarpment of the Sycamore Canyon Wilderness.

If you're used to the mountains, plateaus may make for tame trekking, but the Kaibab Plateau provides access to the precipitous heads of great hiking canyons like Saddle, Nankoweap, North, Jumpup, and Kanab Creek on the North Rim and, far to the south, Sycamore Canyon in the Williams District. Hiking in Kaibab National Forest is not all canyoneering, however. In addition to excellent winter ski touring, there are three significant mountaineering objectives: nipple-shaped Kendrick Peak, named after Major H. L.

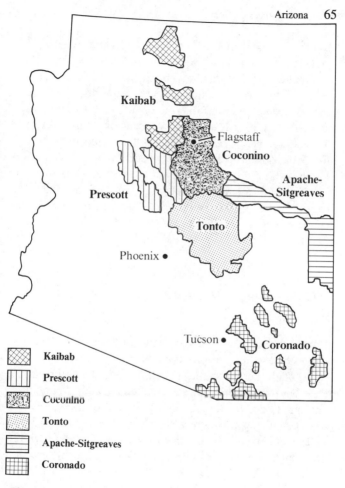

The national forests of Arizona.

Kendrick who, in 1851, escorted Captain Lorenzo Sitgreaves on an ambitious expedition to follow the Zuni, Little
Colorado, and Colorado rivers to the Gulf of California;
rolling Sitgreaves Mountain, which from afar looks more
like a frozen blue waterfall lying on its side than a mountain;
and Bill Williams Mountain, whose snow-fed creeks form
the headwaters of the Verde River. Of the three, only 10,418-
foot Kendrick Peak lies in proposed wilderness. Sitgreaves
Mountain (9,388 feet) doesn't have a trail or road to its
summit, but its roadless state may not last indefinitely in
logging country. Bill Williams Mountain (9,341 feet) has
not been wilderness since the days before the ski lodge, radio
transmitters and receivers, and roads.

Williams Ranger District

Kendrick Peak

If the 4,310-acre environs of Kendrick Peak receive the wilderness classification proposed by Congress under RARE
II, it would be one of the smallest wilderness areas in the
state but one of the highest. This lone island of ponderosa
and mixed conifer thrusts 3,000 feet out of the 7,000-foot
Coconino Plateau, the greatest topographic relief to be found
in the southern section of Kaibab National Forest, providing
backcountry travelers with the finest view in northern Arizona.

To reach Kendrick Peak, drive north from Flagstaff on
U.S. 180 for 17 miles to Forest Road 193. Turn west on
Road 193 and drive 4½ miles to Forest Road 171. Turn west

again and take Road 171 nearly 3 miles to Road 171A. Turn right and follow Road 171A for 1 mile to a dead end. This is the Kendrick Peak Trail (#22), the most popular hiking trail on the mountain. The way to the summit is obvious along all of its 4 miles, during which the trail climbs 2,500 feet to a USFS lookout. A half mile below the lookout you come to the Bull Basin Trail (#40). This seldom used trail drops from the cold, northern exposure of Kendrick Peak for 4 miles to meadows 2,000 feet below. If you're backpacking or ski touring, the densely wooded ridgeline just below the summit offers a lofty yet sheltered place to camp.

On the summit of Kendrick Peak, you have an uninterrupted 360-degree panorama of the region—rivaled only by its southern Arizona counterpart, Mt. Wrightson. Immediately to the east the San Francisco Peaks dominate the horizon. To the north is the great gash of the Grand Canyon; several of its Coconino sandstone temples are identifiable below the North Rim. To the west, if visibility is good, you can see all the way to the Hualipai Mountains near the California border. And looking from southwest to southeast, you can spend an hour naming landmarks in central Arizona.

From Kendrick Peak, return by the same route or take the Pumpkin Trail (#39) down the west ridge to Pumpkin Center. The Pumpkin Trail, which drops 3,200 feet in 4½ miles, is a fine way to complete a traverse Kendrick Peak.

ELEVATION:	7,200 feet to 10,418 feet
VEGETATION:	Ponderosa pine to mixed conifer
WATER:	None except for seasonal snow
NEAREST SUPPLY POINTS:	Flagstaff, Williams

SEASONS:	All year
MAPS:	Kendrick Peak and Moritz Ridge (7.5 minutes); Kaibab National Forest Recreation Map
STATUS:	RARE II
ACTIVITIES:	Cross-country skiing

For further information and up-to-date conditions write:

Forest Supervisor
Kaibab National Forest
Route 1, Box 142
Williams, AZ 86046

COCONINO NATIONAL FOREST

The vast deserts, narrow canyons, and snow-clad peaks of the Colorado Plateau form a mosaic of color and geological diversity, from the imposing sandstone walls of Oak Creek Canyon to the tundra- and bristlecone pine-covered summits of the 12,000-foot San Francisco Peaks. An intricate network of ancient Indian trade routes and modern trails crosses much of this land, waiting to lead the backcountry traveler to a variety of natural wonders. Comprising some 1.8 million acres above and below the Colorado Plateau, the land of the Coconino National Forest was first inhabited and farmed by the ancient Sinagua as long ago as 600 A.D. Many of their largest and most famous ruins—Walnut Canyon, Wupatki, Tuzigoot, and Montezuma Castle—are national monuments, while smaller, though no less important, sites are scattered throughout the high desert and forest of the Coconino National Forest. All indicate a refined culture that still can teach much to modern man. How better to explore a land rich in cultural legacy than on foot, allowing you to feel the country as the earlier inhabitants must have?

Elden Ranger District

The San Francisco Peaks

To many, these lofty, forested peaks represent the Forest Service multi-use concept of "sustained yields of wood, water, forage, wildlife, and recreation." To traditional Navajos, however, the 12,633-foot San Francisco Peaks are *Dook' o' oslid,* the Sacred Mountain of the West, one of four cardinal mountains that border *dinetah,* the country called "Navajoland" in tourist brochures. The San Francisco Peaks also hold religious significance for Hopis, Walapais, and Yavapais. "The Peaks," as many northern Arizonans call them, were once a volcano rising to over 15,000 feet; they are still the highest summits in Arizona. Providing the backcountry traveler with many high-altitude recreational opportunities, the Peaks are included in a 17,940-acre area being considered for wilderness designation under RARE II.

Rising for more than 5,000 feet from dwarf forests of pinyon and juniper to the alpine tundra of their highest point, Humphreys Peak, the San Francisco Peaks provide residents of nearby Flagstaff with a panorama of colors changing with the seasons, and naturalists with a wide spectrum of plant types. It was in these mountains that pioneer ecologist C. Hart Merriam developed the concept of life zones; six of his seven are found on the slopes of the Peaks.

Most people who climb these mountains ride the Snow Bowl ski lift to 11,608 feet before scrambling the last ½ mile to the 12,346-foot summit of Agassiz Peak or hiking the 2 miles to Humphreys Peak. For those who enjoy the rigors and rewards of high-altitude hiking, cross-country skiing, and winter mountaineering, several alternative routes ascend the Peaks. Each is different, though each is appropriate to the nature of these mountains. Probably the most heavily used is the Weatherford Trail (#102), which is actually an old road that provided access for automobiles during the 1920s. There is no danger of losing the trail from base to summit, and with its moderate switchbacks, it makes an excellent winter ski tour or midsummer wilderness run.

To reach the beginning of the Weatherford Trail, drive north from Flagstaff on U.S. 180 for 3½ miles to the Schultz Pass turnoff, Forest Road 420. Follow Road 420 for 6 miles to Schultz Pass. Park here and start walking up Forest Road 522. One-quarter mile north, you come to the Transwestern Gas Pipeline access road running generally east-west. Cross this road and you come to a fork in Road 522. Take the left fork. The right fork is a spur road which ends in Weatherford Canyon ½ mile beyond. In the next mile Road 522 climbs 500 vertical feet through a rolling meadow to a junction. From this junction Road 522 contours west around the base of the Peak, but you take the right fork, the start of the Weatherford Trail. Unfortunately, it's still a jeep road here, and it's not uncommon to encounter vehicular traffic. Stay on the trail as it switchbacks 4½ miles up the southeast flank of Fremont Peak through forests of Douglas, white, and subalpine fir, and Englemann spruce, to 10,000-foot Doyle Saddle. Vehicle traffic is prohibited beyond this point. From Doyle Saddle you get your first view of the Inner Basin, a subalpine meadow that once sheltered an ice age glacier and is Flagstaff's most important watershed. The trail turns west and skirts the north slope of 11,969-foot Fremont Peak for a mile before switchbacking up 500 feet in a mile to Fremont Saddle. Near this saddle are several good spots to camp in the trees out of the wind. Looking around, you'll find the remains of the old Weatherford Cabin, its wood stove dating from the time when its stalwart occupants looked down on the logging and railroad town of Flagstaff, 7 miles away.

From Doyle Saddle, the Weatherford Trail switchbacks 1½ miles up the east face of Agassiz Peak to join the trail (#104) that traverses the ridge spanning Humphreys and Agassiz peaks from north to south. This junction is at 12,000 feet.

If you're short of time or weather conditions are deteriorating, you may opt to climb Agassiz. It's only ½ mile to the south, and the trail is easier and better defined than the Humphreys section is. Or you may want to camp on this ridge before continuing to Humphreys Peak the next morning. It's not as close as it may look, especially if you're not acclimated to the thin air. Depending which way the wind is blowing—and it always blows on the Peaks—several spots on either side of the ridge can shelter a tent or two. The best of these is ¼ mile north in the obvious notch at 11,800 feet. Camp below the notch itself, because the wind can get particularly fierce here. More than one person has perished on this ridge through being unprepared for the bitter winds that whip across the Peaks summer and winter.

From this notch, the trail climbs 800 feet in 1½ miles to Humphreys Peak, meandering a bit more than the Agassiz Peak section and exposed to winds much of the way. The trail has developed variants in places, which is unfortunate considering the fragility of the alpine flora; stay on the main trail. Two crude bivouac shelters on the summit of Humphreys provide protection from the wind while you brew a pot of tea and gnaw a piece of frozen chocolate. If you should be caught in a severe storm on the ridge and can't reach the summit shelters or return to your tent, it's little more than a ½-hour descent to the protection of the treeline on the west slope. Avoid the east slopes in whiteout conditions, as they're more precipitous and, in heavy snows, susceptible to avalanches.

One might expect the views from the summit of Arizona to be the best in the state, but this is no longer true. While on a clear day you still may be able to see forever, clear days are now the exception. Though the poor visibility can sometimes be attributed to the winds typical of the vast Colorado Plateau, usually it's due largely to the coal-burning power plants and generating stations at Joseph City, Four Corners, and Page. Though the fumes are rapidly bringing the air quality of northern Arizona down to that of Phoenix, you should be able to pick out the lone deep blue hump of Navajo

Mountain to the northeast, the North Rim of the Grand Canyon to the northwest, and, to the west, Bill Williams Mountain, Sitgreaves Mountain, and Kendrick Peak. More than 400 cinder cones and dormant volcanoes fringe the base of the Peaks; Sunset Crater, to the east, last erupted around 1200 A.D. The view to the south is blocked by the Humphreys-Agassiz ridge and Agassiz Peak itself. To identify the innumerable other landmarks encircling the Peaks, bring the Arizona Office of Tourism Recreational Maps #3 through #7 or a road map of Arizona, preferably one that displays in shaded relief prominent geographical features.

Return to Schultz Pass by the same route.

Flagstaff Ranger District

There are three other approaches to the San Francisco Peaks: the Abineau Canyon Trail (#127), off Forest Road 418 near White Horse Hills; the Inner Basin routes, off U.S. 89 at the end of Forest Road 522; and the old Philomena Spring Trail. The Abineau Canyon Trail ends in a cul-de-sac at the end of Forest Road 141 near 10,400 feet on the densely wooded north slope of Humphreys Peak. The Inner Basin approach offers challenging winter routes for mountaineers, enervating boulder-strewn talus routes for backpackers and dayhikers, and steep mountain skiing under the right conditions. Camping is not permitted in the basin itself, because of its status as critical Flagstaff watershed. Of the three trails, the Philomena Spring route is probably the most adventuresome; though undeveloped, it's marked much of the way by a waterline and is the route to take when traversing the Peaks from north to south.

To reach the Philomena Spring trail, drive north from Flagstaff on U.S. 180 approximately 20 miles to the White Horse Hills turnoff (Forest Road 151). Turn right and follow 151 past Forest Roads 418 and 418B for 3½ miles to Forest Road 627. Turn left and follow 627 for 1½ miles to Bismarck Lake. Park here if conditions permit and hike cross-country to the east-northeast for ¾ mile. The Philomena Spring Trail is on the north side of the first major drainage west of White Horse Canyon. It's marked by the rusty remains of a 4-inch steep pipe and several water tanks, which were hauled up the mountain by an ambitious cowboy. Following this old pipeline trail shouldn't be a problem; it parallels the drainage to Philomena Spring, 3 miles away and 2,800 feet higher. If you should lose the trail and cannot relocate it, gain the ridge crest above and follow it until it breaks through sparse stands of gnarled bristlecone pine. Philomena Spring is in a depression ¼ mile south at 11,800 feet. After rehydrating, you'll find a number of flat platforms away from the spring in the trees where you can pitch your tent.

San Francisco Peaks Natural Area is located immediately below Philomena Spring. Museum of Northern Arizona scientists and researchers have conducted valuable natural history and environmental studies and cultural history research here and throughout much of the Colorado Plateau.

Humphreys Peak is 800 vertical feet above, and whether you take a mile or a half mile for the ascent depends on how directly you approach the final boulder-strewn slope. There is no trail, but the way is obvious.

If you camp near Philomena Spring and reach Humphreys' summit early in the morning and conditions are favorable, you should be able to descend the Weatherford Trail to Schultz Pass. A more adventurous descent involves following the crest from Agassiz Peak to Fremont Saddle, Fremont Peak, Doyle Saddle, Doyle Peak, and Schultz Peak before descending to Schultz Pass. As on most forested ridges, blown-down timber can impede your progress, but there are several interesting hermit camps en route. The way is not precipitous, though one section on the east ridge of Fremont Peak requires care when descending to Doyle Saddle. This outstanding, infrequently explored ridgeline is, combined with the Weatherford Trail, a fine way to traverse the Peaks from Philomena Spring.

ELEVATION:	7,000 feet to 12,633 feet
VEGETATION:	Pinyon-juniper to arctic-alpine
WATER:	Philomena Spring, Beard Spring, Flagstaff Spring, Snowslide Spring, Doyle Spring, and seasonal snow
NEAREST SUPPLY POINT:	Flagstaff
SEASONS:	All year, depending on activity
MAPS:	Sunset Crater West, Humphreys Peak, White Horse Hills (7.5 minute); Coconino National Forest Map

MANAGING AGENCY:	U.S. Forest Service
STATUS:	RARE II
ACTIVITIES:	Mountaineering, cross-country skiing

Important: Because of the religious significance of the Peaks to several Native American tribes, these mountains should be treated as sacred. *Do not disturb or photograph any religious shrines or offerings you may discover!*

Beaver Creek Ranger District

General Crook Trail

The historic General Crook Trail traverses the southern part of Coconino National Forest from Camp Verde to the Mogollon Rim, a stone's throw from Zane Grey's cabin. Constructed in the 1870s, the 200-mile Crook Trail linked the Military Department of Arizona at Fort Whipple with the outpost of Fort Apache. Today this old military and civilian wagon road has been redeveloped as a 133-mile recreation trail that traverses parts of Prescott, Coconino, and Sitgreaves national forests. Thanks to the Boy Scouts of America, the Forest Service, and a dedicated band of students and citizens, the General Crook Trail was the first designated Arizona State Historic Trail. These people beat the bush looking for the old trail, then marked and developed it.

Due to the trail's proximity to its successor, Highway 87, it is no longer a wilderness route. But the 53 miles within Coconino National Forest skirt the very lip of the Mogollon

Rim and offer the hiker and equestrian a unique opportunity to taste Arizona history while experiencing high desert and mountain country.

Two key points offer access to the Coconino National Forest section of the General Crook Trail: Fort Verde State Historic Park, in Camp Verde, and Thirteen Mile Rock on Highway 87. Thirteen Mile Rock is preferable, as it does not involve a crowded museum trailhead. To reach Thirteen Mile Rock, drive east from Camp Verde on the General Crook Highway (FH-9) for 15 miles to the Thirteen Mile Rock Historic Marker; park here. The trail is across the highway.

The 7-mile hike to the Clear Creek Campground is a good introduction to this rugged trail. The first mile west of Thirteen Mile Rock is the steepest on the entire trail, dropping almost 1,000 feet off the southwestern escarpment of the Mogollon Rim and another 1,000 feet in the last 5 miles to the campground. But it has some of the finest views on the entire trail. As you circle the south slope of Thirteen Mile Rock Butte, the entire Verde River Valley is revealed before you. Pine Mountain Wilderness is the high country on the Verde Rim to the southwest; West Clear Creek is the deep drainage immediately to your north; and the imposing wall of the Black Hills is due west.

Cross a jeep trail after 1½ miles and stay on the old wagon road to mile 10. An attraction of hiking from Thirteen Mile Rock to Clear Creek Campground is experiencing this dramatic landscape from two perspectives: by driving a modern highway and by hiking the parallel historic wagon road.

Perhaps no other hiking trail in Arizona has this intriguing juxtaposition of old and new, which permits the hiker to step back through time while confronting the present. This feeling is nowhere more apparent than in the 2½ miles beyond mile 10, where no more than 50 yards of desert lie between trail and highway. Between miles 7 and 6 you come to the top of a small hill, and West Clear Creek is at your feet. Climb a fence, and after crossing West Clear Creek head west ½ mile to the campground.

ELEVATION:	3,574 feet to 5,500 feet
VEGETATION:	Desert shrub to pinyon-juniper
WATER:	West Clear Creek (purify)
NEAREST SUPPLY POINT:	Camp Verde
SEASONS:	Fall through spring
MAPS:	Walker Mountain, Hackberry Mountain, and Camp Verde Quadrangles (7.5 minute)
MANAGING AGENCIES:	United States Forest Service, Arizona State Parks Board, and Camp Verde Historical Society

Sedona Ranger District

Red Rock–Secret Mountain Area

Oak Creek Canyon is a 16-mile long, 2,500-foot deep gorge that drains much of the Coconino Plateau, the famous red-rock country north of Sedona. Red Rock–Secret Mountain is a 47,480-acre RARE II area of such outstanding beauty that the National Park Service was directed to study the area for possible inclusion in the National Park System. The area is bordered on the east by Oak Creek Canyon, on the north by the West Fork of Oak Creek, on the west by Sycamore Canyon Wilderness, and on the south by the town and ranches of Sedona.

First inhabited by the southern Sinagua around 1200 A.D., the area saw its first white settlers in 1879. Since that time, people have come to live in, develop, and enjoy Arizona's red-rock country. Fortunately, the area is presently protected pending RARE II evaluation. Many longtime Sedona residents would prefer wilderness classification to national park status, with the attendant crowds, traffic, fast-food stands, curio shops, and billboards that characterize many national park gateways.

The serpentine West Fork of Oak Creek is 20-odd miles long. Because of its diverse riparian woodland, 1,717 acres near the lower end of the West Fork was set aside as Oak Creek Canyon Natural Area. A hike through this deciduous tree-filled gorge, as charming a walk as any in Arizona, can take from a few hours to several days. It is the natural gateway to the Red Rock–Secret Mountain area.

To reach the mouth of the West Fork of Oak Creek, drive north from Sedona on U.S. 89A for 9½ miles to an indistinct turnout on the right side of the road. If you reach Cave Springs Campground, you've gone too far; the West Fork of Oak Creek is ¾ mile back down 89A. The turnout was once marked by the grand Mayhew Lodge, which was acquired by the Forest Service but burned down while under their care. A USFS paved path descends between private driveways to Oak Creek. Cross the creek and skirt to the left of a fence, which once guarded Mayhew Lodge. The trail begins beyond this fence.

The West Fork Trail is developed for 2½ miles, as it winds along the bottom of the canyon through hanging gardens of maidenhair fern, Arizona cypress, and Gambel oak, beneath spectacular sandstone and limestone walls. The trail is easily followed—except after a flash flood—and marked every ½ mile with painted stumps; it crosses the stream a half-dozen times in the 2½ miles. There are numerous places to picnic, but camping is not permitted in the natural area. With leaves changing colors, fall is a particularly pretty time to hike along the West Fork; consider this when planning your visit.

The 2½-mile mark is a good destination for a day hike; beyond there is no maintained trail. The pieces of trail you're likely to find generally skirt the right bank on a bench above the streambed. The route follows the streambed to its head, which Forest Road 231 crosses in Section 15, about 13–14 miles from the trailhead. A hike to this crossing makes an excellent 2-day backpack. Don't attempt the trip during winter or spring, when high water floods the canyon floor. The West Fork can be dangerous and even impassable at times of high runoff. The creek is also susceptible to flash floods, even when no rain is falling in the immediate vicinity.

An experienced canyoneer can find exhilarating, 1,000-foot routes out of the West Fork below East Buzzard Poi.

Class 3 and class 4 climbing is required as you pick your way up broken slabs of Coconino sandstone, through ponderosa pine and Douglas fir. From East Buzzard Point head west along the ridge until you reach a spur road; this is Forest Road 792. Follow it for 4 miles to Forest Road 231. From this junction it's another generally level 4½–5 miles to 7,196-foot East Pocket Knob. Under favorable conditions the hike from East Buzzard Point to East Pocket Knob should take no more than 3 or 4 hours. East Pocket Knob is a good place to camp; it overlooks Oak Creek Canyon and is a good place to watch the sunrise.

You can return to your car at the mouth of the West Fork of Oak Creek without retracing your steps to East Buzzard Point or descending back into the West Fork. From the Forest Service lookout tower on East Pocket Knob, zigzag east until you reach the AB Young Trail, which heads east-northeast through ponderosa and scrub oak for a mile before breaking out of the trees. From the lip of the Mogollon Rim, the trail dives 1,600 feet in 1½ miles to Bootlegger Campground on the east side of Oak Creek. The silk-tassel, yucca, and mountain mahogany en route make a striking contrast to the deciduous growth along the West Fork and the ponderosa pine and Douglas fir on the rim above. Your vehicle is a mile north of Bootlegger Campground. This loop makes an exciting 2 to 3-day backpack and a comprehensive introduction to the diverse nature of the Red Rock–Secret Mountain area.

The 2½-mile AB Young Trail itself is a breathtaking day hike to the top of the Mogollon Rim.

ELEVATION:	5,200 feet to 7,196 feet
VEGETATION:	Yucca, deciduous woodland, ponderosa pine, Douglas fir
WATER:	West Fork of Oak Creek (purify) and Buzzard Spring (unreliable, call CNF district ranger for information)
NEAREST SUPPLY POINTS:	Flagstaff and Sedona
SEASONS:	Summer and fall
MAPS:	Munds Park, Dutton Hill and Wilston Mountain Quadrangles (7.5 minute); CNF Recreation Map
MANAGING AGENCY:	U.S. Forest Service
STATUS:	RARE II; being studied by NPS for inclusion in National Park System
ACTIVITIES:	Rock climbing

For further information and up-to-date conditions write:

Forest Supervisor
Coconino National Forest
1100 North Beaver St.
Flagstaff, AZ 86001

PRESCOTT NATIONAL FOREST

Prescott can mean two things to Arizonans escaping the midsummer desert heat: the raucous night life of the city's historic Whiskey Row, and the refreshingly cool, ponderosa-clad mountains and contrasting canyon country of the 1,250,000-acre Prescott National Forest.

From the spectacular sandstone and limestone walls of the Sycamore Canyon Wilderness Area to the broad, lazy stretches of Chino, Skull, and Lonesome valleys, from the history-filled Bradshaw Mountains and their gold-flecked creeks to the stark, sometimes inhospitable Weaver Mountains, Prescott National Forest is a land of many moods and seemingly inexplicable contrasts, beckoning the hearty to explore its 337 miles of developing trails.

Bradshaw Ranger District

Thumb Butte Trail (#33)

Two trails are in contention as the most popular in Prescott National Forest: the Thumb Butte Trail and the Granite Mountain Trail. Involving but a 2½-mile roundtrip to and from the butte's basalt summit, the Thumb Butte Trail is the easier of the two and makes an excellent introductory or conditioning hike.

To reach the trailhead, take the Thumb Butte Road 3 miles west from Prescott to the national forest picnic area. The famous butte is to the south; a sign marks the beginning of the trail.

In the first mile, this well-maintained trail gradually climbs 600 vertical feet to the Thumb Butte Saddle. A half-mile up the trail are the remains of a rough-hewn log cabin once used by a "glory holer" who prospected nearby Miller Creek. Placards are positioned along the trail to help identify such local flora as Gambel oak, emory oak, and agave.

From the saddle, scramble another ¼ mile up a secondary trail to Thumb Butte's 6,522-foot summit. From both the saddle and the summit you'll see monolithic Granite Mountain to the north, the standing wave of the Sierra Prieta rim to the west, and elusive 7,971-foot Mt. Union in the maze of green peaks to the southeast. Carry water and return to the picnic area by the same route or by the new, well-marked variation.

ELEVATION:	5,800 feet to 6,522 feet
VEGETATION:	Scrub oak, juniper, and ponderosa pine
WATER:	Miller Creek (unsafe to drink)
NEAREST SUPPLY POINT:	Prescott
SEASONS:	All year
MAPS:	Iron Springs (7.5 minute); Prescott National Forest recreation map
MANAGING AGENCY:	U.S. Forest Service
ACTIVITIES:	Cross-country skiing, rock climbing

Granite Mountain Trail

Because of its "unique geological, historical, and recreational value" and "its close proximity to an urban area," Granite Mountain Trail was designated by Congress in 1979 as a National Recreation Trail, an official category that includes the 2,610-mile Pacific Crest Trail and the 2,023-mile Appalachian Trail.

Even before this designation, Granite Mountain Trail was the most heavily used trail in Granite Basin Recreation Area. It is the main artery into the proposed 8,500-acre Granite Mountain Wilderness and is used by rock climbers who come from afar to climb the 60 routes that ascend Granite Mountain's sculptured buttresses and clean south-facing slabs. Even if you're not a rock climber, the popular hikes up to the Granite Mountain Saddle and the overlook make an exhilarating day's outing.

To reach the trailhead, take Iron Springs Road 3 miles west to the Granite Basin Lake turnoff. Turn right and follow Forest Road 374 for 5 miles to the Granite Mountain trailhead.

From the trailhead proceed west for over a mile to the Blair Pass junction. The trail leading left is the Little Granite Mountain Trail (#37), which crosses, with many ups and downs in 4 miles, the west slopes of Little Granite Mountain and Two Rock Mountain on its way to the trailhead near the Iron Springs summer home area. Another trail (#39) continues straight from the junction, heading west for ½ mile before turning south to join Trail #38 a mile later. If you follow Trail #38 for 3½ miles, you come to the Buckman

Flat wildlife enclosure. En route you may see the desert pig, the javelina, munching a thorny mouthful of prickly pear.

The trail to the right is the fork to take to reach the top of Granite Mountain. Walk through the wooden chute and climb 1½ miles of moderate switchbacks to Granite Mountain Saddle. You can make camp in the trees or continue another mile to the Granite Mountain overlook. There, amid house-sized granite boulders, the early afternoon winds whipping through the alligator juniper, you have achieved a sense of remoteness in a short 4 miles. Whether you plan to camp or head down to the trailhead, take a moment to admire the rugged country surrounding Granite Mountain, habitat to one of the densest populations of mountain lions in Arizona.

The Forest Service is considering extending the trail "from its present summit end to continue along the north rim then south to return to the trailhead near Granite Basin Lake." This extension would be a first-rate conclusion to the present 4-mile hike to the overlooks.

Return by the same route.

ELEVATION:	5,600 feet to 7,089 feet
VEGETATION:	Prickly pear to ponderosa
WATER:	Seasonal at Clark Spring (purify)
NEAREST SUPPLY POINT:	Prescott
SEASONS:	All year, though summer and winter can be harsh
MAPS:	Iron Springs (7.5 minute); Prescott National Forest Recreation Map

MANAGING AGENCY:	U.S. Forest Service
STATUS:	RARE II
ACTIVITIES:	Rock climbing, horseback riding

Groom Creek Loop Trail (#307)

Spruce Mountain (7,696 feet) was named by an early visitor who mistook its Douglas and white fir for spruce. While there isn't a spruce on the mountain, the area abounds with gray squirrels and white-tailed deer. Occasionally, primarily during winter when Spruce Mountain sees few visitors, the tracks of mountain lions can be seen shadowing those of its quarry, the deer.

To reach the trailhead at either end of the Groom Creek Loop, take the Senator Highway 6 miles south from Gurley Street in Prescott to the first Groom Creek Loop Trail sign. The west leg of the trail (#307) is to your left. If you take this leg, the steeper of the two, it's 2½ miles and 1,400 vertical feet to the Spruce Mountain fire lookout. The south loop of the trail begins 0.7 miles farther south on the Senator Highway; it takes a more leisurely 5½ miles to reach the fire lookout. Old mining roads cross the two trails, but frequent yellow blazes make going astray all but impossible. The two trails, which are receiving more frequent use (albeit illegally) from dirt bikes, are pockmarked from glory holes of days of yore and are occasionally rocky. The commanding view of Pine Mountain Wilderness, the San Francisco Peaks, Granite Mountain, and Thumb Butte makes the effort worthwhile.

Ski touring through Spruce Mountain's lovely stands of fir and ponderosa is better experienced than described.

ELEVATION:	6,400 feet to 7,696 feet
VEGETATION:	Ponderosa pine, fir
WATER:	Seasonal, but scarce
NEAREST SUPPLY POINT:	Prescott
MAIN SEASON OF USE:	May through October
MAPS:	Groom Creek (7.5 minute); Prescott National Forest Recreation Map
MANAGING AGENCY:	U.S. Forest Service
ACTIVITIES:	Cross-country skiing

Chino Valley Ranger District

Juniper Mesa

The proposed 10,000-acre Juniper Mesa Wilderness borders the eastern edge of the historic Luis Maria Baca land grant. Approximately 7 miles long and 3 miles wide, this isolated mesa doesn't seem like much of a wilderness area. But once atop the wooded mesa, you see that it has the primeval qualities of Arizona's largest wilderness areas.

Two short trails climb to the summit of the mesa, which stands alone 1,000 feet above the surrounding cow country, escarped on three sides by 100-foot basalt cliffs. The 2½-mile Juniper Spring Trail (#2) ascends the eastern edge of Juniper Mesa, while the 3-mile George Wood Canyon Trail

(#3) reaches the mesa's western periphery. Between these two trails is high desert country of pinyon and juniper trees, with small clusters of ponderosa on the north slopes. Rusted barbed wire and weathered fence posts have been over-grown. Care, compass work, and route-finding ability are needed to follow the trail (#20) that once linked the two maintained trails.

To reach either the Juniper Spring Trail or the George Wood Canyon Trail, take the Williamson Valley Road north from Prescott for 24 miles, where it turns to dirt. Continue north on Forest Road 6 for 15 miles to the Walnut Creek Work Center turnoff (Road 95). Head west on Road 95 for 3 miles to Forest Road 150. The Juniper Spring trailhead is across from the work center at the end of Forest Road 95F (a spur of Road 95). The George Wood Canyon Trail begins 7 miles west of the work center, off Road 150.

ELEVATION:	5,100 feet to 6,400 feet
VEGETATION:	Century plants to ponderosa
WATER:	Seasonal in Juniper and Bull Springs (purify)
NEAREST SUPPLY POINT:	Prescott
SEASONS:	Fall and spring
MAPS:	Camp Wood (15 minute); Prescott National Forest Recreation Map
MANAGING AGENCY:	U.S. Forest Service
STATUS:	RARE II

Woodchute Trail (#102)

Imagine 30-foot lengths of ponderosa thundering down a giant wooden trough from the top of a forested mountain to a burgeoning mining town 5 miles away and several thousand feet below. When Jerome, now a National Historic Site, claimed a population of 15,000 (served by four groceries, six lodging houses, eleven restaurants, seventeen saloons, and a bank), such a Bunyanesque chute existed. It supplied Jerome's smelters with fuel from 7,834-foot Woodchute Mountain.

To reach the Woodchute Trail take U.S. 89A from Prescott to the Mingus Mountain Inn. From the Inn, it's less than ½ mile to the Potato Patch Campground. From the campground, follow Forest Road 107 to Powerline Tank. The Woodchute trailhead, several hundred yards beyond this stockpond, is marked by a wooden sign.

The Woodchute Trail soon ducks to the right of a small forested knob, then follows the exposed south ridge of Woodchute Mountain. It's 2 miles from the trailhead to Woodchute Tank and another gradual mile uphill to the summit of Woodchute Mountain. Woodchute really isn't a peak; it's more of a forested tableland of bunch grass and pines.

Where the trail breaks out of the trees, much of northern Arizona is in sight: the Sedona red-rock country and the Verde Valley are at your feet, and from this isolated, north-facing viewpoint, you can see into the mouth of Sycamore Canyon. Camping here in midsummer, you can sometimes watch cobalt blue lightning dance from one red-rock escarpment to the next. From this summit plateau, marked by a sign, the Woodchute Trail drops quickly through vicious stands of buckthorn almost 2,000 vertical feet in 3 miles to Sheep Camp. A spectacular hike, but one that requires a car shuttle from Jerome on Forest Road 318A—the line in 1893 for the United Verde and Pacific, "the crookedest railroad in the world."

ELEVATION:	5,500 feet to 7,834 feet
VEGETATION:	Buckthorn to ponderosa pine
WATER:	Seasonal, Woodchute tank (scarce, purify)
NEAREST SUPPLY POINTS:	Jerome and Prescott
SEASONS:	All year
MAPS:	Hickey Mountain and Munds Draw (7.5 minute); Prescott National Forest Recreation Map
MANAGING AGENCY:	U.S. Forest Service
STATUS:	RARE II

Camp Verde Ranger District

Pine Mountain Wilderness

At 7,621 feet, Pine Mountain is the high point of both the Verde Rim and the Pine Mountain Wilderness, which is administered jointly by Prescott and Tonto national forests. Comprising only 17,500 acres, Pine Mountain is a small wilderness but is nevertheless a wild area, with steep canyons and heavy brush to contend with if you stray from any of its 10 developed trails. It's also one of the more difficult Prescott National Forest hiking areas to reach.

To reach Pine Mountain Wilderness, take the Dugas Road Exit from I-17 (6 miles north of Cordes Junction). Head east on Forest Road 68 for 22 miles to the Pine Mountain trailhead. A vehicle with high clearance is best for this road.

Having parked at the Pine Mountain trailhead, you enter a primeval mountain forest explored by few people, though still prowled by a diminishing mountain lion population.

Pine Mountain Wilderness may be seen by a short hike to the summit of Pine Mountain itself; or you can make a broad loop that skirts much of the lofty Verde Rim. To begin either hike, follow Trail #159 for 3 miles to its junction with Trail #12. The footing on Trail #159 is good, the walking mostly level, and the vegetation mainly virgin ponderosa and scrub oak. The water in Willow and Pine springs is usually reliable. Take Trail #12 for 1½ miles to its junction with Trail #161. A half-mile of steep switchbacks up Trail #161 brings you to the summit of Pine Mountain.

Pine Mountain makes a good destination for a day hike or a splendid camping area before you continue into such remote southeastern sections of the wilderness as Yellow Jacket Canyon and Skeleton Ridge. If visibility is good, look for the withered volcanic finger of Weaver's Needle, 60 miles southeast in Superstition Wilderness; even without good visibility, you should be able to make out the 30-mile-long crest of the Mazatzal Wilderness to the east.

Return by the same route or any of several well-marked variations. If you have the time and like cross-country travel,

Turret Peak (5,840 feet) at the southwestern end of the wilderness is worth exploring. In 1872, Major George Randall and his troops surprised a group of Apaches encamped on Turret. Overwhelmed by Randall's daybreak attack, the Indians hurled themselves off the mountain rather than be murdered by federal troops.

ELEVATION:	5,000 feet to 7,621 feet
VEGETATION:	Desert shrub, chaparral, and ponderosa
WATER:	Willow and Pine springs, both permanent
NEAREST SUPPLY POINTS:	Camp Verde and Cordes Junction
SEASONS:	Fall through spring
MAPS:	Tule Mesa (7.5 minute); Prescott National Forest Recreation Map
MANAGING AGENCY:	U.S. Forest Service
ACTIVITIES:	Cross-country skiing

Sycamore Canyon Wilderness

Highlighted by a deep, 25-mile-long gorge cutting through the Coconino Plateau's southern edge (the Mogollon Rim), Sycamore Canyon Wilderness has the unique distinction of being simultaneously administered by Prescott, Kaibab, and Coconino national forests. Sycamore Canyon is a rugged riparian wilderness guarded by alluring walls of red sandstone and white limestone at its upper end and bluffs of brown lava at its lower end. Bordering the proposed Red Rock–Secret Mountain Wilderness of the west, it comprises 47,762 acres of primitive canyon and mountain terrain. Wildlife includes black bear, mountain lion, and deer, while vegetation ranges from cactus and mesquite to walnut and sycamore to Douglas fir and ponderosa pine.

To reach the southern end of Sycamore Canyon, the main point of entry into this wilderness, take Forest Road 161 for 10 miles from Clarkdale to the Sycamore Canyon trailhead, located on the canyon rim. You can hike along the canyon bottom as far as you're prepared to.

If you enjoy watching golden eagles or red-tailed hawks soaring on summer thermals, take the Packard Trail (#66) for 5 miles to the edge of Packard Mesa, where the entire canyon is in view. After an August thunderstorm, when the sun breaks out of the mist and clouds, the breadth of Sycamore Canyon may be spanned with a luminescent rainbow.

If you prefer to be in Sycamore Canyon, the 3-mile jaunt to Parsons Springs makes an enjoyable day hike. Allow yourself an hour and a half for the descent from the trailhead to this verdant spring, which is nestled in mesquite, sycamore, and cottonwood.

It can take up to a week to explore the length of Sycamore Canyon as far as White Horse Lake. The months of April through June are best for arduous backpacking, since water is scarce and unreliable the rest of the year. Allow more time to hike a mile than you normally might. As in many canyon bottoms in Arizona, entire sections of the trails were washed away by the particularly heavy runoff that flooded Sycamore Canyon during the spring of 1979. Footing can be uncertain while you hop from one boulder to the next.

If you want to climb out of the deep gorge, Sycamore Trail (#116), Taylor Cabin Trail, and Trail #7 take you to the top of Sycamore's precipitous eastern rim. If you're an ardent canyoneer, you can scramble out of Sycamore Canyon in many places.

Rather than carrying a tent, you can find a comfortable cave or protective overhang in many places along the canyon bottom. Many of these caves were inhabited by Indians as long ago as 1200 A.D.

ELEVATION:	3,000 feet to 7,000 feet
VEGETATION:	Cactus, walnut, sycamore, fir
WATER:	Summers Spring, Parson Spring (purify)
NEAREST SUPPLY POINT:	Clarkdale
SEASONS:	April through June, September to mid-November
MAPS:	Bill Williams Mountain (15 minute), Loy Butte, Sycamore Point, Cathedral Caves, Picacho Butte S.E. (7.5 minute); Prescott National Forest Recreation Map
MANAGING AGENCY:	U.S. Forest Service
ACTIVITIES:	Swimming

Crown King Ranger District

Castle Creek (proposed wilderness)

Rising abruptly from elevations of 3,000 feet in Black Canyon on their eastern flanks and 4,000 feet in Peeples Valley on their western slope, the 8,000-foot Bradshaw Mountains are a formidable mountain chain that stretches from man-made Lake Pleasant in the south to Prescott in the north. At 6,704 feet, Horsethief Lookout provides the adventuresome traveler with an unparalled view of the southern half of these historic, gold-bearing mountains and much of the proposed Castle Creek Wilderness.

The size and ruggedness of the Bradshaws, combined with their charming history, might result in the Crown King District being overcrowded were they not remote and difficult to reach. Even the numerous trails that penetrate the Bradshaws' scruffy periphery begin at trailheads reached only with tenacity and a stout vehicle. To get into the heart of Crown King's backpacking and horseback-riding country, take Forest Road 259 from the Bloody Basin interchange on I-17 to Crown King. From Crown King, take Road 52 south-southeast to Kentuck Springs Campground, which offers access to a variety of canyon and mountain forest trails—trails ranging in length from a playful 1¼ miles to a more fatiguing 11 miles.

To witness the aftermath of the devastating 26,000-acre Castle Fire—the awesome, disheartening beauty of the charred skeletons of stately pines—take the Castle Creek Trail (#239), which leads into the middle of the proposed Castle Creek Wilderness. It's just under 5 miles to Bench Well, usually a good water source, though the water should be treated. From the Bench Well junction, continue on the Castle Creek Trail for 2 miles to the Lower Dead Cow Spring junction. If you turn right, Trail #240 takes you in 3 rocky miles past Bill Arp Spring and Bill Arp Mine to the Howard Silver Mine in Black Canyon.

If you turn left at Lower Dead Cow Spring, you'll be on the Twin Peaks Trail, which eventually brings you back to your car. After climbing for 2 miles to Upper Dead Cow Spring, you can see Poland Creek, a massive, boulder-strewn drainage dropping from the southeastern Bradshaws and forming the northern boundary of the proposed Castle Creek Wilderness. If you wish to explore the intricacies of this awesome gorge, do so in the fall, when the water is low and temperatures are moderate. From Upper Dead Cow Spring, it's 1.2 miles to Twin Peaks—at 6,881 feet the high point of the Castle Creek area. From this vantage you can see into the mouth of Horsethief Canyon and Hell's Hole several thousand feet below. Trail #223 takes you through Horse-thief Canyon to Poland Creek, an enjoyable hike in late spring or fall but best avoided in summer. From Twin Peaks, it's slightly over 2 miles on Trail #240 back to Kentuck Springs Campground.

Before returning, take a moment to look at the view to the east. It's the plateau country of Black Mesa and Crooks Mesa, cut by the drainages of Bishop, Silver, and Black Canyon Creeks. When heavy spring runoff or August monsoons fill these normally dry washes with roaring flash floods, they feed the Agua Fria River, which drains into Lake Pleasant, periodically washing out highway bridges en route.

From Kentuck Springs Campground, you can make a rewarding 1¼-mile hike south up Trail #217 to Horsethief Lookout. You can contour another 1½ miles from the lookout to Coal Camp Spring on Trail #696. Endurance riders use the corral and cool spring water at Coal Camp and Ben springs to refresh their horses on daylong rides from Black Canyon City to Crown King.

Several other trails can be reached from Coal Camp Spring. The 3-mile Tip Top Trail follows Boulder Creek beyond the national forest boundary. The mile-long East Fort Trail leads to a former Indian encampment with a commanding view of Black Canyon. The Willow Spring Trail quickly descends into the chaparral-covered basin below the forested Horsethief massif. And the ¼-mile South Fort Trail leads to another Indian lookout, a forested knob with one of the most spectacular views in the southern Bradshaws. From South Fort, you can see the Sonoran Desert ranges 50 miles south: the Sierra Estrella, the White Tanks, the Big Horns, and the Eagle Tails.

ELEVATION:	3,000 feet to 6,881 feet
VEGETATION:	Desert shrub to ponderosa pine
WATER:	Coal Camp Spring, Bench Well, Bill Arp Spring, Lower and Upper Dead Cow Springs, Ben Spring, and Willow Spring. Seasonal. *Check with district ranger beforehand.*
NEAREST SUPPLY POINTS:	Crown King, Black Canyon City, Cordes Junction, Mayer

SEASONS:	Depending on access point, all year, though primarily spring through fall
MAPS:	Crown King, Bumble Bee (7.5 minute); Prescott National Forest Recreation Map
MANAGING AGENCY:	U.S. Forest Service
STATUS:	RARE II
ACTIVITIES:	Cross-country skiing, horseback riding

This is only a selection of recreation trails in Prescott National Forest. For further information and up-to-date conditions write:

Supervisor's Office
Prescott National Forest
P.O. Box 2549
Prescott, AZ 86302

TONTO NATIONAL FOREST

"It is the most beautiful region I ever remember to have seen in any part of the world. A vast forest of gigantic pines, intersected frequently with open glades, sprinkled all over with mountain meadows and wide savannas, and covered with the richest grasses. . . ." It was well over 100 years ago when Lieutenant Edward Beale, of Beale's Wagon Road fame, spoke so glowingly of the northern half of the 2.9 million acres that now constitute Tonto National Forest. This is the Mogollon Rim country, southern escarpment of the Coconino Plateau, and the primeval forest lands immediately below. Much of the Tonto's southern half is austere Sonoran Desert terrain, including Bloody Basin, the New River Mountains, Apache Leap, the Black Jacks, and the Goldfield Mountains: cow and mining country, country with deep roots in Arizona history.

Tonto National Forest is notable for incorporating vast acreages of arid desert and semi-desert lands, as well as the timbered lands normally associated with a national forest. Of special interest are the largest national forest wilderness in the state, the mountainous 205,000-acre Mazatzal Wilderness, and the most publicized wilderness, the legendary Superstition Wilderness, comprising 124,117 acres of desert interrupted by volcanic rock pinnacles.

Mesa Ranger District

Superstition Wilderness

> Granted that they did not find the riches of which they had been told; they did find the next best thing—a place in which to search for them.

> PEDRO DE CASTENADA, 1545

Over the years people have died of thirst in the scorched, undifferentiated terrain of the Superstition Mountains. Others have died from snakebite. Still others have been murdered, their skulls shattered from ambush. But whether modern

Argonauts or simply curious travelers, they had something in common. Each was drawn into the Superstitions by the tyrannical magic of Jacob Waltz and his Lost Dutchman gold. Thirty-seven mysterious deaths have taken place in the Superstitions since that white-bearded, gold-pilfering immigrant skulked around the box canyons and precipitous ridges.

Most hikers are lured to the Superstitions—for either a day hike or an extended backpack—as much by its aura of mystery as by its awesome beauty and ruggedness. Is it possible to travel through such country and live to tell about it? Yes, if you go prepared, avoid the parched summer months, and can resist the inexplicable lure of the Lost Dutchman legend, which so pervades these mountains.

Of the 21 trailheads providing access to Superstition Wilderness, First Water and Peralta Canyon are the most heavily used. On weekends during the peak seasons of fall and spring, Tonto's Wilderness Information Specialists register up to 500 people a day at these trailheads. Of the numerous routes worth exploring in the Superstitions that take you far from the crowds of metropolitan Phoenix, none is more rewarding or less frequently traveled than the Superstition Mountain traverse.

To reach the start of this hike, take U.S. 60 (also 80/89) from Apache Junction to Florence Junction, where Highway 80/89 turns south. Continue on U.S. 60 for 2 miles to the Peralta Road turnoff. Turn left and follow this improved dirt road (Forest Road 77) 7 miles to Carney Springs Road. Turn left and proceed another mile to Carney Springs Campground and the West Boulder trailhead.

In the first mile, the steep West Boulder Trail climbs over 1,000 feet to an unnamed pass at 3,600 feet. Avoid camping on this saddle, a former Indian encampment sacred to the Apaches, who once inhabited the Superstitions. From the saddle, you can follow the West Boulder Trail 2½ miles to Willow Spring and beyond, or you can picnic at the saddle before turning back.

To continue the traverse of Superstition Mountain, head southwest from the saddle following a prominent ridge to Superstition Mountain's 5,057-foot south summit. It's a steep, trailless 2½ miles to the summit, but you can see the entire route from saddle to summit. Stay as close to the ridgeline as the alien-looking dacite pillars permit.

Several good camping spots are found a few hundred yards southwest of the south summit. To the northeast is the withered finger of Weaver's Needle. This well-known landmark figures in the legend of the Lost Dutchman Mine, because it was the last thing mentioned by Jacob Waltz on his deathbed: "There's a great stone face looking up at my mine. If you pass three red hills, you've gone too far. The rays of the setting sun shine on my gold. Climb above my mine and you can see Weaver's Needle." Naturally, many modern treasure seekers begin their search near the Needle.

Beyond Weaver's Needle stands the entire jagged skyline of Superstition Wilderness. To the north you can see the snow-capped 7,657-foot summits of Four Peaks, the southern extension of the Mazatzal Mountains and a mountain sacred to the Fort McDowell Indians.

The 5 miles of ridge between the south summit and Superstition Mountain's 5,024-foot north summit is an exhilarating trek, though not particularly difficult, as most of the climbing is behind you. Stay on the ridge or just below it on the west side until you reach Summit 4,402 about 4 miles along. (On the Goldfield quadrangle, Summit 4,402 is at the north end of Section 16.) Here you must find a passage through the notch ahead; it's an unexposed and nontechnical scramble down a series of rock steps, though you may choose to pass packs by hand. From the notch, it's another mile to the north summit. The descent begins between Summits 5,024 and 4,861 with a steep, trailless—though unexposed—scramble down talus into Siphon Draw. Siphon Draw is one of the prettiest canyons on the mountain. Generally follow the left-hand side of the drainage for the first mile, until a trail appears on the right-hand side, taking you the last ½ mile to the road. From the trail's end, it's another 1½ miles to Goldfield, if you didn't leave a vehicle here before the hike. Goldfield is 5 miles north of Apache Junction on the "Apache Trail," Highway 88.

There is no water on this route, so carry enough for the 1½ to 2 days the traverse requires. Hike in the fall, or in early spring when golden poppies are in bloom. Summer is too hot, and snow often precludes a safe winter trip.

To reach the heart of Superstition Wilderness, avoiding the crowded Peralta Canyon and First Water trailheads, take U.S. 60/89 from Apache Junction to Florence Junction. Drive east from Florence Junction for 2 miles and turn left onto the Queen Valley Estates Road. Follow this road 3½ miles to Whitlow Dam, take the left fork *below* the dam; ½ mile later the Milk Creek Ranch Road begins. Drive, hike, or run 7 miles north on this road to the confluence of Milk Creek and Whitlow Canyon. The Coffee Flat Trail to Whitlow Corral is a 2-mile hike up Whitlow Canyon. Avoid this otherwise charming stretch during the spring flash flood season.

From the Whitlow Corral you can head east or west. If you head east, it's about a mile on the Coffee Flat Trail to Reed's Water, a good camping spot with generally reliable water. The 2 miles from Reed's Water up Randolph Canyon to Dripping Springs are easy walking in the creek bed, though the trail periodically washes out. You can usually find water at Dripping Springs, which is below the confluence of Randolph and Fraser canyons south of the streambed.

From Dripping Springs you can head east up Fraser Canyon to the seldom explored east end of Superstition Wilderness, or you can circle Coffee Flat Mountain, eventually returning to Whitlow Corral. The springs are normally flowing on this enjoyable 12-mile hike. Take the Red Tanks Trail 4 miles to La Barge Canyon. Stay on the north side of the stream bed when heading down the upper canyon for 2 miles to a junction with the Whiskey Springs Trail. From this junction the route back to Whitlow Corral is obvious; a trail now links the Miner's Trail and the Coffee Flat Trail.

With some 150 miles of developed trails in the Superstitions radiating from 21 trailheads, endless variations of loops, figure-eights, and hikes between trailheads can be devised. However, few are as rewarding as the hike and scramble up Fish Creek Canyon. It's one hike sure to bring you in touch with the Superstition's natural history—if you avoid spring vacations, when the first mile of Fish Creek is crowded with sunbathers and day hikers.

From Apache Junction, drive northeast up Highway 88 for 14 miles to Canyon Lake. From Canyon Lake, it's another 10 miles to the mouth of Fish Creek Canyon, which is at the end of the third mile-long switchback as you descend Fish Creek Hill. Park on either side of the bridge.

While no developed trail penetrates the awesome canyon, the route is obvious, though it requires scrambling over boulders. Numerous caves in the dark rhyolitic walls high above Fish Creek invite exploration. To walk the length of Fish Creek Canyon to its confluence with Rogers Canyon, allow the better part of a day, especially if carrying a pack. It's 7 or 8 miles to Rogers Canyon, with the going slower than on developed trails. The Rogers Canyon Trail shown on the Iron Mountain quadrangle exists mostly in the minds of the cartographer who drew the line. In Rogers Canyon are several excellent places to camp before turning back or continuing farther into the Superstitions.

If you plan to continue, pack enough water to reach Mullin Spring or Randolph Spring, and don't count on finding water at either spring. This trip is best done *after* the heavy spring runoff or during a spell of fair weather between winter rains.

If you know the trail system, you can spend an enjoyable week going from Fish Creek Bridge to the Peralta Canyon trailhead. There is nothing like a moonlit night in the heart of the Superstitions, when a delicate white glow covers the desert and the towering century plants and rock pinnacles cast eerie shadows.

ELEVATION:	2,000 feet to 6,265 feet
VEGETATION:	Southern desert shrub to chaparral, unexpected clusters of ponderosa at the highest elevations
WATER:	Unpredictable and unreliable, check with Mesa District Ranger
NEAREST SUPPLY POINTS:	Superior, Apache Junction, and Tortilla Flat
SEASONS:	Fall through spring
MAPS:	Goldfield, Weavers Needle, Iron Mountain, Florence Junction, and Horse Mesa Dam (7.5 minute); Tonto National Forest Recreation Map
MANAGING AGENCY:	U.S. Forest Service
ACTIVITIES:	Rock climbing
REFERENCE:	*Superstition Wilderness Guidebook,* by Michael F. Sheridan. Publishers Press, Inc., Phoenix, AZ
OTHER DATA:	Avoid the Superstitions during summer. Carry more water than you think you'll need. Leave a detailed itinerary and don't stray from it.

Pleasant Valley Ranger District

Sierra Ancha Wilderness Area

The curiously shaped Sierra Ancha Wilderness, which lies west of the Fort Apache Indian Reservation, would benefit from proposed RARE II additions. The area is only 11 miles long from north to south and at its widest, southern end, only 6 miles across; at its narrowest, it's no more than a mile wide. The borders of this 20,850-acre mountain wilderness exemplify the problems of wilderness preservation when mining, timber, and ranching interests take precedence. Of the 49 miles of trails in the Sierra Ancha, 15 miles consist of old jeep trails built during the uranium rush of the 1950s. Yet exciting hiking can be done while nature slowly tries to undo the intrusions of man. The area abounds with cliff dwellings first inhabited by the Salados around 1200 A.D. and is prime bear and mountain lion habitat. The topography is rugged, varying from 3,500 feet along Workman Creek to 7,733 feet near Aztec Peak. Heavy growths of manzanita and mountain mahogany make cross-country travel difficult at lower elevations, and precipitous box canyons restrict off-trail travel at higher elevations. Don't underestimate the primeval nature of this wilderness despite its narrow borders.

You can reach the Sierra Ancha by driving south from Young for 20 miles on the dirt "Globe-Young Highway," Highway 288, to Forest Road 487 or by heading north from Roosevelt Dam for 21 miles on 288 to Forest Road 487. Aztec Peak Lookout, almost 8 miles up Road 487, is a good place to pause and survey the terrain before striking out.

Trail #140 begins from Road 487 a mile below Aztec Peak Lookout. This trail is difficult to follow in places as it cascades 4,000 feet in 8 miles to Cherry Creek. A vehicle may be left on the Cherry Creek Road (203) only if you know that sometimes swollen Cherry Creek can be crossed. If you're not ready for the strenuous hiking this route demands, begin near the Cherry Creek Road, climb Aztec Peak, and spend the night. This hike is also a challenging introduction to the Sierra Ancha.

A less demanding though equally pleasant alternative is a hike along Trail #139 through small clusters of ponderosa for 4 miles from its junction with Trail #140 to Edwards Spring. The hiking is fairly easy, and the panoramas of the country to the east and west are excellent. You can discern the blue tableau of the White Mountains to the east, the craggy 7,000-foot ridge of Mt. Ord, Boulder Mountain, and Four Peaks to the west, and, if you're high enough, the jumbled mass of the Superstitions to the southwest. The Edwards Spring hike makes an exhilarating day hike or a more relaxed overnight introduction to this rough-hewn country.

ELEVATION:	3,500 feet to 7,733 feet
VEGETATION:	Semi-desert, pinyon-juniper, sparse mixed conifer
WATER:	Check with Pleasant Valley Ranger District
NEAREST SUPPLY POINTS:	Young and Globe
SEASONS:	All year, depending on access

MAPS:	McFadden Peak (15 minute)
MANAGING AGENCY:	U.S. Forest Service
ACTIVITIES:	Cross-country skiing
OTHER DATA:	Wildland management research program undertaken in Sierra Ancha Experimental Forest adjacent to the wilderness area.

Cave Creek Ranger District

Mazatzal Wilderness

Wilderness is an idea as much as a place, with modern man learning to pass like the shadow of a cloud across what he did not make and cannot improve.

GILBERT M. GROSVENOR

According to legend, a Paiute Indian pointed to the space between his extended fingers and exclaimed "Mazatzal," meaning "empty place in between," to describe the Mazatzal Mountains. Though white settlers have altered the Mazatzals with haphazard mineral exploration and large herds of cattle, the 205,000-acre Mazatzal Wilderness is hardly an "empty place in between." Rising from 2,600 feet north of Bartlett Lake to 7,888-foot Mazatzal Peak, the wilderness includes every life zone from Lower Sonoran to Canadian, providing cactus for the javelina at lower elevations and berries for the timid black bear at higher elevations. Golden eagles soar over inaccessible scarps of granite, where ancient Sinagua once protected themselves from marauding enemies. Screams of the furtive mountain lion remind local ranchers and visiting hikers alike that this is big, wild country that still demands to be known and understood on its own terms.

Much of the Mazatzal's 180 miles of trails is kept in aboriginal condition by fierce winter snows and summer monsoons. An exception is the well-used Barnhardt Trail (#43). To reach the trailhead, drive 65 miles north from Mesa on Highway 87 to Barnhardt Road (USFS Road 419). Turn left and drive 5 miles to the end of this road, where the Barnhardt Trail starts. Head west past the wilderness boundary and uphill through agave, sotol, and Emory oaks for an easy 1½ miles. The trail begins to steepen here, switchbacking up the south side of deep Barnhardt Canyon, swinging in and out of shaded nooks, and crossing brooks. Four miles out, this trail meets the Sandy Saddle Trail (#231). Follow the Barnhardt Trail, the left fork, another ¾ mile to the Gila/Yavapai county line.

To climb Mazatzal Peak, launch your assault here. You can avoid bushwhacking through manzanita and turbinella oak by locating an old fire road that parallels the county line. Follow it for a mile or so up the northwest ridge of Mazatzal Peak. Here it disappears, but you are most of the way through the burned-over thicket. Another ½ mile up the ridge are level places among wind-blasted ponderosas where you can camp. The summit is a mile farther; the route should be obvious. Avoid the precipitous west face by skirting the ridge crest to the east. From the summit, you can see north to Zane Grey's storied Mogollon Rim country.

To encircle Mazatzal Peak rather than climb it, continue

west from the Gila/Yavapai county line on the Barnhardt Trail for another mile to the Divide Trail junction. If you continue straight ahead at the junction, the Davenport Wash Trail (#89), takes you into the Mazatzal's seldom-hiked outback. This rugged trail is 15 miles long, dropping almost to 2,000 feet where it finally reaches the upper end of the Horseshoe Dam Road (Forest Road 205) after passing the South Fork of Deadman Creek (perhaps named for an errant traveler who attempted this hike in midsummer).

To continue circling Mazatzal Peak, turn south at the Divide Trail junction onto the Divide Trail (#23). Pass the Brody Seep junction, skirt the imposing 1,000-foot west face of Mazatzal Peak—an ice climber's winter delight— and admire the Verde River basin to your west. After 3 miles on the Divide Trail, turn left onto the Y Bar Basin Trail (#44). Drink from Windsor Spring, then hike a mile to the Y Bar Basin Saddle. Turn left again and cross Mazatzal's islands of Canadian zone Douglas fir before plummeting down the last 4½ miles of the Y Bar Basin Trail below Suicide Ridge to the Barnhardt parking area.

The Mazatzal Divide Trail, which crosses the Divide Trail junction, skirts much of the Mazatzal's crest from north to south. Though most of the springs are reliable for a fall or spring backpack, this trail is longer and more difficult than the Chiricahua Crest. Allow 3 to 4 days for the 29-mile traverse. To reach the northern trailhead, drive west from Payson on the East Verde River Road (Forest Road 406) for 10 miles to the City Creek trailhead. The Divide Trail is to your left. Reaching the southern trailhead requires as much route-finding ability as the trail itself does. From the Sunflower Work Center drive north on Highway 87 for 2 miles to Forest Road 201. (On the Reno Pass quadrangle, this intersection is just north of the Cross F Ranch, near BM 3758 in Section 25.) If this road is closed (call Cave Creek District Ranger for information), USFS Road 201 can also be reached from a turn 2½ miles farther north on Highway 87. Stay on Road 201 until you reach its end on the south slope of 7,030-foot Mt. Peeley. The last few miles is an easy place to get your car stuck during winter or spring, so you may choose to hike. Once on the Mazatzal Divide Trail, you'll realize it's one of the better multi-day hikes through the range, even though the trail is in places overgrown.

ELEVATION:	2,600 feet to 7,888 feet
VEGETATION:	Lower Sonoran to Canadian
WATER:	Barnhardt Canyon, Windsor Seep, Club Spring, Davenport Wash, Deadman Creek, Mountain Spring, and Willow Spring (check with Cave Creek District Ranger)
NEAREST SUPPLY POINTS:	Payson, Sunflower, Scottsdale
SEASONS:	All year, depending on access point; even upper elevations can get hot in summer and harsh in winter

MAPS:	Mazatzal Peak, Table Mountain, and Reno Pass (7.5 minute); Payson (15 minute); Tonto National Forest Recreation Map
MANAGING AGENCY:	U.S. Forest Service
ACTIVITIES:	Mountaineering

For further information and up-to-date conditions write:

Supervisor's Office
Tonto National Forest
P.O. Box 13705
Phoenix, AZ 85002

APACHE-SITGREAVES NATIONAL FOREST

Mountain, forest, valley, and streams are blended in one harmonious whole. . . . Few worldwide travelers in a lifetime could be treated to a more perfect landscape, a true virgin solitude, undefiled by the presence of man.

CAPTAIN GEORGE M. WHEELER, 1873

Many people think of Arizona as a lone saguaro cactus protruding from a stark sweep of desert, and a turkey vulture roosting on the bleached bones of a poor migrant who didn't reach the next waterhole. They don't think of subalpine forests, open meadows, or mountain streams running with clear water. They don't envision Apache-Sitgreaves National Forest, which encompasses 2,000,000 acres of mountain country in east-central Arizona. Apache-Sitgreaves National Forest can claim more lakes, reservoirs, and watercourses than any other national forest in the Southwest. Administered as one national forest from Springerville, Apache-Sitgreaves includes the eastern half of the largest continuous stand of ponderosa pine in the nation. It is prime habitat for elk, bear, turkey, deer, and antelope as well as a summer haven for droves of human visitors escaping the stifling heat of the saguaro-and-vulture country to the south.

Springerville Ranger District

Mount Baldy Wilderness

Situated on the northeast slopes of 11,403-foot Mt. Baldy, an extinct volcano that is the second highest mountain in Arizona, is Arizona's loftiest wilderness. Here are the headwaters of the Little Colorado River, which winds across northern Arizona to join the Colorado River at the east end of the Grand Canyon. Mount Baldy is also the state's smallest wilderness, yet its 6,975 acres contain the only subalpine vegetation in an Arizona wilderness. Most visitors come for the unparalleled summit view, while others come to fish the 5 miles of streams for brook, rainbow, and cutthroat trout. The two developed trails in the wilderness are among the best maintained in Arizona, rivaled only by the Chiricahua Crest Trail.

To reach Mount Baldy Wilderness, drive east from McNary on Highway 260 for 16 miles to a junction with Highway 273. Turn right on 273 and proceed southeast for 11 miles to Sheep Crossing. Turn right before crossing the West Fork of the Little Colorado River onto a Forest Service spur road. The West Fork trailhead is ½ mile beyond.

The West Fork Trail is an outstanding 2-day backpack, though most people who travel it—or the East Fork Trail—do so in a day, which minimizes the impact of camping in this small, verdant wilderness. This trail is soft underfoot, almost devoid of the rocks that characterize most other Arizona trails. The pitch of the West Fork Trail (#94) is gradual for the first 2 miles, as it parallels the West Fork of the Little Colorado through a narrow meadow, an ideal place to fish or picnic. A serene ½ mile farther are fine views of Mount Baldy, 1,500 vertical feet above. Where you see a small natural pond on your left, the trail begins climbing through stands of blue and Englemann spruce and corkbark fir. This trail is easily followed, except possibly in winter, when the Mount Baldy Wilderness receives more than half of its 45 inches of annual precipitation, in the form of snow. Continue up the switchbacks, and a mile beyond is the junction of the West Fork and East Fork trails. You will have climbed 1,500 feet in 6 miles.

The treeless ½ mile above the trail junction—as well as the north, west, and south slopes—lie within the Fort Apache Indian Reservation. A permit is required for hiking on the Reservation. (Write Apache Tribal Headquarters, P.O. Box 218, White River, AZ, for information; call 602-338-4385.) To traditional Apaches Mt. Baldy is *Dzil Ligai* ("white mountain") and sacred; it's common to encounter Indians on a religious pilgrimage. Respect their feelings, and you'll be rewarded with the finest views in eastern Arizona.

"The view from the summit was the most magnificent and effective of any among the large number that have come

under my observation. Outstretched before us lay the tributaries of seven principal streams, . . . four main mountain
peaks, . . . and valley lands far surpassing any I have before
seen." Captain George M. Wheeler, leader of U.S. government survey expeditions in the 1870s, was not exaggerating.
After identifying the streams and peaks he was referring to,
try to pick out the Ord/Hurricane Creek route, which traverses the Mount Baldy massif from Snake Spring to Hurri-
cane Lake. It's a seldom done hike on more primitive trails,
and it traverses the range's wilder country. Since it crosses
Indian land, hiking it requires a permit, but it's an excellent
3-day backpack through the heart of the range.

From the West Fork/East Fork trail junction, you can
return the way you came or descend the East Fork Trail 6½
miles to the Phelps Cabin. From Phelps Cabin to Sheep
Crossing is a 4-mile hike along Road 273. It's a fine way
to conclude one of the best high-altitude loops in the state.

ELEVATION:	9,000 feet to 11,400 feet
VEGETATION:	Aspen, ponderosa pine, Engle-mann and blue spruce
WATER:	First 3 miles of the West Fork Trail and miles 1 and 5 descending on the East Fork Trail
NEAREST SUPPLY POINTS:	McNary, Springerville, Greer
SEASONS:	June to September; excellent cross-country skiing in winter
MAPS:	Mt. Ord (7.5 minute)

MANAGING AGENCIES: U.S. Forest Service and Bureau
                       of Indian Affairs
ACTIVITIES: Fishing, cross-country skiing

For further information and up-to-date conditions write:

Springerville Ranger District
P.O. Box 640
Springerville, AZ 85938

CORONADO NATIONAL FOREST

Coronado National Forest has the unique distinction among
Arizona's national forests of including 12 mountain ranges.
Spread across half of southern Arizona, they are the Peloncillo, Chiricahua, Dragoon, Whetstone, Patagonia, Santa
Rita, Winchester, Galiuro, Santa Theresa, Pinaleno, Rincon, and Santa Catalina mountains. These "islands in the
sky"—some rising to over 9,000 feet—enable isolated ecosystems to thrive high above the desert floor and rolling grass
savannahs. They provide a habitat for numerous species of
specially adapted plants and animals, while challenging the
wilderness traveler to adapt to the physical rigors and elevation changes of crossing many life zones.

Douglas Ranger District

Chiricahua Wilderness

Rising spectacularly from 3,000-foot elevations in the San
Simon, San Bernardino, and Sulphur Springs valleys, the
forested Chiricahua Mountains are one of the more sub-

lime—and cooler—mountain chains in the Southwest. Crowning the range's 9,000-foot crest, Chiricahua Wilderness comprises some 18,000 acres. Steep canyons radiate from higher summits like Monte Vista, Fly, and Chiricahua peaks, in places bounded by towering cliffs. Of the 74 mammal species found in this woodland sanctuary, only the rare Chiricahua fox squirrel is endemic to the Chiricahua Mountains. Ponderosa and Chihuahua pine, Douglas fir, and Englemann spruce are a few of the 18 species of trees providing nesting sites for the 244 species of birds that inhabit these mountains.

Of the 111 miles of developed trails that facilitate travel in these craggy mountains, 49 miles lie within the Chiricahua Wilderness. The 4 major access points to Chiricahua Wilderness all have Forest Service campgrounds: Rustler Park, Cave Creek, Bucker Lake, and Turkey Creek. If you're interested in just a taste of the Chiricahuas, use Turkey Creek. From Wilcox, drive south on Highway 186 for 32 miles to the entrance to Chiricahua National Monument. Proceed past the Monument turnoff on Highway 181 for 11 miles to the West Turkey Creek Road (Forest Road #41). Follow Road 41 for 11 miles to the Morse Canyon Campground, which has been abandoned. Morse Canyon Trail (#43) climbs 1,400 vertical feet in 2 miles to Johnson Saddle. From this saddle, you can scramble up Johnson Peak, a satellite of 9,357-foot Monte Vista, or continue up Trail #219 nearly 2 miles to Monte Vista Lookout.

From Monte Vista Lookout, you can see everything that

lies between the southern end of the Chiricahua Wilderness and northern Sonora: the golden grasslands of the San Bernardino Valley; the bristling Pedregosa Mountains, southern extension of the Chiricahuas; and the 6,000-foot Peloncillo Mountains, a RARE II area at the southeastern corner of Arizona. In the right season you may have the fortune of seeing a rare twin-spotted rattlesnake, which is occasionally found near 8,000 feet in Chiricahua Wilderness.

Probably the best way to see the rest of Chiricahua Wilderness is to hike the Crest Trail (#270) from Monte Vista Lookout to Fly Saddle. This 6-mile trail essentially follows the ridge crest of the Chiricahuas, affording the hiker glimpses of Sulphur Springs Valley to the west and San Simon Valley to the east. The Crest Trail skirts both 9,796-foot Chiricahua Peak, the high point of the range, and 9,666-foot Fly Peak, farther north, though short side trails lead to the summits of these peaks. The Crest Trail intersects a half dozen other marked trails worth exploring; most are canyon trails which plunge out of the wilderness area. Although you usually can't find water right on the Crest Trail, such sources as Anita Spring, Bear Wallow Spring, and Bear Springs can be reached by following side trails. But a profusion of trails with occasionally confusing trail signs can cause problems orienting yourself in Chiricahua Wilderness.

No tour of the Chiricahuas is complete without a hike into Bear Canyon. From Monte Vista Lookout, follow the Crest Trail for 1 mile to the Raspberry Ridge Trail (#228). Turn right and traverse Raspberry Ridge for 1½ miles before descending into Bear Canyon. The trail plummets 2,000 feet in the next 2 miles to Rucker Lake Campground and is comparable to hiking halfway into the Grand Canyon. Alternatively, consider hiking up the Raspberry Ridge Trail from Rucker Lake Campground, spending the night near Monte Vista Peak, and hiking back down. Either way, a hike through Bear Canyon enables you to experience how precipitously this "island in the sky" rises from base to summit.

ELEVATION:	6,000 feet to 9,796 feet
VEGETATION:	Upper Sonoran to Canadian
WATER:	Anita, Bear Wallow, and Bear springs (usually available)
NEAREST SUPPLY POINTS:	Douglas and Wilcox
SEASONS:	Spring through fall; also beautiful in winter
MAPS:	Chiricahua Peak (15 minute); Coronado National Forest Recreation Map, Douglas Ranger District
MANAGING AGENCY:	U.S. Forest Service
ACTIVITIES:	Hiking, fishing and cross-country skiing
REFERENCE:	*Hiking Trails and Wilderness Routes of the Chiricahua Mountains,* by Cachor Taylor, Rainbow Expeditions, 1977
OTHER DATA:	American Museum of Natural History research station in Cave Creek

Safford Ranger District

Galiuro Wilderness

The Galiuro Mountains, twin parallel chains of exceptionally rugged mountains in southeastern Arizona, are a wilderness area as primeval in character as any in the United States. Seldom visited, the Galiuros can be difficult both to travel in and to reach. Uncompromising topography, dense stands of catclaw and manzanita, and massive uplifted red blocks limit travel to Forest Service trails and rocky creek beds.

Summer temperatures can soar to 100 degrees in lower canyons like Copper Creek, Redfield, and Pipestream, while heavy winter precipitation can bury the northern exposures of 7,000-foot Bassett, Sunset, and Kennedy peaks under a half dozen feet of snow, resulting in flash-flood conditions in the spring. Rattlesnakes, scorpions, and the rare gila monster may be encountered during the warmer months. You may obtain glimpses of bear, mountain lion, javelina, and white-tail and desert mule deer at cooler times of the year.

The few roads that probe these mountains usually require a 4-wheel-drive vehicle. Except for the abandoned Pride Ranch at the chain's southern end and Power's Garden in the Galiuro Corridor, few man-made improvements are encountered, giving the impression that the Galiuro Wilderness has been affected exclusively by the forces of nature.

Two major trail systems parallel the Galiuros: the Redfield/Rattlesnake Canyon route, which passes between the twin crests; and the East Divide/Rattlesnake Canyon route, which combines ridge and canyon hiking. The East Divide route is the more spectacular of the two and has more than one access point.

From Wilcox take the Fort Grant Road (650) north for 22 miles to its junction with Graham County Road 651. Turn west and follow Road 651 approximately 14 miles to Forest Road 660. Proceed through the gate and park ½ mile beyond.

Follow this 4-wheel-drive road 3.6 miles to the Ash Creek Trail (#287) and hike 3 miles up the Ash Creek Trail to its junction with the Bassett Trail (#277). (Water is usually available at Lower and Upper Ash Creek springs.) The Ash Creek Trail is obvious throughout this climb of almost 3,000 feet. If visibility is good, you can see the 10,000-foot Pinalenos to the east, the Santa Theresas to the northeast, the Rincons and Santa Catalinas to the west, and pyramid-shaped Mt. Wrightson to the southwest. Ascending the final 1 mile and 700 vertical feet to the 7,094-foot summit of Bassett Peak makes a fine introductory hike to the Galiuros.

To see more of Galiuro Wilderness, continue north along the length of the range. At the Bassett Peak junction, turn right and follow the East Divide Trail (also #287), 5½ miles to the base of Sunset Peak. The route is obvious, though the trail is not. It's overgrown with brush but can usually be found just below the crest. (There is no water along this stretch.) Historians say Coronado traveled a little "east of north through the Galiuro Range and across Aravaipa Valley to the foot of Eagle Pass."

At a junction at the base of 7,094-foot Sunset Peak, take the left fork and continue on the East Divide Trail. The fork to the right is the High Creek Spring Trail (#290). The next

2-mile stretch is rocky, devoid of water, and elusive—like many Arizona trails, whether in mountain or desert. Thick brush in the Sunset Peak area, mixed with dense stands of ponderosa, Mexican, and Chihuahua pine, can make relocating a lost trail difficult. Should you lose the faint track, stay on the ridgetop and you should eventually find it.

When you reach a junction and turn from the East Divide Trail onto Trail #285, the way becomes more obvious, with better footing, as the trail drops 1,000 feet in the next mile. The section of Trail #285 that drops to Rattlesnake Creek is overgrown with acacia and manzanita, so make sure you're on the trail before attempting this merciless jungle. The next 3 miles, in which Trail #285 tumbles another 1,000 feet as it winds along Rattlesnake Creek, provide some of the most rewarding hiking in the Galiuros. (Water can usually be found.) At the old Powers Mine Road, now Trail #96, turn right (north) and follow Trail #96 for 3½ miles to Power's Garden.

In 1918 Power's Garden was the scene of a fatal shootout, which started one of the largest manhunts in the history of Arizona. Several structures are still standing, including the Power's Garden Cabin, which is open for public use; it is also periodically used by the Forest Service and by a local rancher for a camp during roundup. (Check with Safford District Ranger for availability.) Power's Garden is situated in the Galiuro Corridor, a narrow strip 9½ miles long by 1½ miles wide, which is not wilderness but is undergoing further review under RARE II.

Continue north from Power's Garden down Trail #96 (actually an abandoned road), much of which is washed out. Stay in the bottom of Rattlesnake Canyon until you reach the base of Power's Hill, 5½ miles from Power's Garden. Ascend the precipitous road for a mile to the top of Power's Hill and follow it another 11 miles to the Aravaipa Road. A 4-wheel-drive or other high-centered vehicle can usually be driven as far as Power's Hill, though, and left as a shuttle, eliminating this long waterless stretch.

ELEVATION:	4,000 feet to 7,671 feet
VEGETATION:	Semi-desert grassland to mixed conifer
WATER:	Power's Garden, Mud Spring, Corral Spring, Holdout Spring, Cedar Spring, Jackson Cabin, Lower and Upper Ash Creek Springs (*Check beforehand; purify*)
NEAREST SUPPLY POINTS:	Klondike and Wilcox
SEASONS:	Spring through fall
MAPS:	Reddington, Galiuro Mountains, and Sierra Bonita Ranch (15 minute); Coronado National Forest Recreation Map, Safford Ranger District
MANAGING AGENCY:	U.S. Forest Service

Santa Catalina Ranger District

Pusch Ridge Wilderness

Of the three designated wilderness areas in Coronado National Forest, Pusch Ridge is the most accessible, though as rugged and perhaps more precipitous than Galiuro Wilderness. Only 10 miles north of downtown Tucson, its 56,430 acres include much of the "Front Range" of the Santa Catalina Mountains. Pusch Ridge is the newest wilderness in Coronado National Forest, designated in 1978. It is perhaps the one wilderness area in Arizona that, when winter snows encrust its granite towers, gives you the enchanted feeling of being somewhere other than in the Southwest, perhaps in the Sierra Nevada.

Eight trailheads provide access to several hundred miles of trails, some well maintained, others more primitive. Heavily used paths offer southern Arizona's hikers, backpackers, mountain runners, and rock climbers an escape from metropolitan Tucson several thousand feet below. Swimming has traditionally been popular in the area, but a tragic flash flood late in the summer of 1981 claimed several victims.

Three major trail systems climb to the 9,000-foot crest of Pusch Ridge Wilderness from the desert floor: the Bear Canyon/Palisades route, the Sabino Canyon/Spencer Ridge route, and the Esperero Canyon/Romera Pass route. However, only one trail system, the East Fork/West Fork/Romero Canyon route, traverses the entire wilderness area from east to west. It intersects each of the other 3 systems, offering the hiker interesting variations.

To reach the east end of the traverse, take the Mt. Lemmon Highway about 3 miles past the Molino Basin picnic area to the abandoned Federal Honor Camp. Park here. (The trailhead at the west end of the traverse is near Rancho Romero, 16 miles north of Tucson on U.S. 80/89, the old Florence roadway.)

Hike along a dirt road west of the Prison Site 1½ miles

to the Sycamore Reservoir trailhead. Follow the Sycamore Reservoir Trail 1 mile, descending almost 600 feet, to the reservoir. The reservoir is a good place for a picnic on a day hike, providing a dramatic view of the West Fork all the way to Romero Pass. From the reservoir, continue north for approximately 50 yards, cross a stream bed, and locate the remains of an old fire road, which forks after ½ mile. Take the left fork and continue west another ¾ mile to the East Fork Trail (#29). Follow it west almost 2 miles to the Box Camp Canyon/Sabino Canyon trail junction. Footing up to this point is excellent.

From the junction proceed 6.8 miles northwest up the West Fork Trail (#24), which climbs 3,000 feet by moderate switchbacks to Romero Pass. (Water is available in Hutch's Pool.) Fortunately, the trail is easily followed. Just below 6,000-foot Romero Pass, the West Fork Trail switchbacks veer to the right, giving the impression that you're headed to the top of Mt. Lemmon, perhaps tempting you to turn left at a junction onto Trail #26. But unless you're going to Cathedral Rock, stay on the switchbacks, which soon trend back left.

Romero Pass makes an ideal camp if you're going to return the way you came. If you are continuing into Romero Canyon, proceed southwest along the crest of the pass for 50 yards. The Romero Canyon Trail (#8) drops over the northwest side of the Cathedral Rock ridge. The descent is trickier than the trail you've hiked: this section hasn't been maintained recently and is washed out in places, so that both trail location and footing are uncertain. The trail avoids the stream bed itself, tending to hug the right (north) bank. From Romero Pass to Rancho Romero is 7 miles; water can usually be found en route.

ELEVATION:	2,800 feet to 8,000 feet
VEGETATION:	Sonoran desert to mixed conifer
WATER:	Romero Creek, Hutch's Pool, Sycamore Reservoir, and others (seasonal; call for information)
NEAREST SUPPLY POINT:	Tucson
SEASONS:	All year, but avoid flash-flood season in spring and late summer
MAPS:	Bellota Ranch and Mt. Lemmon (15 minute); Coronado National Forest Recreation Map; Santa Catalina Ranger District
ACTIVITIES:	Rock climbing, cross-country skiing

Nogales Ranger District

Mt. Wrightson

Three isolated areas in Coronado National Forest are recommended for RARE II wilderness classification: the 7,344-foot Santa Theresa Mountains, north of Galiuro Wilderness and east of Aravaipa Canyon Primitive Area; 9,466-foot Miller Peak, between the Fort Huachuca Military Reservation and the Sonoran border; and 9,453-foot Mt. Wrightson. Of the three, the most eye-catching is pyramidal Mt. Wrightson. Bordered on the south by the historic Luis Maria Baca Land Grant and on the north by the Santa Rita Experimental Range and Wildlife Area, Mt. Wrightson rises a startling 5,000 feet from base to summit. Some 200 bird species are known to nest in Mt. Wrightson's Madera Canyon, including Mexico's colorful coppery-tailed trogon. Like Chiricahua Wilderness, the Mt. Wrightson area is an ideal place for bird watchers, and also for hikers and backpackers. The 12-mile round-trip hike from the end of the Madera Canyon Road to the wind-swept summit of Mt. Wrightson makes an invigorating day's outing or overnight backpack.

From Tucson drive south on I-19 to the Madera Canyon turnoff, near Continental. Head southeast on Road 62 for 7 miles to its junction with Road 70. Turn right on Road 70 and drive another 6 miles to the Roundup Campground.

Follow Trail #134, the "Super Trail," a little over 2 miles to a saddle near 6,400 feet, below the Little Shot Mine, which overlooks Madera Canyon. Here you get your first look at the craggy summit cap of Mt. Wrightson. Climb 1½ miles to Sprung Spring (water) and another ½ mile to Josephine Saddle at 7,000 feet. A memorial erected on this saddle for three Boy Scouts who died in an autumn snowstorm in 1958 is a grim reminder of the drastic weather changes that can overcome an unwary hiker.

Bellows Spring is a mile up the Old Baldy Trail (#94). From Bellows Spring, it's another 1½ miles to 8,800-foot Baldy Saddle. Turn south at the trail junction and climb the northeast ridge of Mt. Wrightson to its summit. You may camp here and witness an Arizona sunrise, but if the wind is blowing, the trees below Baldy Saddle offer a more sheltered site.

From the summit of Mt. Wrightson, with the best panoramic view in southern Arizona, you can identify a half dozen mountain ranges: the Chiricahuas, Dos Cabezas, Galiuros, Rincons, Santa Catalinas, and, most prominent, the granite dome of 7,864-foot Baboquivari Peak 40 miles west. Baboquivari is *I'toi,* the sacred mountain of the Papagos.

ELEVATION:	4,000 feet to 9,453 feet
VEGETATION:	Prickly pear and agave to Mexican and Chihuahua pine
WATER:	Sprung Spring, Baldy Springs, Bellows Spring (purify; check with Nogales District Ranger)
NEAREST SUPPLY POINTS:	Green Valley, Sahuarita, and Tucson
SEASONS:	Spring through fall, though winter's excellent if you're prepared for harsh weather
MAPS:	Mt. Wrightson and Sahuarita (15 minute); Coronado National Forest Recreation Map; Nogales Ranger District
MANAGING AGENCY:	U.S. Forest Service
STATUS:	RARE II
ACTIVITIES:	Bird watching

For further information and up-to-date conditions write:

Supervisor's Office
Coronado National Forest
301 W. Congress
Tucson, AZ 85701

AREAS NOT INCLUDED IN THIS GUIDE

There are four U.S. Forest Service RARE II Areas not covered in this chapter. They are:

Coronado National Forest

   Miller Peak (22,280 acres)
   Santa Teresa (27,160 acres)

Kaibab National Forest

   Kanab Creek (73,170 acres)
   Saddle Mountain (39,190 acres)

   One U.S. Forest Service Primitive Area also falls in this category:

Apache National Forest

   Blue Range Primitive Area (173,000 acres)

National Parks and Monuments

GRAND CANYON NATIONAL PARK

Few natural wonders on the planet have been written about more than the Grand Canyon of the Colorado River. Yet few of the books and articles concerning the Grand Canyon discuss hiking in the Canyon. The opportunities for foot travel in the Canyon are both incredibly rich and unusually challenging. Rather than attempt to condense a world of vital information into a few pages, this book will direct you to sources of detailed information.

The half dozen guidebooks to hiking in the Grand chiefly detail the crowded trails. Most of these guides borrow heavily from J. Harvey Butchart's two-volume *Grand Canyon Treks,* but none addresses itself to *inner* Canyon hiking and trekking better than these two volumes, written by a former math professor who has hiked over 25,000 miles in the Canyon. These small books, pamphlets really, are invaluable aids for the hiker interested in avoiding the more popular and crowded rim-to-river trails detailed in the other guides; they provide the information needed for traveling safely off the beaten path through the inner Canyon. Butchart, more than any other person, has worked out the complex, potentially dangerous peculiarities of the labyrinth on foot. He discovered 96 rim-to-river routes, though in 1882 geologist Clarence Dutton proclaimed that only four existed. In addition, Butchart pioneered 154 breaks through the Redwall Formation, the most formidable and rotten of the Grand

Canyon's major barriers. *Grand Canyon Treks,* Vols. I and II, are published by La Siesta Press, Box 406, Glendale, CA 91209.

The shaded relief map of the National Park, printed by the U.S. Geological Survey, and Bradford Washburn's new map, "Heart of the Grand Canyon," produced by the Cartographic Division of the National Geographic Society, are valuable supplements when you plot a course with Butchart's guides.

Also recommended is *Grand Canyon Perspectives: A Guide to the Canyon Scenery by Interpretive Panoramas,* by Kenneth Hamblin and Joseph R. Murphy. *Grand Canyon Perspectives* interprets the Canyon's seemingly infinite spatial dimensions simply and succinctly. (*Grand Canyon Perspectives* is published by H&M Distributors, Box 7085, University Station, Provo, UT 84602.)

No book puts the Grand Canyon into better historical perspective than J. Donald Hughes' classic *The Story of Man at the Grand Canyon.* It's a colorful, annotated history that will make your Canyon wanderings more enjoyable because it gives humanity a place in this overwhelming natural wonder.

For a more complete listing of references on the Grand Canyon, see *Bibliography of the Grand Canyon and the Lower Colorado River, 1540–1980,* by Earle E. Spamer with George H. Billingsley, William J. Breed, Robert C. Euler and Grace Keroher, Grand Canyon History Association Monograph Number 2. This is a comprehensive bibliography covering periodicals, series, theses, dissertations, popular works, geography, geology, hydrology, ecology,

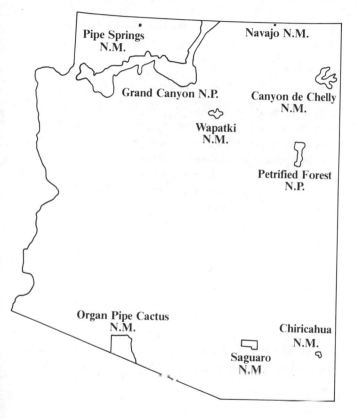

The national parks and monuments of Arizona.

archaeology, history, maps and charts, and miscellaneous entries.

PETRIFIED FOREST NATIONAL PARK

Of the estimated one million people who annually visit Petrified Forest National Park in northeastern Arizona's Painted Desert, fewer than 1% take the time to visit the backcountry. The remainder snap a photo or two and hurry on—or instead of taking a picture, they take "just a small piece" of petrified wood in purse or pocket. That habit started in 1879, when General William T. Sherman carted off a log to Washington, D.C.—a log the Navajos considered to be the bones of the giant Yietso, slain by their forefathers. Bad habits die hard, and each year some 25,000 pounds of petrified wood are smuggled out of the park.

But there is more to do in this park than take pictures or "souvenirs." Over half of Petrified Forest National Park has official wilderness status. Two separate sections, the Painted Desert and Rainbow Forest wilderness areas, provide modern man with the matchless opportunity to step beyond the scenic vistas and explore the subtle beauty of this timeless land.

Southern Half

Rainbow Forest Wilderness

Established in 1970, Rainbow Forest Wilderness is located in the southern half of Petrified Forest National Park. With

7,240 acres, this wilderness is the second smallest in Arizona and one of the smallest in the United States. The gentle topography makes it a splendid area for becoming acquainted with the rigors of cross-country walking. With no trails penetrating its interior and no natural springs, the wilderness retains its primeval nature. For variety, explore this enchanting area by the light of a full moon. Long shadows on the land, curious sounds, and the bright night sky turn Rainbow Forest Wilderness into an otherworldly place.

Fires are not permitted in Rainbow Forest Wilderness—hardly an inconvenience since there's no wood to burn. Camping is not permitted in this area either, and you must register for hikes at the Park Ranger's office.

To reach Rainbow Forest Wilderness, drive 19 miles southeast from Holbrook on Highway 180 to the Petrified Forest National Park entrance. Turn north from 180 and proceed 3 miles to the park museum. Drive or walk the next ½ mile to the Long Logs and Agate House parking area.

Head east from the parking area for ½ mile, to a major drainage. Descend into this drainage and follow it generally east-northeast for 2 miles to the southwestern edge of Puerco Ridge. Continue, following one of several drainages to the top of the ridge. One drainage, the identity of which you must discover for yourself, crosses one of the finest pot shard scatterings to be found in a natural setting. Resist the temptation to pocket pottery or petrified wood. It's rude, and it's a federal offense.

Stay atop Puerco Ridge and proceed northeasterly for 3 easy miles. Unless you're using a compass or have an uncanny sense of direction, the lack of any striking geographical features makes orientation difficult, but if you stray too far east, you meet the East Boundary Road, which eventually connects with the paved Park Road. If you stray too far west, you also reach pavement. Use the Tepees, the Haystacks, the Battleship, and Blue Mesa to maintain your bearings.

Pronghorn abound in the area. If you're fleet of foot, try running with them for 50 yards. If not, look south and try to pick out 10,877-foot Escudilla Mountain or 11,403-foot Mt. Baldy 70 miles away. Pilot Rock (6,235 feet), the highest point in Petrified Forest National Park, is 20 miles to the north.

Puerco Ridge eventually merges with Crystal Mesa. Where it does, turn north and skirt the eastern edge of Crystal Mesa for 4 or 5 miles until you meet an old road. This is the Wallace Tank section of the East Boundary Road, which at this point should be angling northeast. Follow this track another mile or 2 to the Park Road. If you're walking or running from one end of Rainbow Forest Wilderness to the other, park a shuttle vehicle at this junction, which is ¼ mile south of Blue Mesa Loop Drive in the southwest quarter of Section 34.

ELEVATION:	5,300 feet to 5,700 feet
VEGETATION:	Desert grassland
WATER:	None
NEAREST SUPPLY POINT:	Holbrook
SEASONS:	Fall through spring
MAPS:	Petrified Forest National Park (1:62,500)

MANAGING AGENCY: National Park Service
ACTIVITIES: Orienteering

Northern Half

Painted Desert Wilderness

Unlike the narrow, J-shaped Rainbow Forest Wilderness, which is constricted by roads, the broad Painted Desert Wilderness is true wildland not dissected by scenic access roads. Its 43,020 acres of weirdly eroded badlands occupies most of the northern half of Petrified Forest National Park. A natural petrified-log bridge, Indian ruins, fossilized bones, and a clay, silt, and sandstone rainbow of rugged topography offer something for both the day hiker and backpacker.

To reach Painted Desert Wilderness, drive to the Chinde Point picnic area 1½ miles north of the park headquarters. Pick your way north down off Chinde Point ¾ of a mile to Lithodendron Wash. (Camping is permitted north of Lithodendron Wash.) Follow the sandy wash southwest for a mile to the lower end, its confluence with Chinde Wash. The footing is excellent both in the wash and along its rim. Head northwest for ¾ mile, then turn north up Chinde Wash and head for Chinde Mesa. About 1½ miles up this wash, you are west of the Black Forest and Onyx Bridge—one of two petrified-log bridges in the park. A hike to this bridge, then back to Chinde Point, makes a rewarding day hike.

To explore the seldom visited north end of Painted Desert Wilderness, continue north up Chinde Wash all the way to the southern foot of Chinde Mesa. You should be able to find petroglyphs at the 5½-mile mark and ruins ½ mile beyond. Keep your eyes open for antelope and deer. A mile north of the ruins, in the northeast quarter of Section 16, Chinde Wash forks. Take the left fork and follow it 1½ miles to the foot of Chinde Mesa. (In this fork are the remains of a 1920s-vintage Ford truck.) Take care in gaining the 6,008-foot summit of Chinde Mesa. The fluted mounds look softer than they are, and only a 10-foot slide would make you realize how much like ball bearings the surface is. And even if you left your itinerary with a friend or ranger, they'd not quickly find you if you broke a leg. This country is best hiked with a companion.

From the top of Chinde Mesa, locate the Chinde Point picnic area 5½ miles south and plot your return route. If you are planning to loop Pilot Rock rather than return by the same route, memorize your course through the intervening badlands, so that after you descend from the mesa you know where you're going. A loop including Pilot Rock is exciting either as a day hike or overnight trip, because you realize how alone you are in this immense, austere landscape.

Several ridges descend the southwest side of Chinde Mesa; use the most prominent to gain the valley floor. Once on the floor, 1½ miles southwest of the mesa, head west toward Pilot Rock for about 3½ miles. Even without a trail, the footing is good and the brush sparse. At the right time of the year you might find a few potholes with water, but don't count on them. The summit of Pilot Rock is perhaps best approached from the northeast, where there are Indian ruins.

These ruins are unusual in being made from blocks of the black lava prevalent on the summit of Pilot Rock.

The Chinde Point picnic area is 7½ miles due southeast of Pilot Rock, though on foot it's at least 10 miles. Again, visualize your route before starting and use care descending the southeast ridges of Pilot Rock. A mile southeast of Pilot Rock you reach the north fork of Digger Wash. Follow this fork south for ½ mile, then leave it and turn southeast. Descend the northwest fork of Lithodendron Wash 4 miles to its confluence with the main channel of Lithodendron. From the confluence, it's 2 miles back to the Chinde Point picnic area if you return by the route by which you began the hike. If you try a shortcut, you may end up on Pintado Point and walk an extra mile on pavement back to your vehicle.

If you're backpacking, the 24-mile Chinde Mesa to Pilot Rock loop can take from 1½ to 3 days. Remember that you must carry all the water you need. But stay out of washes during flash-flood danger.

ELEVATION:	5,400 feet to 6,235 feet
VEGETATION:	Desert grassland
WATER:	Seasonal potholes at the base of Chinde Mesa and Pilot Rock
NEAREST SUPPLY POINT:	Holbrook
SEASONS:	Fall through spring
MAPS:	Petrified Forest National Park (1:62,500)
MANAGING AGENCY:	National Park Service

ORGAN PIPE CACTUS NATIONAL MONUMENT

Organ Pipe Wilderness

The largest wilderness area in Arizona is 299,600-acre Organ Pipe Wilderness, which constitutes much of 516-square-mile Organ Pipe Cactus National Monument. Bordered on the west by the stark Cabeza Prieta National Wildlife Range and on the east by the vast Papago Indian Reservation, its southern boundary is the Sonora border. Its desolate mountains, broad stretches of desert flats, dry washes, and alluvial fans mark the convergence of three deserts: the California Microphyll Desert, the Central Gulf Coast phase of the Sonoran Desert, and the upland Arizona Succulent Desert. This overlapping desert biota results in unusual mixtures of boojum tree, senita cactus, teddy bear cholla, prickly pear, bur-sage, and creosote bush. Two-hundred-fifty species of birds have been observed in Organ Pipe, many of them at Quitobaquito Springs, a historic watering hole and prehistoric settlement. Of the seven large mammals that live in the wilderness, perhaps the rarest is the small Sonoran pronghorn, with a population of about 500 in Mexico and 75 in the United States. While there have been no official sightings, the Mexican jaguar and the gray wolf are also believed to roam through Organ Pipe. The list of mammals, reptiles, and amphibians numbers over 100, a striking testimony to life's ability to adapt to a harsh desert environment.

The Organ Pipe region saw its first human habitation at least 12,000 years ago; it was much later inhabited by the Sand Papagos. From the 1500s through the 1700s, it was traversed by most of the prominent Spanish missionaries and explorers, including Melchoir Diaz on his way to the Colorado River, Father Francisco Garces en route to the Gila River, Padre Eusebio Kino linking his Mission San Marcelo in Sonoyta with Yuma, and Juan Bautista de Anza blazing a route from California to Mexico. Of all the historic routes that crossed the area, none is more infamous than *El Camino del Diablo,* The Devil's Highway. Pioneered by Padre Kino during the late 1600s, *El Camino del Diablo* paralleled the present southern border of Organ Pipe and traversed the merciless Tule, Lechuguilla, and Yuma deserts. Because *El Camino del Diablo* was the only route across southern Arizona not subject to attack by hostile Indians, it was used heavily during the 1800s. This notorious desert track claimed the lives of over 250 Argonauts en route to the California gold fields.

Foot travel through Organ Pipe Wilderness has changed little and can be just as unforgiving during the brutal summer months. As there are few established trails in Organ Pipe, most of the hiking is cross-country. Because of the nature of the land, hiking is not particularly difficult if you come prepared for desert travel and visit the area between late fall and early spring. The few trails that do traverse the area are clandestine migration routes heavily used by northward-surging Mexican nationals en route to employment opportunities. One of these trails, linking several permanent springs, indicates how hiking should be approached in Organ Pipe. There is little permanent ground water, except when the *tinajas* fill after sudden rains, so you either have to carry all

the water you need—a gallon per person per day, *minimum*—
or design your trek around the location of the springs. Even
if your plans are no more ambitious than a spring day hike,
carry an automobile survival kit.

To reach Organ Pipe Cactus National Monument, drive
south from Ajo on Highway 86 for 11 miles to Why. Turn
south on Highway 85 and drive 26 miles to the visitor center.
You must secure a permit here before venturing into the
backcountry. Both developed roads in the monument are
loops: the 21-mile Ajo Mountain Drive and the 51-mile Puerto
Blanco Drive. Both begin at the visitor center, and both
provide access to unparalleled desert hiking and trekking.

If you're interested in something longer than the popular
Bull Pasture and Montezuma's Head day hikes, a good 2- to
3-day backpack crosses Organ Pipe's seldom explored west
end. Most of the hiking is on an old jeep trail, and as it links
three waterholes, it's a good introduction to desert hiking.
From the visitor center, drive 4 miles south on Highway 85
to the southern leg of Puerto Blanco Drive. Turn west and
drive 15 miles to Quitobaquito Springs and a picnic area.

Park near Puerto Blanco Drive and hike north on the road.
Looking west after a mile, you can see the drainage leading
up to Burro Springs at the southern end of Quitobaquito
Hills and, ¼ mile north, the drainage leading to Williams
Spring. These two springs are often reliable, but camping
is not permitted in this entire area, as wildlife rely heavily
on these waterholes. At mile 2 is a fork in the road. Take
the left fork, which is the primitive road you'll be hiking
on. If you don't enjoy walking on this track, parallel it on

either side. Cipriano Pass is at mile 4; once across this pass, you are in the California Microphyll Desert of bur-sage and creosote bush flats. Near mile 6, Pozo Nuevo is to your left, marked by an old shack, a windmill, and a stock tank. This is a good place to obtain water or to camp. Don't camp closer than ½ mile to the waterhole, though, as wildlife depend on it. At BM 1,247, about mile 8, Cipriano Hills are east of you. The hills were named for a local hombre named Cipriano Ortega, who made "little ones out of big ones" at the Victoria Silver Mine. At mile 10, cross a series of braided washes. To scramble up 3,197-foot Kino Peak, head east, either down a major wash or along the T.15S/T.16S boundary line 3½ miles, or just beyond I,1,438. Follow this drainage north 3 miles to a prominent notch east of Kino Peak. From the notch, scramble up ledges to the summit. There's a register on top, and the view puts the immense desert in better perspective. Unless you are doing this climb during the wet season, though, Kino Peak is better approached from Bates Well (see below).

Looking west from mile 11 at the open country, you begin to understand what confronted the early explorers. At mile 16, near the Bates Well junction, you can get a taste of *El Camino del Diablo* by following its track for 3 miles to the west boundary of the Organ Pipe Wilderness. You can follow this track all the way to Yuma, and some people still do each year, in 4-wheel-drive caravans. Driving or walking, the trek across Cabeza Prieta National Wildlife Refuge requires a permit, as some of the route is subject to periodic shelling from the Luke Air Force Gunnery Range. (Applications for permits should be directed to the U.S. Fish and Wildlife Service, P.O. Box 418, Ajo, AZ 85321.)

To reach Bates Well from mile 16, turn east at the junction and hike 6 miles to this former mining settlement. There should be water here, but obtain information beforehand from monument headquarters. Bates Well is a good place to leave a shuttle car. It's 20 miles south of Ajo on the Bates Well Road.

During spring, if you have the time, hike north from mile 17 (BM 1,198) across a series of washes paralleling Growler Wash on the north to Peak 1,787. The spring flowers, the birds, and the isolation provide a desert experience few people have. It's a 6-mile round-trip, perhaps best approached by leaving your vehicle at BM 1,242, near the end of the Bates Well Road, then hiking the 2 miles to BM 1,198 before striking north.

To reach Kino Peak from Bates Well, head southwest down Growler Wash for nearly 2 miles. Scramble out of the wash and head south-southeast for 1 mile to a prominent east/west drainage. Follow this drainage until it forks about ¾ of a mile later. Take the south fork and follow it for 2½ miles to the prominent notch east of Kino Peak. There are places to camp in this notch, though burning firewood is not permitted in Organ Pipe Wilderness. From the notch, scramble up a series of interconnecting ledges to the summit. Kino Peak makes a long day hike or a good overnight backpack.

There are also numerous hikes and treks in the section of Organ Pipe east of Highway 85. Most involve ascents to the Ajo Range, which is the geographical boundary between the

Papago Indian Reservation and Organ Pipe Cactus National Monument. As in the west half of Organ Pipe, little ground water is to be found, so most hikes from Ajo Mountain Drive are limited to 1–3 days, or by the amount of water you can carry. But detailing all the hikes in so vast an area as the Organ Pipe Wilderness is beyond the scope of this guide.

ELEVATION:	1,100 feet to 4,808 feet
VEGETATION:	Creosote bush to elephant tree
WATER:	Call for information
NEAREST SUPPLY POINTS:	Ajo and Why
SEASONS:	Late fall through early spring
MAPS:	Organ Pipe Cactus National Monument (1:63,500); National Park Service Recreation Map
MANAGING AGENCY:	National Park Service
REFERENCE:	*Routes to Desert Watering Places in Papago Country, Arizona,* by Kirk Bryan. Water-Supply Paper 490-D, U.S. Government Printing Office, Washington, DC.

For further information, write for the 3-page "Hiking and Mountaineering Guide to Organ Pipe Cactus National Monument" to:

Organ Pipe Cactus National Monument
Box 38
Ajo, AZ 85321

SAGUARO NATIONAL MONUMENT

The 78,720-acre Saguaro National Monument was established to protect the incomparable stands of leviathan saguaro cactus that have been growing in this part of the Sonoran Desert for thousands of years. To further protect the area, 71,400 acres were designated official wilderness. While the desert scrub and grassland-transition plant communities dominate the small western section of Saguaro National Monument, the much larger—and higher—eastern section includes both of these communities, as well as oak woodland, oak/pine woodland, ponderosa pine forest, and Douglas fir/white fir forest. Both the Tucson Mountain Unit (the western section) and Rincon Mountain Unit (the eastern section) provide the backcountry traveler with rugged wilderness adventures despite their proximity to sprawling Tucson.

Tucson Mountain Unit

To reach the Tucson Mountains, drive west from I-10 (Speedway) 10 miles to the Bajada Loop Road. Turn right and drive a mile to the Hugh Norris trailhead. The 11-mile round-trip hike described here begins at approximately 2,600 feet. The trail is well marked and heavily used; there should be no difficulty following it to the 4,687-foot summit of Wasson Peak, except during winter when snow may be encountered as low as the trailhead. The trail climbs steeply in the first ¾ mile, then begins switchbacking. Some of the switchbacks are steep, but level sections give your legs a chance to recover. After 3 miles you reach an intersection.

Continue across it and climb toward Amole Peak. From the exposed trail, you can pick out Baboquivari Peak and Kitt Peak to the south, Mt. Wrightson and Miller Peak to the southeast, and—from the summit of Wasson Peak a few miles farther—the entire Santa Catalina Range and the 8,000-foot high Mica Mountain and Rincon Peaks crowning the eastern section of Saguaro National Monument. There is no water on this trail; carry enough for your needs. If you plan to camp, get a permit at the Tucson Mountain Visitor Center.

ELEVATION:	2,600 feet to 4,687 feet
VEGETATION:	Saguaro-ocotillo to desert grassland
WATER:	None
NEAREST SUPPLY POINT:	Tucson
SEASONS:	All year
MAPS:	Avra and Jaynes quadrangles (7.5 minute)
MANAGING AGENCY:	National Park Service
OTHER DATA:	The Arizona-Sonora Desert Museum is located in this section of Saguaro National Monument (see last section of this chapter).

Rincon Mountain Unit

To reach the Rincon Mountains, which constitute most of the eastern half of Saguaro National Monument, drive east from Tucson on the Old Spanish Road to Freeman Road.

Turn south; the national monument headquarters are ½ mile south on the left. If you plan an overnight hike into the Rincons, get a backcountry permit at headquarters. The Mica Mountain trailhead is a mile south of headquarters on the south side of a picnic area. The trail is well maintained, but unless you're in excellent condition, you'll need to camp before reaching 8,666-foot Mica Mountain. The 15-mile trail climbs more than a vertical mile through six life zones.

From the picnic area, head south for 1 mile to the foot of Tanque Verde Ridge. Here the trail begins climbing in earnest to Juniper Basin, at mile 6, where some enterprising hermit hauled up enough cement to construct a cabin. You can usually find water in this drainage during spring runoff. After dropping into Juniper Basin and climbing out its right side, you begin climbing the southwest ridge of Tanque Verde Peak. You reach the top 2 miles later, before descending a moderate grade to 6,400-foot Cow Saddle and a trail junction, 10½ miles from your trailhead. If you are low on water, you can make a steep 4-mile round-trip hike to Grass Shack Spring. But Manning Camp is 4½ miles closer to your objective, and you can almost always find water in the creek. Manning Camp is a good place to camp, as is Spud Rock Cabin, which usually has dependable water as well.

Being a ridge route, the hike up Mica Mountain affords unparalleled views from base to summit of much of southern Arizona.

ELEVATION:	3,200 feet to 8,666 feet
VEGETATION:	Saguaro to Douglas fir/white fir
WATER:	Douglas Spring (contaminated), Juniper Basin, Grass Shack, Manning Camp, Spud Rock
NEAREST SUPPLY POINT:	Tucson
SEASONS:	Fall and spring
MAPS:	Rincon and Happy Valley (15 minute)
MANAGING AGENCY:	National Park Service

National Wildlife Refuges

Theodore Roosevelt started the National Wildlife Refuge system in 1903, setting aside Pelican Island, Florida, as a "preserve and breeding ground for native birds." The system idea indicates the president's concern over the fate of wildlife in a growing America and his recognition of the need for undisturbed habitat set aside for the survival of certain species. Approximately 400 refuges in the United States today embody the belief that people should allow all living things their place in the world. Refuges are spread from coast to coast and include arctic tundra, marshlands, desert, plains, mountains, and islands. Most of the habitats contain both land and water areas.

Refuge managers strive to maintain a balanced program for migratory birds, big game animals, endangered species, and nongame species. Southwest refuges have special programs for unusual wildlife: the Kofa Game Range in West Central Arizona hosts the endangered desert bighorn sheep; the Bosque del Apache National Wildlife Refuge in New Mexico participates in a unique experiment in which chicks of the endangered whooping crane are given sandhill cranes as foster parents. Other special Southwest wildlife needing protection are the ocelot, jaguarundi, eagle, peregrine falcon, pronghorn, beaver, and red wolf.

National Wildlife Refuge managers also supervise research aimed at assuring the perpetuation of each native animal and plant, as well as interpretive programs and other services intended to broaden our understanding and appreciation of our environment and our role in it. In addition, National Wildlife Refuges have recreation goals: to assure people opportunities to participate in the wilderness experience.

Most of the refuges can be considered wilderness areas, and most are open to wildlife enthusiasts. But few trails are maintained for hikers, who must study their maps and plot their own adventures. Each refuge is administered differently and should be contacted by mail or phone before you make final plans to trek through the area.

Refuges in Arizona include Cabeza Prieta NWR, Havasu NWR, Kofa NWR, and Imperial NWR.

CABEZA PRIETA NATIONAL WILDLIFE REFUGE

Cabeza Prieta, established in 1939, encompasses 940,000 acres of desert in Yuma and Pima counties, on the Mexican border. Larger than Rhode Island, it includes 12 mountain ranges, which contain desert bighorn sheep, Sonoran pronghorn, desert tortoises, desert kit fox, and a great variety of reptile life. Over 200 species of birds have been recorded in this refuge.

Granitic and lava mountain ranges are separated by broad desert valleys—the typical Basin and Range Province profile. Elevations vary from 200 feet to 3,000 feet. Summer is extremely hot and dry, but winter temperatures are moderate. Vegetation consists of Lower Sonoran zone creosote and mesquite, other desert shrubs, cactus, and a few unusual plants found nowhere else: the elephant tree, sinita cactus, and Kearney sumac. Waterholes and wells are scarce, though some have been developed by the Bureau of Sport Fisheries and Wildlife.

The refuge lies in the path of spring bird migrations that pass around the head of the Gulf of California. These migrations can be observed from February to June. In summer, flocks of white-winged doves swoop down onto mountain waterholes.

Since rainfall varies from 3 inches per year at the western edge to more than 10 inches on the eastern edge, a great variety of resident birdlife frequents the *charcos*, dugout-type waterholes in the Growler Valley. In especially wet years, atypical bird species, such as the horned lark and meadowlark, breed in the range. Proximity to the Gulf of California results in the occurrence of such birds as white pelican, osprey, and ring-billed gull.

Most roads in the area are scarcely more than trails, so travel can be hazardous. Motorized travel is permitted only on designated roads, and 2-wheel-drive vehicles may not get through some of the sandy washes encountered on these roads. Off-road vehicles are prohibited. There are no facilities for gasoline, sanitation, or drinking water.

Early visitors crossed this extremely arid environment to seek fortunes in gold and other minerals in California. *El Camino del Diablo,* the Yuma-Caborca Trail, which stands virtually untouched since men with wagons and horses attempted the bleak crossing, bears testimony to the hardships endured by these hardy pioneers.

The values of hiking, photography, and nature observation are recognized; they are permitted in all areas except where military gunnery ranges operate. Camping is permitted, though state laws prohibit camping within ¼ mile of waterholes and within 50 feet of designated roads. Campfires are permitted, but firewood is scarce.

Applications for entry permits and other inquiries should be directed to one of the following offices:

Main Arizona/New Mexico Office
U.S. Fish & Wildlife Service
2953 W. Indian School Road
Phoenix, AZ 85017

Cabeza Prieta NWR
P.O. Box 418
Ajo, AZ 85321

U.S. Fish and Wildlife Service
P.O. Box 1032
Yuma, AZ 85364

KOFA NATIONAL WILDLIFE REFUGE

The Kofa and Castle Dome mountains and the intervening King Valley make up most of this refuge, located northeast of Yuma, south of Quartzsite, and east of U.S. 95. This 660,000-acre home for desert bighorn sheep is situated in the hottest part of the Sonoran Desert, though temperatures are pleasant in winter. Sparse desert shrub is scattered over the landscape. Rough dirt roads cross the reserve; some require 4-wheel-drive vehicles.

The Kofas and Castle Domes provide the main habitat for the bighorn, where this reclusive mammal can escape increasing pressures from man. The ranges are also home for mule deer, coyote, kit fox, gray fox, ringtail cat, badger, bobcat, and mountain lion. Birdlife includes Gambel's quail, owls, Gila woodpecker, flycatchers, verdins, hawks, and the omnipresent vulture. Water dictates their activities. Rainfall varies from traces to 5 inches yearly, but the U.S. Fish and Wildlife Service has improved existing waterholes and built artificial tanks to help overcome dry seasons.

Signal Peak in the Kofas is over 4,000 feet high, an "island" rising from the desert floor and displaying higher-elevation plant life, such as simmondsia and scrub oak. The views are outstanding from many peaks in both the Kofas and Castle Domes, with vistas reaching into California and Mexico.

Famous Palm Canyon is located below Signal Peak on the west edge of the refuge. In the spectacular setting of this rugged canyon the native palm tree, unique to the Arizona desert, once prospered. Sadly, vandals burned out these stands several years ago; a few remaining palms can be seen in the precipitous drainages high above the floor of Palm Canyon.

Hiking, photography, sightseeing, and wildlife observation are permitted in all areas of the refuge except private land-holdings. Campers select their campsites but must abide by the waterhole laws and not camp within 100 feet of the road. Camping is limited to 14 days. For information, contact:

Refuge Manager
Kofa NWR
P.O. Box 1032
Yuma, AZ 85364

HAVASU NATIONAL WILDLIFE REFUGE

Havasu National Wildlife Refuge is located between Needles, California, and Lake Havasu City, Arizona, along the Colorado River. It was created in 1941 to manage and protect wildlife near the area flooded when Parker Dam was built. The refuge is divided into three units: Topock Marsh, Topock Gorge, and the Bill Williams Delta. The Colorado River provides over 300 miles of shoreline within the 41,500-acre refuge.

Open water, narrow river channels, extensive sloughs, and aquatic and semi-aquatic habitats abound with beaver, muskrat, and raccoon. The desert runs down to the edge of the water, providing an interesting overlap of riparian and desert habitats. Kangaroo rats, desert cottontails, jackrabbits, ground squirrels, and gophers live in close proximity, along with many bat species, which inhabit the surrounding caves. Desert bighorn sheep and wild burros and horses share the area with coyotes, gray and kit foxes, porcupines, and badgers.

Birdlife includes shore birds, water birds, wading birds,

gulls, terns, and other fowl that either spend the winter or migrate through the refuge. Two of the bird species are threatened, at least in this area: the peregrine falcon and Yuma clapper rail. Adjacent uplands contain Gambel's quail, roadrunners, and several dove species.

The Topock Marsh Unit is located north of Topock, Arizona, which is where I-40 crosses the river. The marsh, lying east of the river, features an extensive network of channels and ponds. The eastern side of the marsh forms a 4,000-acre lake.

The Topock Gorge Unit, accessible most easily by boat, is the outstanding scenic area along the lower Colorado River, affording the canoe or raft traveler close views of jagged canyon walls and hidden side canyons. Hiking is possible in the uplands but takes careful preparation due to the rugged topography.

The Bill Williams Delta, which includes a mud delta surrounded by towering volcanic cliffs, contains a Research Natural Area of over 400 acres.

A self-guided boat tour explains natural history to travelers through Topock Gorge, and a waterfowl feeding area near the refuge farm offers visitors a chance to see wintering geese at close range. An observation tower provides even better viewing.

No specific maintained trails have been developed for hiking, but in the Topock Marsh Unit are 16 miles of road open to the public for foot and bicycle travel. Other than certain areas closed to protect wintering waterfowl, all the units in the Havasu NWR are open to hiking throughout the year.

Camping is allowed in two areas in the Refuge, Five-Mile Landing and Catfish Paradise, and directly below the south boundary of the Topock Gorge Unit. Off-road driving is prohibited.

For additional information, contact:

Refuge Manager
Havasu NWR
1406 Bailey Ave.
Needles, CA 92363

IMPERIAL NATIONAL WILDLIFE REFUGE

Imperial NWR is superimposed on BLM land 24 miles north of Yuma. Situated on both the California and Arizona sides of the Colorado River, it was established in 1941 to manage the wildlife attracted to the backwaters that formed behind Imperial Dam. It extends about 30 miles along the river and contains 26,000 acres of backwater lakes, marshes, ponds, and sloughs, plus a few mountain ranges. Summer weather is extremely hot, but water for cooling off is plentiful. Winters offer ideal conditions for observing Canadian geese and other waterfowl. Ducks, coots, and swans are among the more than 200 bird species recorded in this refuge. Many shore birds and transients frequent the wet area in July and August. Spring and fall offer the greatest avian variety when both land bird and water bird migrants are numerous. Blue herons, green herons, least bitterns, clapper rails, and white-winged doves nest in these exotic desert/riparian habitats. Spectacular concentrations of swallows are also frequently observed.

Hiking, sightseeing, and photography are permitted in most areas of the refuge. There are no maintained hiking trails; the hiker must use maps and plan his own trek. A self-guided interpretive trail about 1¼ miles long, presently under construction, will acquaint the visitor with Lower Sonoran zone natural history.

Overnight camping is not permitted in the refuge in order to avoid conflicts with wildlife and sanitation problems. There are, however, camping areas in the BLM-administered lands and in nearby Yuma. Most of the refuge is accessible only by boat or foot. Little potable water is available except at Picacho Peak headquarters and the Martinez Lake area. No off-road vehicular travel is permitted.

For further information contact:

Refuge Manager
Imperial National Wildlife Refuge
P.O. Box 2217
Martinez Lake, AZ 85364

Bureau of Land Management Primitive Areas

The 1964 Classification and Multiple Use Act gives the Secretary of the Interior authority to designate natural areas with outstanding scenic and primeval characteristics as primitive areas. Paria Canyon and Aravaipa Canyon, with a combined area of 32,662 acres, were the first places in Arizona to be designated Bureau of Land Management primitive areas. In 1979, 35,092 acres of the "rugged, geologically complex" Virgin Mountains were incorporated as part of Paiute Primitive Area.

Primitive areas like Paria, Aravaipa, and Paiute supplement our system of wilderness areas without requiring authorization by Congress, and offer the backcountry traveler the same opportunity to step outside of mechanized society long enough to discover his natural environment and, perhaps, himself.

Safford District

Aravaipa Canyon Primitive Area

The Apache word *Aravaipa* means "little running water," and Aravaipa Creek is one of the only free-flowing perennial streams crossing Arizona's Sonoran Desert. Recommended for wilderness classification in 1979, Aravaipa Canyon was a primary migration route for prehistoric Hohokam and Salado Indians. The 4,044 acres of lush riparian habitat, sheltered by the high walls of this deep wilderness gorge, support a variety of both threatened and endangered species. Among the endangered species are the bald eagle, peregrine falcon, and Gila top minnow, which was reintroduced in the area in 1978. The long list of threatened animals includes the gray hawk, snowy egret, zone-tailed hawk, black hawk, beardless flycatcher, buff-breasted flycatcher, desert bighorn, coatimundi, rock rattlesnake, Gila monster, desert tortoise, loach minnow, round-tailed chub, and spikedace. Yet the BLM still permits grazing along the fragile canyon bottom. Horse flies are abundant and aggressive, water has to be treated, and much of the vegetation has been trampled. Twice during the last eight years a vehicle was authorized to haul a pump 3 miles into the proposed wilderness. Still, Aravaipa endures.

Two trailheads provide access into Aravaipa. To reach the West Entrance, drive south from Superior on Highway 177 to Winkleman. Turn south onto Highway 77 and proceed 10 miles to the Aravaipa Canyon Road turnoff. Take this road 13 miles to the West Entrance parking lot. To reach the East Entrance, drive north from Wilcox 33 miles to Bonita. From Bonita continue north on the Aravaipa Valley Road 31 miles to Klondike and from Klondike to the East Entrance.

A permit is required for hiking in Aravaipa, available by writing the Safford District Office, 1707 Thatcher Blvd., Safford, AZ 85546. When deciding which entrance to use, consider, along with driving distance, that 30 permits are issued per day for the West Entrance, 20 for the East Entrance. Whichever entrance you use, there are 3 hiking strategies:

a day hike, a 2 to 3 day trip to the other end and back, and a one-way hike between entrances. The last requires a time-consuming, fuel-wasting car shuttle, unless two groups start at opposite ends and exchange keys as they pass.

Aravaipa's sycamores, cottonwoods, and willows invite the second look afforded by the return leg of a round trip. The 14-mile round trip from one entrance to the other and back isn't physically demanding; little elevation is gained or lost, and the footing is generally excellent—though high shoes are best for the stream-bed hiking.

Don't hurry through Aravaipa. If you have time, explore Booger Canyon, Painted Canyon, and other canyons. There are ruins to explore near Horse Camp Canyon, once inhabited by an early settler. Across from Hell Hole Canyon is the Dugway Trail, which leads to the south rim of Aravaipa and gives a good view of the entire canyon. At the east end of Aravaipa is Turkey Creek, which in a week can be explored all the way into Galiuro Wilderness. Turkey Creek was once a migration route, and you may find evidence of ancient journeys. Whether you spend a day or a week in Aravaipa, you soon realize why several hundred Apaches chose to farm the fertile west end of the canyon during the late 1800s, before 132 Indians, mostly women and children, were massacred there by local vigilantes. While the Dugway Trail is the only developed trail in Aravaipa, route-finding is not a problem. Follow a stream bed to your destination, though doing so may prove an adventure during spring runoff or summer flash-flood seasons.

ELEVATION:	2,640 feet to 3,060 feet
VEGETATION:	Desert shrub to chaparral
WATER:	Aravaipa Creek, though mercury often exceeds "recommended maximum levels for drinking water"
NEAREST SUPPLY POINTS:	Hayden, Wilcox, Safford
SEASONS:	All year, though fall through spring is most popular
MAPS:	Klondike (15 minute)
MANAGING AGENCY:	Bureau of Land Management

Kanab District

Paria Canyon Primitive Area

> Difficult as it is to imagine and to appreciate, Grand is, none-theless, more manageable than the canyon country upstream from it in Utah. From one rim of the Grand Canyon, you can easily see the opposite rim eight to ten miles away. Standing on the edge of canyon country in Utah, you would be one hundred miles away from the opposite side—a hundred miles of canyons, mesas, buttes, reefs . . .
>
> C. GREGORY CRAMPTON, *Standing Up Country*

Once used as an access route by Pueblo Indians, Paria Canyon begins on Utah's Pausaugunt Plateau and drains into the Colorado River 85 miles downstream at Lee's Ferry, Arizona. Paria Canyon Primitive Area includes the lower 35 miles, of which the first 7 are in Utah, the remaining 28 in Arizona. The narrow sandstone defile cuts and twists through a land as sublime in its own way as the Grand Canyon.

To take a 3- or 4-day backpack—or a long day's run—through Paria Canyon Primitive Area, begin at the White House Ruin trailhead at the north end of the primitive area. The Kanab District office will not issue permits to hike the length of Paria Canyon upstream from Lee's Ferry, because you should have up-to-date weather information when you pass through the 5-mile "Narrows," which begin 4.2 miles from the top. If you left from Lee's Ferry, by the time you trekked the 25 miles to the Narrows, your weather information would be two days old and the Paria could be flooding. Don't be in the Narrows during a flash flood.

To reach the trailhead, drive west from Page on Highway 89 for 28 miles to the primitive area turnoff. Turn left and proceed 3 miles on a dirt road to the homestead site called White House Ruins.

The way is obvious—stay in the stream bed until you reach Lee's Ferry—but some of the highlights might not be so obvious. In the 5 miles above the Narrows, you discover that much of the walking entails following one bank or the other; by the time you reach Lee's Ferry you will have crossed the shallow Paria River innumerable times. These crossings are normally through water from 6 inches to 2 feet deep and are not cold except in winter. In spite of the fords, Paria Canyon has some of the best footing of any canyon in Arizona; it's hardpacked sand, in or out of the water. High shoes, however, are recommended; they keep out irritating pebbles.

A mile from the trailhead, you pass the primitive area

boundary and 3 miles farther, the last good camping area before entering the Narrows. The Narrows are 5 miles long, and by the time you're halfway through them you'll be looking for possible escape routes should a black wall of water come barreling down the gorge. There are no escape routes from the Narrows, though there is an arch at the 6-mile mark of the trail. Beyond this arch, the footing improves from good to better.

At the 7-mile mark, Buckskin Gulch comes in from the west. It's a 16-mile gorge as spectacular as the Paria itself. A hike down the Paria to this confluence, then back up Buckskin is a good 2- or 3-day loop and much easier to arrange a car shuttle for than the Paria hike. However, Buckskin is blocked by rockfall 1½ miles up from its confluence with the Paria, and ropes are required to negotiate this 30-foot high obstacle. There are two approaches to the head of Buckskin: the first 4 miles south of Highway 89 on the House Rock Valley Road and the second 4 miles farther south on the same road. Both approaches require a permit. Buckskin has clear running water, so it's a good idea to fill up here before crossing into Arizona a few hundred yards downstream.

Should you negotiate the Narrows *after* a flash flood, a ½-mile-long lake near the Paria/Buckskin confluence could require a flotation device such as an air mattress.

About 9 miles down, there should be a seep on the right side of the canyon. At mile 10, with the psychological pressure of the Narrows behind, you can relax. A few miles farther, the walls lean back periodically to reveal the edge of Poverty Flats and the Paria Plateau. This country was first inhabited by the *Anasazi* (ancient ones), who scratched out an existence farming what land they could till. Then the Paiutes came and, according to one anthropologist, so refined running that they could run antelope to death. Neighboring Utes started preying on Paiute children and selling them to New Mexican slave traders. Mormon polygamists found it ideal country for hiding from the law. Historic country, and backpacking country as fine as any in the Southwest.

Near Judd Hollow, 16 miles down, are scattered some weathered boards and rusted machinery. According to a BLM brochure, they're the "remains of old water station used by early Mormon ranchers attempting to pump water from river up 1,000-ft. high escarpment to dry Paria Plateau"—no small undertaking. Between the Buckskin confluence and Judd Hollow are four good seeps on the right side of the stream bed. Below Judd Hollow are usually enough springs and seeps to get to Lee's Ferry. Good camping spots also become more frequent from this point on. Eighteen miles down, Wrather Canyon enters from the west. Half a mile up this canyon is a 200-foot arch in the Navajo Sandstone that's worth a side hike. There's also free-flowing water in this canyon.

Twenty miles down, the channel enters the Moenave and Kayenta rock formations. About 23 miles out, a side canyon comes in from the south; 100 yards up this canyon is a spring. The last spring is in verdant Bush Head Canyon another mile downstream.

The last 10 miles to Lee's Ferry can be oppressive on a warm spring day. The canyon opens and swings abruptly to the southeast, becoming exposed to the sun until mid-afternoon. Early morning is a good time to hike this stretch. Once the canyon does open up, you can see the 5,538-foot Echo Peaks, the high point of Echo Cliffs. Echo Peaks were named by John Wesley Powell and his men, who climbed to the top, shot a pistol, and counted 22 echoes.

Take your time hiking the last 5 miles in order to savor the history: the old ranch site with a boardwalk hanging above the Paria River, Lee's Ferry Cemetery, and the Lee's Ferry Ranch, or "Lonely Dell," as John D. Lee's wife called it.

If you don't have the time or the vehicle shuttle necessary for hiking the length of Paria Canyon Primitive Area, or if you're waiting to leave on a river trip through the Grand Canyon, hiking up from the Lee's Ferry Ranch makes a rewarding afternoon's outing. Hiking up to Bush Head Canyon and back is a good introductory backpack, but don't hike beyond, because of the flash-flood threat.

To reach the trailhead at Lee's Ferry Ranch, turn right from Highway 89A at Marble Canyon onto the Lee's Ferry Road. It's 6 miles of blacktop to the Lee's Ferry Ranch turnoff, which is before the wooden bridge spanning the Paria River. Turn left, and the trailhead is ½ mile beyond.

ELEVATION:	4,400 feet to 3,200 feet
VEGETATION:	Deciduous riparian
WATER:	Buckskin Gulch, Wrather Canyon, Bush Head Canyon, numerous springs and seeps (call beforehand); in emergencies, the Paria (filter and purify)

NEAREST SUPPLY POINTS: Page, Kanab
SEASONS: Fall, winter, early summer
MAPS: Paria, Paria Plateau, and Lee's Ferry (15 minute); BLM Recreation Map
MANAGING AGENCY: Bureau of Land Management

For further details and up-to-date information write:

Kanab District Office
Bureau of Land Management
Kanab, Utah 84741

St. George District

Paiute Primitive Area

Situated between the Colorado River and the Nevada and Utah borders, the Arizona Strip is a wild, desolate piece of land 140 miles long and 80 miles wide. It's more closely associated with Utah and Nevada, because you have to drive through one of those states to reach this hidden sliver of Arizona. Only three main roads traverse the Strip; all of them are dirt, and two deadend at remote overlooks on the north rim of the Grand Canyon. The towns that serve the Strip are located on its northern periphery: Jacob's Lake, Fredonia, and Colorado City, Arizona; St. George, Utah; and Mesquite, Nevada. When you head south into this outback, you're on your own in a land as untamed as any nonwilderness area in the United States.

Rising more than 6,000 feet from the Mohave Desert along the Virgin River to isolated clusters of Douglas fir above 8,000 feet on Mt. Bangs, Paiute Primitive Area is tucked away in the northwest corner of the Strip. Comprising 35,092 acres of the Virgin Mountains, Paiute Primitive Area may be the wildest tract of backpacking terrain in Arizona, except for the west end of the Grand Canyon. Just getting there is a wilderness experience, but once there, you realize the wildness is also inherent to the area.

To reach Paiute Primitive Area, drive west from St. George on I-15 to the Bloomington exit. Turn left and drive south on the Quail Hill Road beyond the Bloomington Hills sub-division. Stay on the Quail Hill Road to Wolf Hole. Turn right at Wolf Hole and drive to the South Trailhead, which is north of Cougar Spring.

Belying the term "trailhead," there are no trails in the primitive area, only bulldozer grades and, according to the BLM brochure, "wagon ruts." However, the only wagons that traveled here creaked and groaned along the Honeymoon Trail, a historic Mormon trail that skirts the base of the Virgins, in the late 1800s. The "wagon ruts" must be those of prospectors and seismologists who are occasionally seen 4-wheel-driving on the bulldozer tracks. Once you reach Cougar Spring, you have the choice of bushwhacking or following the swath left by technology.

A good introduction to the Virgin Mountains is a hike over 8,012-foot Mt. Bangs that combines bushwhacking and track-following. From Cougar Spring, zig-zag through the buckbrush toward any of several prominent ridges heading up to the Virgin Ridge. Stay out of the drainages because of the vicious brush. The ridges climb steeply; after a mile or so, the chaparral gives way to outcroppings of granite boulders and ponderosa. The hiking becomes less of a struggle, and a mile to the northwest you gain the crest of the Virgin Ridge. Here you get your first view of the Mohave Desert, a view more reminiscent of the southern California ranges than of any other Arizona range. Some scrambling is involved in following the Virgin Ridge 2 miles to the summit of Mt. Bangs, but you can minimize it by taking your time and planning your route. There is no shelter from the wind on the stark, craggy summit of Mt. Bangs, only a weathered, wooden surveyor's mast.

Descend Mt. Bangs by the northeast ridge for ½ mile, or until you see a safe descent line to a bulldozer grade several hundred feet below. Follow this well-traveled grade 1 mile to the Littlefield Reservoir. From the Littlefield Reservoir, head north along a track that follows the Virgin Ridge for 5 miles. The ridge is waterless, but in fall or spring it is probably the most breathtaking hike in the Paiute. To make a loop, follow the Virgin Ridge north of Littlefield Reservoir 3 miles to the Atkin Spring bulldozer trail. It's a steep 2 miles down to Atkin Spring, but there's usually water and a good view down Sullivan Canyon. To finish this loop, head southwest from Atkin Spring up another bulldozer trail. It's 3 miles from Atkin Spring back to Littlefield Reservoir by this track.

To complete the Mt. Bangs loop, the Virgin Ridge walk, or the Atkin Spring loop, follow Cottonwood Wash south from Littlefield Reservoir 2½ miles to Cougar Spring. This section also follows a track but is more esthetically pleasing than some other tracks by virtue of the colorful riparianlike habitat of Cottonwood Wash.

Explored by bulldozer tracks or by your own route, Paiute Primitive Area has a special way of defining solitude; it only takes a few miles to grasp its meaning of the word.

ELEVATION:	2,000 feet to 8,012 feet
VEGETATION:	Prickly pear to Douglas fir
WATER:	Cougar and Atkin springs
NEAREST SUPPLY POINTS:	Mesquite, Nevada; St. George, Utah
SEASONS:	Spring through fall, depending on elevation
MAPS:	Littlefield (15 minute); BLM Recreation Map
MANAGING AGENCY:	Bureau of Land Management, St. George, Utah
ACTIVITIES:	Orientation, trail construction

State, County, and City Parks

STATE HISTORIC PARKS

The Arizona State Historic Parks were developed to show-case the people and events that shaped the state's past. They are visited primarily for their historic values rather than for recreation. The system includes Fort Verde, Jerome, McFarland, Painted Rocks, Tombstone Courthouse, Tubac Presidio, and Yuma Territorial Prison.

STATE RECREATION PARKS

The Arizona Recreation Parks offer a variety of environments. Many parks include small artificial lakes, which attract outdoorspeople year-round. *Established* hiking trails are few, but many paths, old roads, and animal trails can be followed on these state lands. Use the USGS topographic maps of an area.

All but one of the state recreation parks are described below. For further information on all Arizona state parks, including fees and regulations, contact:

Arizona State Parks
1688 W. Adams
Phoenix, AZ 85007

Alamo Lake State Park

Alamo Lake, located in an unspoiled area of desert lowland in the Bill Williams River Valley, offers a somewhat isolated experience. The 500-acre flood-control lake contains warm-water fish, including bluegill, bass, and catfish. Summers are hot and winters mild.

The lake is surrounded by low, rolling hills, upon which may be observed plant and animal life typical of Lower Sonoran zone deserts.

Facilities include primitive and modern campsites, showers, a dump station, a boat-launching ramp, a swimming beach, and picnic areas. The lake level can vary up to 50 feet depending on rain runoff.

To reach Alamo Lake take U.S. 60/70 to Wenden, then drive 38 miles north to Alamo Crossing.

For further information, contact:

Supervisor
Alamo Lake State Park
P.O. Box 38
Wenden, AZ 85357

Buckskin Mountain State Park

Buckskin Mountain Park is located on a bend in the Colorado River, surrounded by rugged desert cliffs and hills. Its desert habitat, which represents the Lower Sonoran life zone, lies adjacent to exotic riparian habitat. The park mainly serves water-sport enthusiasts, but the surrounding topography offers high-quality hiking within short distances of the campsites.

Facilities include campsites with picnic tables and grills,

tent campsites, a boat-launching ramp, rest rooms with showers, and a small museum and visitor center. A store open from February through November sells groceries, camping supplies, and gasoline.

Summers being hot, the best hiking times are from November through May.

The park, which comprises 1,676 acres, is 12 miles north of Parker on Highway 95.

For further information, contact:

Supervisor
Buckskin Mountain State Park
P.O. Box 664
Parker, AZ 85344

Dead Horse Ranch State Park

This 300-acre park is located at an elevation of 3,300 feet in the heart of lush Verde Valley, a major riparian habitat running through central Arizona. The park, which provides access to the Verde River, consists of flat farmland sloping up to steep hills cut by many drainages. A mixture of flora and fauna inhabits this area. Bird life is abundant. Desert shrub, chaparral, and oak woodland combine with riparian habitat to provide the hiker with a variety of experiences and scenery. The park serves as a convenient center from which to explore the national monuments and other attractions of central Arizona.

A 4-acre fishing lake is stocked with bass and catfish. Campsites and picnic areas with water and electricity are available, along with a dump tank. Supplies and gasoline are available in Cottonwood.

To reach the park, turn off 5th Street in Cottonwood, 20 miles west of I-17.

For further information, contact:

Supervisor
Dead Horse Ranch State Park
P.O. Box 144
Cottonwood, AZ 86326

Lake Havasu State Park

Located adjacent to Lake Havasu City, this park, with 13,000 acres, is the largest in the state system. There are 45 miles of shoreline hiking and large areas of primitive desert shrub country to explore. The boundaries of the park extend from the shore of Lake Havasu east to Highway 95 and from Lake Havasu City south to the Bill Williams River. Pittsburg Point is a boat-launching and swimming-beach area. Cuttail Cove, 15 miles south of Lake Havasu City, offers boat facilities, campground accommodations, restrooms, showers, and a dump station. Supplies can be obtained in Lake Havasu City.

For more information contact:

Supervisor
Lake Havasu State Park
P.O. Box 645
Lake Havasu City, AZ 86403

Lyman Lake State Park

This 160-acre park, the smallest in the system, is oriented toward fishing in 1500-acre Lyman Lake. This lake is fed by snowmelt from Mt. Baldy and Escudilla Mountain in the White Mountains. The surrounding area is vegetated with typical desert grassland mixed with the pinyon-juniper community and provides expanses of rolling hills for hiking. Summers are mild at the lake's 6,000-foot elevation; winter can be cold and windy. The park is open all year but is at its best in spring and summer. A small herd of buffalo browses near the park entrance.

Facilities include boating areas, a campground with showers, a dump station, and a store.

Largemouth bass, walleye, northern pike, and channel and blue catfish are the predominant fish.

Lyman Lake is located 11 miles south of St. Johns on U.S. 666.

For further information, contact:

Supervisor
Lyman Lake State Park
Box 39
St. Johns, AZ 85936

Picacho Peak State Park

Forty-five miles northwest of Tucson, near I-10, Picacho Peak shoots up nearly 1,500 feet above the Lower Sonoran vegetation of the 2,000-foot desert floor. This spectacular pinnacle, which has guided desert travelers since prehistoric times, also looms above the site of the only Civil War battle fought in Arizona. It is popular with rock climbers.

The 3,400-acre park offers an interpretive exhibit and self-guided nature trail, as well as ramadas, picnic sites, and restrooms.

For further information, contact:

Supervisor
Picacho Peak State Park
P.O. Box 275
Picacho, AZ 85241

Roper Lake State Park

This 240-acre park, located 6 miles south of Safford on U.S. 666, was developed with a primitive campground (no overnight camping except by special permission) and day-use facilities for fishing, picnicking, swimming, and hiking. At 3,000 feet, the park is warm in summer and mild in winter. Spring and fall offer warm days and cool nights. The park is situated at the base of the Pinaleno Mountains, with 10,717-foot Mt. Graham soaring above. The Pinalenos are one of the desert "islands" that contain a variety of life zones and microhabitats.

For further information, contact:

Supervisor
Roper Lake State Park
P.O. Box 1351
Safford, AZ 85546

Lost Dutchman State Park

The notorious Superstition Mountains form the backdrop for newly created Lost Dutchman State Park. Situated at 1,700 feet in the Lower Sonoran life zone, the park is covered with cactus communities, ocotillo, palo verde trees, and desert shrub. Here you may absorb the legends of gold mines, Apache raids, and recent attempts to find the Lost Dutchman Mine. It is an ideal base from which to explore Superstition Wilderness. The park offers picnic tables, ramadas, and restrooms. Supplies are available in Apache Junction, 5 miles southwest by Highway 88.

For further information, contact:

Supervisor
Lost Dutchman State Park
P.O. Box 1561
Apache Junction, AZ 85220

Patagonia Lake State Park

Located 16 miles northeast of Nogales on Highway 82 is another state park centered on a lake. Situated in historic Sonoita Creek Valley in the heart of southern Arizona grassland country, the 275-acre man-made Patagonia Lake nestles between two sections of Coronado National Forest, which offers open spaces for hiking and backpacking. The park's 4,000-foot elevation means a mild climate all year; spring and fall are the most popular seasons.

Patagonia Lake is stocked with largemouth bass, bluegill,

crappie, channel catfish, and winter rainbow trout. The 640-acre park is furnished with ramadas and primitive campgrounds. A concession is operated at the lake.

For further information, contact:

Arizona State Parks
1688 W. Adams
Phoenix, AZ 85007

MARICOPA COUNTY PARKS

Maricopa County—Phoenix's county—has one of the largest county park systems in the country; 14 regional parks and recreation areas, comprising 118,000 acres, surround the city. Few hiking trails are maintained, except in the White Tanks Mountain Regional Park, but hiking and backpacking opportunities are limited only by your imagination and map-reading ability. Many dirt roads, horse trails, animal trails, jeep trails, and cattle trails cross these desert parks, and all are open to hiking. Most are wilderness parks with limited facilities; their virtue is their proximity both to Phoenix and to the major desert ranges surrounding the city.

A brief description of the major parks and hiking areas follows.

Lake Pleasant Regional Park

This 14,400-acre park northwest of Phoenix is a favorite place for escaping the summer heat because of the lake created by Waddel Dam, which impounds the Agua Fria River. The lake is surrounded by shady picnic areas, camping facilities, and boating facilities. Supply concessions and restrooms are available in the park. There is water but no electricity in the campgrounds. A park entrance fee is charged. Hikers and horse-packers can use the lake as a trailhead when exploring the higher deserts and foothills.

To reach Lake Pleasant, take the Black Canyon Freeway north of Phoenix about 30 miles to the Lake Pleasant turnoff. Travel west for 10 miles to the park.

Estrella Mountain Regional Park

The Estrella Mountains are a prominent landmark, rising to an elevation of 4,337 feet from the desert floor southwest of Phoenix. They are little explored and contain rugged terrain worthy of the experienced backpacker. Little water is available, and typical low desert vegetation covers the slopes, giving way to Upper Sonoran zone chapparal towards the tops of the peaks.

This recreation area comprises 56 acres of grassland with picnic tables, grills, and restrooms. Seven ramadas are equipped with electricity. Sites to accommodate 25 tents are available at the east end of the park. A desert camping area with no water is available; advance reservations are necessary. An archery range is located in the southwestern corner of Estrella Mountain Regional Park. Water is available in the picnic areas. This 18,600-acre park is located 3 miles south of Goodyear via Bullard Road, south of Highway 85.

McDowell Mountain Regional Park

This wilderness park contains some of the lushest Lower Sonoran plant life in the Phoenix area. Bounded by the Fort McDowell Indian Reservation and Tonto National Forest, this 20,941-acre preserve contains over 70 primitive picnic areas and a horse-staging area. McDowell Mountain Regional Park is a good example of farsighted planning. In the winter it is a perfect retreat from the congestion of Phoenix, yet only a 45-minute drive from downtown. Many old ranch and jeep roads beg for hikers to follow them into the McDowell Mountains and the surrounding foothills and rock formations.

Access is from Rio Verde Drive, 10 miles east of Pinnacle Peak Mountain. USGS quadrangles: McDowell Peak and Fort McDowell (7.5 minute).

White Tanks Mountain Regional Park

White Tanks Mountain is the largest park in the Maricopa system with 26,337 acres of desert and mountain wilderness. There are picnic tables with grills, ramadas, and restrooms and a 40-site campground with no water or electricity. Advance reservations are required, and a 14-day camping limit is enforced.

The White Tanks are named for the granite catch basins found at the bases of exposed bedrock outcrops. Write for details of the extensive system of maintained trails.

To reach the park, travel west from Peoria on Olive Avenue for 15 miles to the park entrance.

Usery Mountain Recreation Area

A gateway to the Superstition Mountains, this recreation area includes 3,324 acres of superb Lower Sonoran plant life. Facilities include picnic tables with grills, ramadas, restrooms, a 75-unit campground (14-day limit), and a group campsite (advance reservation required). There is no water or electricity. There is a 28-target archery range.

Old roads provide hiking, and the open desert invites the off-trail trekker accustomed to orienting by landform, time, and distance. The Usery and Goldfield mountains are within hiking distance.

To reach Usery Mountain Recreation Area, drive 12 miles northeast from Mesa via the Apache Trail to Old Bush Highway, which is followed to Usery Pass Road. Follow the signs.

Cave Creek Recreation Area

Cave Creek is a primitive park, at present undeveloped, encompassing 2,752 acres 2 miles west of Cave Creek Road on New River Road. The lush vegetation of this high desert country extends to Tonto National Forest on the north and east. This is excellent hiking and riding country with unlimited open desert and many old roads and jeep trails.

Sun Circle Trail

Better known as the "Canal Bank Trail," this 110-mile horse, bike, and hiking trail makes a loop around Phoenix by linking roads on the banks of irrigation canals. These canals were originally dug by the Hohokam Indians, who lived in the valley around 500 A.D. These ancient waterways were so well engineered that early settlers simply redredged them for their own farms. They are still used today, constituting the Salt River Project Irrigation District. The canals have many side branches that narrow to ditches for residential lawn watering.

The Arizona State Horsemen's Association initiated the movement to obtain rights of way for horsemen on the canal banks. In 1965, the Maricopa County Board of Supervisors, the Salt River Project, and the Department of the Interior signed an agreement designating portions of the canal banks for use as hiking and riding trails. The Sun Circle Trail connects urban, rural, and wilderness landscape; side trails to city and county parks are still being developed.

Further information about the Maricopa County Park system can be obtained by writing:

Superintendent of Maricopa County Parks and Recreation
    Department
4701 E. Washington Street
Phoenix, AZ 85034

THE PHOENIX CITY TRAILS

The City of Phoenix has one of the most enviable park systems in the country. Five mountain parks within the city limits contain hiking trails that lead to summits with hundred-mile vistas. Outdoor recreation is pursued in Phoenix year-round, and these mountain trails are used in both summer and winter. A hiker can spend an hour or a day tramping the city trails. These mountain parks are big enough to give the hiker the same feeling of isolation from the city that he or she would experience on a remote backpack though they are within 15 minutes of home.

The Phoenix Mountain Range stretches for 9 miles across the north slope of the Salt River Valley, from Camelback Mountain on the southeast to Moon Hill on the northwest. The Salt River, Gila, and Guadalupe ranges make up South Mountain Park at the southern limits of the city. Papago Park is located close to the suburbs of Tempe and Scottsdale. The park system totals 23,640 acres (37 square miles). The preserves are microcosms of the Lower Sonoran life zone and provide a preview of larger adventures in the surrounding deserts.

More than 300 plant species grow in the mountain parks, including almost all varieties of Arizona cactus. Saguaro, barrel cactus, hedgehog, pincushion, jumping cholla, Christmas cactus, ocotillo, staghorn cactus, and prickly pear and palo verde, elephant, and ironwood trees are prevalent. The parks also provide habitat for animal life, notably reptiles: snakes, lizards, Gila monsters, horny toads, geckos, and chuckwallas. The mammal population is restricted by man's presence but includes California jackrabbit, mule deer, cottontail rabbit, ground squirrel, various mice, raccoon, coyote, gopher, kit fox, and ringtail cat. The Maricopa

Audubon Society lists over 50 bird species observed throughout the park system.

Squaw Peak Park

Squaw Peak Summit Trail

This favorite trail begins at the first picnic ramada in Squaw Peak Park and meanders up the mountain for 1.2 miles, climbing 1,208 feet to the sharp summit. The views from Squaw Peak give you a feeling of being on a wilderness skyscraper looking down on the surrounding city.

There are enough other trails to this and surrounding summits to occupy a full weekend of hiking.

Squaw Peak Circumference Trail

This trail starts at Squaw Peak Park's northeast parking area and circles Squaw Peak, surmounting several passes en route and intersecting two summit trails. The 4-mile loop is fairly strenuous and takes a good half day.

North Mountain Park

North Mountain Park Trail

Begin in the parking area at the northwest end of North Mountain Park and ascend North Mountain. From the top, the trail loops back to the picnic area. Remnants of mining activity are visible along the trail, which climbs about 1,000 feet in one steep mile and takes about 1½ hours.

Shaw Butte Trail

An old utility road climbs 2.2 miles to the summit of Shaw Butte. The climbing is fairly strenuous. Evidence of ancient Hohokam Indian civilization has been observed in the rock outcroppings along the route. The trail overlooks the entire western part of the Phoenix Valley.

Echo Canyon Park

Camelback Mountain, 2 miles southeast of Squaw Peak, is a prominent Phoenix landmark that resembles a camel lying down. The beauty and majesty of the mountain are being eroded by development creeping up the steep slopes. Once Camelback was an open mountain, with several trails leading to the 2,704-foot summit, but private development has surrounded the base, and the only point of access remaining is Echo Canyon Park, a small remnant of the former open spaces. The park, salvaged from an attempt to completely cut off the mountain to public access, contains a few short hiking trails in addition to the summit trail.

Camelback Mountain Summit Trail

From the parking lot, the summit trail heads up east toward a tilted rock on a saddle, just below a prominent formation called the Praying Monk. The trail heads south to another saddle, which forms the camel's neck, then ascends to the summit via a series of steep washes. Allow 2 hours for the trek.

Echo Canyon Trails

From the Echo Canyon parking lot, trails lead to other parts of this sloping park land. The main trail leads to an interpretive ramada, then southwest toward Bobby's Rock, a prominent formation. From this rock, the trail goes up to a large saddle from which the Phoenix skyline can be seen.

Other trails starting from the ramada take you to different parts of the park. There are rock climbing opportunities and small caves to explore. There are no picnic facilities, restrooms, or water. The park is open from sunrise to sundown.

South Mountain Park

The largest municipal desert park in the world extends 11 miles from east to west across the southern boundary of Phoenix. With little development, the park's natural environment is preserved as it was when Indians traversed the range. There are over 40 miles of hiking and saddle trails, picnic facilities, and restrooms, electric lights, fire pits, water, and garbage disposal units in selected areas of the park.

South Mountain Park Trail

The park's main trail starts in the parking area in Pima Canyon, which is reached by driving through Guadalupe into the park, passing many petroglyphs on the way. Hike from the parking lot past the natural bridge and into Hidden Valley. Continue following a game trail through Fat Man's Pass and onto the crest of the ridge. Hidden Valley and the section of Pima Canyon near Eagle Pass were considered sacred by Indians and contain petroglyphs that can be viewed by the hiker. From Eagle Pass, follow the crest all the way to the San Juan area. There are hundred-mile vistas from many points along this trail. In many places the trail crosses park roads, where parking is available for those wanting to hike parts of this 13¾-mile trail. This full-day hike requires a car shuttle.

Hieroglyphic Trail

Start at the Boy Scout Pueblo at 19th Street and Dobbins Road and climb to the crest of the range. Follow the South Mountain Trail through Fat Man's Pass and Hidden Valley to its junction with the Mormon Trail. This strenuous loop, 6.5 miles long, takes the average hiker about 4 hours.

Kiwanis Trail

Starting at the main park entrance, traverse through the picnic areas to Telegraph Pass, where the trail joins the South Mountain Trail. From this junction continue west until you find the trail that goes back to the main gate. The Kiwanis Trail is 3 miles long and takes about 4 hours.

Holbert Trail

Start from the stable area just off Central Avenue, at the park's north boundary. Travel southeast and climb to Dobbins Lookout, at an elevation of 2,330 feet. The trail is 1¾ miles long with a 1,000-foot gain in elevation. Three hours are needed for the round trip.

Papago Park

This unique preserve within the expanding metropolitan area of Phoenix, Tempe, and Scottsdale contains the famed Phoenix Zoo, the Desert Botanical Gardens, many picnic ramadas, and various trails wandering through the open desert country. Rock climbing is taught on sandstone and conglomerate buttes and pinnacles.

This park is another example of farsighted city planning as the expanding metropolis fills vacant desert land with development. "Desert islands" preserved within the city limits will provide relief from the urban tempo of the growing city.

Indian Reservations, Museums, Gardens, and Clubs

RESERVATIONS

Indian reservations occupy more than a fourth of the land area of Arizona. Rules and regulations regarding camping and hiking on tribal lands may change on short notice. Each tribal council should be contacted regarding the current status of hiking and backpacking on their respective reservations. Tribal council addresses are included for your information. No hiking and camping should be planned without tribal permission.

Colorado River Agency

Colorado River Indian Tribes	**Rt. 1, Box 9-C, Parker, AZ 85344**
Fort Mojave Tribal Council	Rt. 1, Box 23-B, Parker, AZ 85344
Chemehuevi Tribal Council	P.O. Box 888, Needles, CA 92363
	P.O. Box 1976, Havasu Lake, CA 92363

Fort Yuma Agency

Quechan Tribal Council	**P.O. Box 1591, Yuma, AZ 85364**
Cocopah Tribal Council	P.O. Box 1352, Yuma, AZ 85364
	Bin C, Somerton, AZ 85350

Truxton Canon Agency

Havasupai Tribal Council	**Valentine, AZ 86437**
Hualapai Tribal Council	P.O. Box 10, Supai, AZ 86435
Tonto Apache Indian Tribal Council	P.O. Box 168, Peach Springs, AZ 86434
Yavapai-Apache Community Council	P.O. Box 1440, Payson, AZ 85541
Yavapai-Prescott Board of Directors	P.O. Box 1188, Camp Verde, AZ 86322
	P.O. Box 348, Prescott, AZ 86301

Fort Apache Agency

White Mountain Apache Tribal Council	**P.O. Box 560, Whiteriver, AZ 85941**
	P.O. Box 700, Whiteriver, AZ 85941

Hopi Agency

	P.O. Box 158, Keams Canyon, AZ 86034

Hopi Tribal Council — P.O. Box 123, Oraibi, AZ 86039

Kaibab Band of Paiute Indians — P.O. Box 302, Fredonia, AZ 86022

Papago Agency — **P.O. Box 578, Sells, AZ 85634**

Papago Council — P.O. Box 837, Sells, AZ 85634

Fort McDowell Office — **Rt. 1, Box 700, Scottsdale, AZ 85256**

Fort McDowell-Mohave-Apache Community Council — P.O. Box 17779, Fountain Hills, AZ 85268

Pascua Yaqui Tribal Council — 4821 W. Calle Vicam, Tucson, AZ 85706

Pima Agency — **Sacaton, AZ 85247**

Ak-Chin Indian Community — Rt. 2, Box 27, Maricopa, AZ 85239

Gila River Indian Community — P.O. Box 97, Sacaton, AZ 85247

Salt River Agency — **Rt. 1, Box 117, Scottsdale, AZ 85256**

Salt River Pima-Maricopa Community Council — Rt. 1, Box 216, Scottsdale, AZ 85256

San Carlos Agency — **San Carlos, AZ 85550**

San Carlos Apache Tribal Council — P.O. Box O, San Carlos, AZ 85550

Navajo Tribal Council — **Window Rock, Arizona 86515**

Navajo Mountain

To traditional Navajos, 10,388-foot Navajo Mountain is *naatsin' aan,* "Head of the Earth," one of five sacred mountains which encircle *dinetah,* "Earth Mother." A solitary mountain straddling the Arizona/Utah border, it rises from a labyrinth of deep canyons sliced into its precipitous slopes. Because it is a sacred mountain, a hike should be undertaken with reverence.

Both trails that skirt the rugged flanks of Navajo Mountain lead to Rainbow Bridge, the largest natural arch in the world. Each is 14 miles long and requires endurance, but the reward is not just in seeing the Bridge but in hiking one of the most exciting and rewarding routes in Arizona and Utah. Neither trail is maintained, and both traverse rugged, though incomparable, topography.

To reach either trailhead, drive south from Page for 52 miles on Highway 98 to the Inscription House/Navajo Mountain turnoff. Head north on this dirt road 35 miles to the Rainbow Lodge/Navajo Mountain Trading Post junction. Take the left fork 5 miles to a rock dome. Turn right just before reaching the dome, and follow a rough dirt road another 2½ miles to the old Rainbow Lodge site. Now a burned-out ruin, Rainbow Lodge, once owned by Arizona Senator Barry Goldwater, was the main starting point for horseback-riding tourists visiting Rainbow Bridge. The ruins are still a good place to camp after a long drive. If you're lucky, you may hear the lyrical singing of Navajos south of your camp.

To reach the other trailhead, continue past the Rainbow Lodge turnoff 6 miles to the Navajo Mountain Trading Post.

Gas and supplies are available here. The trailhead is 8½ miles beyond. Stay on the main road for 4 miles to a 4-way intersection. Continue through the intersection to another fork 3 miles farther. Cross the cofferdam to a fork ½ mile beyond. Turn left and head 1½ miles to Cha Canyon. The trailhead is not marked, but the trail begins at an entrance into Cha Canyon.

The Rainbow Lodge Trail begins at 6,300 feet just west of the ruins. There is no water for the first 8 miles; hike this first stretch in the morning. The first 5 miles, similar to a hike along the Grand Canyon's Tonto Formation, swings in and out of 3 major canyons as you skirt the southwest side of Navajo Mountain. Most of the mileposts are marked by stumps of red pipe. At the 5-mile mark, you reach Yabut Pass and get an unbelievable view of Cliff Canyon. The trail drops 1,600 feet in the next 2 miles to 4,800 feet. The first water is a mile farther; fill your canteen before continuing downstream. Redbud Pass is 1½ miles farther. There are places to camp on either side of this pass, which was blasted away by Wetherill and Bernheimer in 1922 during their quest to be the first whites to encircle Navajo Mountain. Ruins are passed en route to mile 11, where Bridge Creek and the Navajo Mountain Trading Post Trail enter from the right. Turn left and stay in the stream bed to mile 12, where the trail skirts the right side of the drainage, passes through a Rainbow Bridge National Monument gate, and continues to Echo Camp at mile 13. Echo Camp has water, from a seep in a rock wall, and several wooden structures remaining from the days of horseback tours. Until a few years ago, it was a good place to camp; visitors making the short walk from Lake Powell have littered the site. Rainbow Bridge is ¼ mile beyond.

Zane Grey, in *Tales of Lonely Trails,* writes:

> Rainbow Bridge was not for many eyes to see. The tourist, the leisurely traveler, the comfort loving . . . would never behold it. Only by toil, sweat, endurance and pain could any man ever look at *nonnezoshe* [Rainbow Bridge]. It seemed well to realize that the great things of life had to be earned.

Grey wrote long before Glen Canyon Dam was constructed and the impounded waters of Lake Powell made possible painless visits by leisurely travelers.

Don't go beyond Echo Camp to the Bridge unless you're prepared for the hordes, the boats, the lake. Before Lake Powell was formed, Navajo medicine men made religious pilgrimages to Rainbow Bridge, the nearby confluence of the San Juan and Colorado Rivers, as well as to perform sacred ceremonies. With the confluence drowned, however, it is impossible for the medicine men to continue their pilgrimages to the male and female rivers, from which the Cloud and Rain People were born. Once the National Park Service authorized the Rainbow Bridge Marina, beer-drinking, picture-taking tourists made the medicine men uncomfortable when they tried to perform the Protectionway Ceremony at the Bridge.

You can return by the same route or take the Navajo Mountain Trading Post Trail. This requires a car shuttle, but it's worth the effort. The Trading Post Trail is described in the direction from Cha Canyon toward Rainbow Bridge.

About 1 mile from the Cha Canyon trailhead, the trail splits; take the left fork. Care must be taken to stay on the correct trail, as it's crossed by footpaths and sheep trails for the next 4 or 5 miles. Water can usually be found in Bald Rock Canyon at mile 3. A half mile beyond, the trail skirts a sweat lodge and climbs to the top of a sand-swept hummock. Nasja Canyon, with good water, makes a fine place to camp. Look for Owl Bridge to your left ½ mile farther. There is water in Oak Canyon, about mile 9, and 1½ miles farther you start down Bridge Canyon, an excellent place to camp amid amazing scenery. To continue to the Rainbow Lodge Trail junction, stay in Bridge Canyon another 2 miles.

The north flank of Navajo Mountain may be climbed from Surprise Valley near Owl Bridge; a steep, nontechnical scramble leads to the summit. The ascent is waterless, though, all the way to War God Spring beyond the mountain's south summit. Leave at daybreak and pack enough water to reach the spring by nightfall. The view from the summit is unparalleled, encompassing the Henry and Abajo mountains, the Kaiparowits Plateau, and the Escalante River, all in southern Utah. This route, however, facing north, is usually buried in snow during winter and spring.

ELEVATION:	3,900 feet to 6,300 feet
VEGETATION:	Desert shrub, pinyon-juniper, ponderosa pine
WATER:	First Water Camp, Cliff Canyon, Bridge Canyon, Echo Camp

NEAREST SUPPLY POINTS: Kayenta, Tuba City
SEASONS: Spring and fall
MAPS: Navajo Mountain (15 minute),
                       Chaiyahi Flat (7.5 minute)
MANAGING AGENCY: Navajo Tribal Council, National
                       Park Service

MUSEUMS AND GARDENS

An outing is more enjoyable when a hiker knows the local geography and natural history. In addition, playing an active role in wilderness preservation depends on knowing how natural forces interact to shape the environment. Environmental education can be obtained by formal schooling, and it can also be obtained informally, at public gardens and museums. These facilities often offer short courses oriented toward those curious about the world around them. Museums usually sell literature that discusses the processes that have led to our present landforms and plant and animal life.

Desert Botanical Garden

Over 100,000 visitors a year enter this unique desert garden, dedicated from its inception to the study of the plant life of deserts and arid lands. More than a thousand cacti and other arid-land plants grow in the garden's natural setting.

The Desert Botanical Garden was founded in 1935 for the purposes of studying, conserving, and educating. It participates in worldwide exchange programs with other botanical institutions and scientists. It offers a growing series of educational programs for children and adults at modest fees. Its Richter Memorial Library contains more than 4,000 books and 170 periodicals that concern the botanical, ecological, and horticultural aspects of the deserts of the world.

A gift shop sells the seeds of succulent plants and information on growing them, starter plants in small pots, books and periodicals for the amateur plant grower.

The garden is open every day of the year from 9 A.M. to sunset. Contact:

Desert Botanical Garden
Galvin Parkway
Papago Park
Box 5415
Phoenix, AZ 85010

Boyce Thompson Southwestern Arboretum

Arboretum in Latin means "a place grown with trees." The word has acquired a more specific connotation in English: a place set aside for scientific research and the study of trees, for education, and for the fostering of an appreciation for plant life. Boyce Thompson Arboretum is, in addition, a small-scale replica of Upper and Lower Sonoran communities traversed by a riparian community. Another area, set aside for exotic trees and shrubs from around the world, provides shade and bird habitat.

Colonel W. B. Thompson, a mining magnate, in 1929 set aside this 30-acre garden as a tribute to the beauty and diversity of desert plant life. It claims one of the world's largest collections of arid-land plants and is also a haven for an amazing cross-section of wildlife, from the residents of the aquatic world of the stream habitat through the land fauna of the desert to the desert bird species, which are provided with an overhead sanctuary.

A self-guided nature trail loops for 1⅓ miles through the various environments. The flora path has identification signs in front of the various plants.

The Arboretum gift shop has a varied and interesting collection of books and literature on Arizona's natural history. An annual plant sale draws people from throughout the state.

It is well worth the hour drive from Phoenix to see this microhabitat masterpiece and learn from its unique display of the natural world.

Contact:

Boyce Thompson Southwestern Arboretum
U.S. Highway 60
Superior, AZ 85273

The Arizona-Sonora Desert Museum

This world-renowned combination museum, zoo, and botanical garden offers an immersion in Sonoran Desert habitat second only to an actual desert trip. A large variety of dryland fauna is displayed in environments constructed to resemble an animal's natural habitat. Artificial rodent burrows, cliff dwellings for various mammals, underwater homes for beaver and otter, and an aviary for desert bird species are a few of the natural enclosures that house desert animals.

Labeled desert plants grow along walkways in real soil next to artificial boulders and rock walls. These "natural habitats" bound the various animal homes.

The museum is set in one of the lushest desert regions in North America: the Sonoran Desert near Tucson. Situated west of the city in Tucson Mountain Park, the museum offers unobstructed desert vistas into Mexico and is surrounded by many-colored mountain ranges that are cut by canyons and *bajadas*.

The museum, open every day from 8:30 A.M. until sundown, is a must for anyone traveling through Arizona.

Contact:

Arizona Sonora Desert Museum
Route 9
Tucson, AZ 85704

Museum of Northern Arizona

This museum is devoted to preserving, exhibiting, and researching the natural and cultural history of the Colorado Plateau. The Colorado Plateau Province, discussed in the Introduction and early in this chapter, is one of the most diverse and scenic geographic regions in the Southwest.

The museum offers exhibits of archaeology, ethnology, geology, and Indian crafts, including special Navajo and Hopi annual shows. The education offerings include a children's program, adult classes, and an expedition program, which involves hikes, ski tours and river trips.

Located 2 miles north of Flagstaff on Highway 180, the

museum is open from 9 A.M. to 5 P.M. except Sundays (1:30 P.M. to 5 P.M.). For further information, contact:

Museum of Northern Arizona
Route 4, Box 70
Flagstaff, AZ 86001

Hiking Clubs

Many local hiking clubs are associated with high schools, churches, businesses and YMCA and YWCA organizations. Other groups, loosely organized, meet informally and plan outings. A few hiking clubs that have been active for a number of years are:

Southern Arizona Hiking Club
P.O. Box 12122
Tucson, AZ 85711

Central Arizona Hiking Club
American Youth Hostel, Inc.
14042 N. 38th Place
Phoenix, AZ 85018

Northern Arizona Hiking Club
Box 15700
Northern Arizona University
Flagstaff, AZ 86011

Arizona State University Outing Club
Women's Physical Education Building
Arizona State University
Tempe, AZ 85281

The Landscape

Nearly 10 million years ago, tectonic deformations of the earth's crust gave New Mexico's topography its fundamental form. Since then, geologic forces have mostly modified details of the basic structure—streams eroding their courses and depositing sediments, ice-age glaciers gouging the higher mountains, volcanoes covering parts of the landscape with a veneer of lava. Volcanic eruptions were occurring 25,000 years ago when man first arrived. The lush grasslands and well-watered forests that then existed were already inhabited by saber-toothed tigers, mastadons, and mammoths.

New Mexico today, like Arizona, is a dry state—a state to be hiked with a filled canteen rather than an empty cup. Like Arizona, though, it is also a state of remarkable contrasts. Six of the seven life zones identified by Merriam—all but the Tropical—occur here. Two of the physiographic provinces that cover Arizona continue into New Mexico, and, in addition, two other provinces extend into the state from the north and east (map, p. 204).

Basin and Range Province

The Basin and Range Province continues east from Arizona across southern New Mexico as far as the Pecos River. As in Arizona, great fault-block ranges extending north and south are separated by desert basins. These ranges are steeper and more rugged than the higher Rocky Mountains in the northern part of the state.

The climate is a typical arid desert climate, most of the moisture coming in the summer from the Gulf of Mexico.

The Chihuahuan Desert extends north into southern New Mexico, bordering the Sonoran Desert, which lies to the west. Elevations range from nearly sea level along the Rio Grande to 6,000 feet in the higher desert plains. Freezing temperatures are more common in the Chihuahuan than in the lower Sonoran.

The familiar creosote bush, mesquite, yucca, and cactus species thrive in the dry climate. The characteristic plant of the Chihuahuan Desert, though, is the *agave lecheguilla,* which grows in great forests on the desert floor.

Animal life is similar to that of the Basin and Range Province in Arizona.

Great Plains Province

The Great Plains that cover the west-central part of North America extend into eastern New Mexico. The Great Plains are characterized by flat grassland with isolated buttes and mesas scattered over the landscape. The cattle country of eastern New Mexico is part of the Llano Estacado or "Staked Plain" of West Texas.

The climate is semi-arid, with more rainfall than the desert but not enough for intensive farming. Scenic hiking is limited to small canyons and watercourses.

Rocky Mountain Province

The Rocky Mountain chain extends north into Canada and

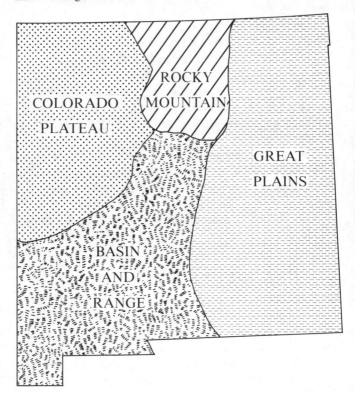

The physiographic provinces of New Mexico.

south as far as Santa Fe. The New Mexico Rockies are split into two sections by the Rio Grande. The Sangre de Cristo Mountains, including 13,161-foot Wheeler Peak—highest point in the Southwest—are east of the river; the San Juan Mountains extend just below the Colorado border west of the Rio Grande, reaching elevations of 11,000 feet. Both ranges contain a large variety of hiking areas.

The Jemez Mountains, just south of the San Juans, are of volcanic origin, created within the last 10 million years. A million years ago, huge eruptions blew out 50 cubic miles of earth, creating great *calderas,* or depressions. One such caldera, Valley Grande, is 18 miles across with Redondo Peak rising in the middle.

Climate is subhumid to humid in the Rocky Mountain Province, which is subject to the same Pacific Northwest storms as northern Arizona, the high mountains creating much of their own weather.

Colorado Plateau Province

The Plateau Province reaches from Arizona into New Mexico. The northwest corner of this state is made up of the same layers of sedimentary rock, eroded into mesas, buttes, canyons, and badlands. Elevations range from 5,000 feet to 11,000 feet. Throughout the province volcanic activity is evident where molten material pushed up through the sedimentary layers and spread over the landscape. The cone of Mt. Taylor is the largest extinct volcano in the region. Some of the lava beds have eroded completely, leaving the cores or vents of the original volcano; Shiprock and Cabezon are notable examples.

The Plateau Province is Navajo country, with its wide expanses of flat, dry landscape. Climate is hot and dry in summer, cold and windy in winter.

Riparian Habitat

Riparian habitat in New Mexico, as in Arizona, is precious topography, sustaining the greatest diversity of plant and animal life found anywhere in the state as well as providing water for agriculture and industry. The mighty Rio Grande, flowing south from Colorado to Mexico, bisects the state and is fed by streams from the Santa Fe, Cibola, and Gila National Forests, via the Rio Chama, the Rio Puerco, and other rivers. The vast majority of New Mexico's population lives in communities founded along the watercourses.

The National Forests

The national forests in New Mexico, as elsewhere, are managed according to the multiple-use concept, with recreation attaining ever-increasing priority as the demand increases for hiking, climbing, and backpacking opportunities in forested mountain areas. The Forest Service has responded with a program of putting trail information into Recreation Opportunity Guides or ROGs, which, when completed, will provide excellent data on trail conditions within each Ranger District. Guides will be kept in each District office and be available to prospective hikers. The ROG program is in its infancy and, with recent budgetary cutbacks, the project may not be completed for some time.

This section introduces you to the important hiking areas in New Mexico's national forests and refers you to local Ranger District offices for the latest trail additions, deletions, and improvements. The five national forests in New Mexico are divided into many districts separated by land not administered by the Forest Service. They are covered here in a rough arc beginning in the northeast part of the state and moving southwest.

Most of the national forests occupy mountain ranges, and most of the trails lead to high country, or "cool country" as it is called in the Southwest. Most national forest trails ascend from lower elevations through varying life zones and climates, forcing you to think in terms of 50- and 60-degree temperature ranges in the course of a long day hike.

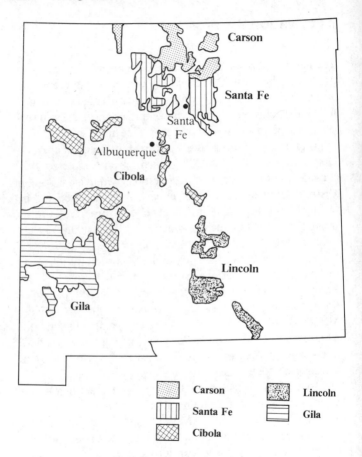

The national forests of New Mexico.

CARSON NATIONAL FOREST

The forest named after trapper and frontier scout Kit Carson is spread over an extensive area that includes New Mexico's share of the San Juan and Sangre de Cristo ranges. A western extension, the Jicarilla District, includes an area of high mesas with juniper and ponderosa pine cover. The seven Ranger Districts include two wilderness areas: Latir Peak Wilderness and Wheeler Peak Wilderness. Some districts have established hiking trails, while others have none. Forest Service maps in most districts refer readers to the more detailed USGS topographic maps, which should be obtained before reaching the trailhead.

Carson National Forest comprises 1.4 million acres at elevations ranging from 6,000 feet to 13,161 feet. The mountains, which flank both sides of the upper Rio Grande valley, are interspersed with high lakes. Recreation opportunities include trout fishing in lakes and streams, elk, deer, and turkey hunting, horseback riding, pack trips, and hiking. The normal season for hiking is from May through September and for cross-country skiing from December through April. Snow lasts at timberline until June. The variation between day and night temperatures can be extreme. Afternoon showers are frequent in July and August. Major nearby towns are Chama, Cimarron, Española, Farmington, Taos, and Tierra Amarilla.

Canjilon Ranger District

The Canjilon Ranger District has no established hiking trails, except for a 0.8-mile nature trail adjacent to Echo Amphitheater Campground, but hikes can be planned using topographic maps and information from District headquarters. Write:

Canjilon Ranger District
P.O. Box 488
Canjilon, NM 87515

The district contains four main campgrounds: Canjilon Creek, which is 10 miles northeast of Canjilon via Highway 110 and Forest Road 130; Canjilon Lakes, 12 miles northeast of Canjilon via Highway 110 and Forest Road 129; Trout Lakes, 10 miles northeast of Cebolla via Forest Road 125; and Echo Amphitheater, 15 miles southwest of Canjilon off US 84.

El Rito Ranger District

The area included in this district contains several deep canyons and high ridges that support spruce-fir-aspen communities. The south end of the district, which is characterized by deep canyons and unusual sandstone formations, blends into desert country around Sierra Negra and Red Wash Canyon. No hiking trails are maintained; you must plan your own outings.

The one campground, El Rito, is located on El Rito Creek 5 miles northwest of the town of El Rito and is reached by Highway 110. For information, contact:

El Rito Ranger District
P.O. Box 56
El Rito, NM 87530

Jicarilla Ranger District

This mesa-covered district is open to hiking and backpack-ing but is without established trails. The two campgrounds are Buzzard Park, 17 miles south of U.S. 64 on Forest Road 310, and Cedar Spring, 11 miles south of U.S. 64 on Forest Road 357. Water is not available in either campground; how-ever, drinking water is available at Bubbling Spring located on Highway 64. Winter snow and rain can make some of the roads impassable. For information, write:

Jicarilla Ranger District
Gobernador Route
Blanco, NM 87412

Taos Ranger District

Immediately east of Taos lies the Taos Ranger District, encompassing part of the Sangre de Cristo Mountains, the Taos Mountains, and the drainages of the Rio Fernando, Rio Chiquito, and Rio Grande del Rancho. Elevations range from 7,000 feet, at Taos, to over 10,000 feet in the Sangre de Cristos. Several hiking trails are maintained.

El Nogal Nature Trail (#131)

From the El Nogal picnic ground on U.S. 64 in Taos Canyon, take ½ hour to walk this trail, on which interesting flora and geology are marked by posts and interpreted by a brochure.

Divisadero Loop Trail (#108)

From the El Nogal picnic ground, a route goes north, traversing Divisadero Peak in a 6-mile, fairly steep and winding loop, mostly through pinyon-juniper vegetation.

South Boundary Trail (#164)

This newly designated National Recreation Trail starts at the El Nogal picnic ground and extends about 20 miles over elevations varying from 7,000 feet to 10,363 feet at Paradise Park. The trail, used both by backpackers and horseback riders, passes through a variety of terrain and flora, with outstanding views across the entire district.

The trail is historically significant as a homesteaders' trail, blazed in the 1800s to drive cattle and sheep to mountain grazing areas; thus its National Recreation Trail designation.

Peñasco Ranger District

Most of the land included in the Peñasco District is mountainous terrain above 10,000 feet. It's great for summer hiking, though the Forest Service discourages winter adventures. The district itself maintains trails irregularly, but four of its campgrounds—Trampas Canyon on Forest Road 207, Santa Barbara on Forest Road 116, and Agua Prieta and Angostura on Highway 3—serve as trailheads for maintained trails leading to the popular Pecos Wilderness. This wilderness, which is dominated by the Truchas Peaks, juts into the southern tip of the Peñasco District, but as most of its area is in Santa Fe National Forest, the entire wilderness is discussed under that forest.

The district includes five other campgrounds open in summer: Hodges on Forest Road 116/270, Comales on Highway 3/75, and Duran Canyon, La Junta, and Upper La Junta, all on Forest Road 76 northeast of Tres Ritos. Always check with the district office on the status of trails.

Tres Piedras Ranger District

The Tres Piedras District has four established camping areas: Hopewell Lake, 20 miles northwest of Tres Piedras on U.S. 64; Lagunitas, 26 miles northwest of Tres Piedras via U.S. 64 and Forest Road 87; Los Pinos, 15 miles southwest of Antonito, Colorado, via U.S. 285 and Forest Road 284; and Laguna Larga, 24 miles north of Tres Piedras via U.S. 285 and Forest Roads 87 and 78.

No established trails are maintained, but there is much open country, grassland parks, and forested land for the adventurous trip planner. For information, write:

Supervisor
Tres Piedras Ranger District
Tres Piedras, NM 87577

CRUCES BASIN WILDERNESS AREA

This wilderness is too new to have an official map. It is located just south of the Colorado border, encompassing the Cruces, Beaver, and Diablo Creek drainages. No trails have been established in the wilderness, but the Brazos Peak (15 minute) and Bighorn Peak (7.5 minute) topo maps are helpful for cross-country planning. Elevations reach 10,000 feet and higher, so good conditioning and equipment are necessary. For details, contact Tres Piedras Ranger District.

Questa Ranger District

Two wilderness areas are situated in the Questa District: the expanded Wheeler Peak Wilderness and the newly designated Latir Peak Wilderness. Hundreds of trails cross this district, many leading to the top of New Mexico's highest summit, Wheeler Peak. There are 14 campgrounds in the district. Six are north of Taos on Highway 150, reaching by way of Highway 3: Lower Hondo Canyon, Cuchilla, Upper Cuchilla, Italianos, Leroux, and Twining. Another six are between Questa and Red River on Highway 38: Elephant Rock, Fawn Lakes, Junebug, Columbine, Eagle Rock, and Goat Hill. Cebolla Mesa is south of Questa on Highway 3, while Cabresto Lake is northeast of Questa, reached by Forest Roads 134 and 134A.

An overview of some of the main trails situated in the two wilderness areas is given in the following table. A more detailed description of the Wheeler Peak Wilderness follows. Topographic or Forest Service maps should be used for detailed planning.

Main Trails in Questa Ranger District

Trail No.	Name	Length, miles	Difficulty
63	Long Canyon	3	Moderate
64	Gold Hill	4.25	Moderate
60	Gavilan	2.35	Difficult
59	Italianos	3.71	Difficult
58	Manzanita	4.25	Difficult
61	Yerba	4.12	Difficult
98	Flag Mountain	2	Moderate
57	Lobo Peak	6	Difficult
71	Columbine	5.7	Easy
69	Deer Creek	5.21	Moderate
72	Placer Fork	4.78	Moderate
65	Goose Creek	7.38	Moderate
WHEELER PEAK WILDERNESS			
55	Sawmill Park	7.58	Easy
56	East Fork	4.73	Easy
62	Williams Lake	1.84	Moderate
91	Lost Lake	8.23	Difficult
90	Bull-of-the-Woods	7	Moderate
LATIR PEAK WILDERNESS			
82	Lake Fork	7.06	Moderate
85	Bull Creek	6.24	Difficult
81	Midnight	5.89	Difficult
102	Cebolla Mesa	1	Moderate

WHEELER PEAK WILDERNESS

Capping the State of New Mexico is Wheeler Peak Wilderness, with summits of the Sangre de Cristo ranging from 11,000 feet to the state's high point, 13,161-foot Wheeler Peak. Subalpine vegetation is mixed with Englemann spruce, corkbark fir, and bristlecone pine. Four fishing lakes and several streams are located in the area. Wildlife to be found in this wilderness includes mule deer, elk, bear, and grouse; marmots, pikas, and martens are prominent among the smaller mammals, and many songbirds are to be heard.

The average annual precipitation is 35–40 inches, about half from summer rains and half from winter snow. Winter storms can quickly drop temperatures below freezing. The best time to visit this area is from June through September. May and June are dry, July and August rainy, typically with afternoon showers. Snowfall begins in early November, when the area opens to cross-country skiing.

A free permit, available at the Taos and Questa district offices, is required to camp overnight in the wilderness.

SANTA FE NATIONAL FOREST

Santa Fe, typical of southwestern national forests, includes a conglomeration of life zones supporting a variety of life forms. The boundaries take in semi-arid grasslands that slope up to subalpine high country. Elevations range from 6,000 feet to 13,000 feet in the 1,580,969 acres that make up this northern New Mexican playground. The forest is divided into two sections by the Rio Grande: east of the river the southern Sangre de Cristo Mountains occupy most of the Pecos Division, while west of the Rio Grande the Jemez and San Pedro mountains rise to nearly 12,000 feet to dominate the terrain.

Four wilderness areas are within the forest boundaries: Pecos Wilderness in the eastern section and San Pedro Parks, Chama River Canyon, and Dome wildernesses in the western section. Over 40 campgrounds and recreation sites are within the forest, most equipped with running water and restrooms; some have trailer hookups. Hiking trails are found near all recreational areas, most of them marked and easy to follow. Again, check with the local office of one of the seven ranger districts; higher trails may be snowed in as late as early July.

Summer temperatures are usually mild, with cool evenings and warm days. Rains occur from July to September. Winters are cold at the higher elevations; snow depths range from 8 to 10 feet.

Road travel is sometimes impeded by summer rains and winter snows. Inquire at the nearest ranger station.

Coyote Ranger District

The Coyote District contains the northeast half of San Pedro Parks Wilderness, the entire Rio Chama Wilderness, parts of the San Pedro Mountains, and the north side of the Jemez Mountains. The 5-unit Rio Puerco Campground has tables, fire pits, and a pit toilet. The nearby Rio Puerco is the water source; the water should be purified. The campground is located 10 miles southwest of Coyote and southeast of Gallina, on Forest Road 103, which is reached by Highway 96.

Rio Chama Wilderness is new, and there are few maps of the area. At present, the boundaries are not even officially determined. The backcountry of this wilderness is strikingly wild and remote. The Rio Chama is suitable for white-water sports.

Rio Puerco Trail (#385)

The trailhead is Rio Puerco Campground, at the end of Forest Road 103. This steep route into San Pedro Parks Wilderness ascends from 8,900 feet to 10,440 feet in its 6-mile length. The trail starts in heavy conifer and passes through many aspen stands. At Vega Redonda, the trail is joined by Trail #43 and joins Trail #32, near the district boundary, on the south end of Bega del Oso. Water is available along the trail.

Hart Trail (#293)

Turn off the Chama Highway (U.S. 84) onto Forest Road 145 and follow it through a piece of Carson National Forest. The road ends at the trailhead, near the northern reaches of Rio Chama Wilderness. This steep 1-mile trail provides access to the Rio Chama for wilderness fishing. The steep, sidehill trail drops at a 15–20 percent gradient. The trail is recommended for summer travel only.

Upper Gallina Trail (#36)

Take the Red Rock Trail (#30; see below) to a point 1 mile into San Pedro Parks Wilderness, where the Upper Gallina Trail begins. The trail is entirely in a wilderness and is for the experienced backpacker only. From the junction at 8,900 feet the trail climbs to 10,350 feet along the side of a hill. The gradient is 15–20 percent for a 0.7 mile section.

LENGTH: 2.9 miles
DIFFICULTY: easy to moderate

Vega Redonda Trail (#43)

From Highway 44 just north of the town of Cuba, turn north onto Highway 96, then south onto Forest Road 103, which is followed for 8½ miles to Forest Road 93, which in turn leads to the trailhead.

This trail is located mostly in San Pedro Parks Wilderness and is for experienced backpackers or hikers only. The trail, which starts at 9,200 feet and reaches a high point of 10,080 feet, is entirely on hillside. Gradients vary from 10–15 percent to 15–20 percent. Water is available in the beautiful high country through which the route passes.

LENGTH: 3.0 miles
DIFFICULTY: moderate to more difficult

Red Rock Trail (#30)

As for the Vega Redonda Trail, take Highway 44 to Highway 96, but continue on Highway 96 to Forest Road 76, just west of Gallina. Road 76 leads to Forest Road 14, and Road 14 to the San Pedro Parks Wilderness boundary and the trailhead.

This wilderness trail is for the experienced only. The starting elevation is 8,300 feet, and the high point 9,700 feet.

LENGTH: 3.2 miles
DIFFICULTY: moderate to most difficult

Rio Capulin Trail (#31)

From Highway 96, 3.8 miles east of Gallina, turn south on Forest Road 76, and take Road 76 to Forest Road 171, then Road 171 to Cecilia Springs. Follow signs to the trailhead. This is wilderness for the experienced backpacker only. Approximately 1½ miles from Cecilia Springs you cross the San Pedro Parks Wilderness boundary. The starting elevation is 8,900 feet and the high point 10,500 feet. The gradients are 0–10 percent for 1.8 miles, 15–20 percent for 4.2 miles, and 20–30 percent for 2 miles. The terrain is sidehill for 2 miles, rolling hills for 1.8 miles, and plateau for 4.2 miles.

LENGTH: 8 miles
DIFFICULTY: easy to most difficult

Cuba Ranger District

The westernmost district of Santa Fe National Forest encompasses parts of the Nacimiento Mountains and San Pedro

Mountains and half of San Pedro Parks Wilderness.

Two campgrounds are located off Highway 126: Clear Creek, with 10 sites and pit toilets, and Rio Las Vacas with 6 sites and pit toilets. Water is available from nearby creeks and springs.

San Pedro Parks Wilderness can be reached by five trailheads to be described—two west of the wilderness off Highways 44 and 96, three off Highway 126 to the South.

There are no official campsites within the wilderness. Camping within ¼ miles of the San Gregorio Reservoir is prohibited.

San Pedro Parks is a high wilderness, with much of the land at 9,000-foot to 10,000-foot elevations. Hikers must be in good condition to venture into this backcountry.

This wilderness is basically a huge meadow surrounded by stands of spruce forests. From the surrounding highway, it appears to be a massive mesa—a mesa inviting exploration.

Los Pinos Trail (#46)

This trail is reached by turning east from Highway 44, within the city limits of Cuba, onto Forest Road 95 and going northeast for 6½ miles to the trailhead. The trail extends 6 miles to junctions with other trails within San Pedro Parks Wilderness.

This is a wilderness trail for experienced backpackers. It starts at 8,060 feet, climbing steeply in places, 2,040 feet in 3 miles. Water is available along the route.

San Pedro Parks is remote and beautiful.

Vacas Trail (#51)

From Cuba, go east on Highway 126 for 12 miles to Forest Road 264. Go north on Road 264 for 2.7 miles to the trailhead parking area.

The trail runs north into the San Pedro Parks Wilderness. The gradient is 0–10 percent for the entire route, which comprises 3.5 miles of stream bed and 5.5 miles of plateau. This picturesque trail is not difficult and is recommended for family outings and backpacking training. Fishing is allowed at San Gregorio Reservoir, which also makes an easily accessible picnic site. Water is available along the route. Large wildlife, such as deer, elk, and bear, and a variety of smaller wildlife inhabit the area. During the winter and early spring, roads to the trailhead may be closed.

LENGTH: 9.0 miles
DIFFICULTY: easy to moderate

Palomas Trail (#50)

From the parking area for the Vacas Trail take Forest Road 70 about 3 miles to the trailhead of the Palomas Trail. It is also feasible to enter the wilderness by the Vacas Trail and return by this trail.

This is a wilderness trail and, with its continually low gradient of 0–10 percent and short length, is recommended for novice backpackers. The peaceful trail is also recommended for family use. Water can be obtained from the Rito De Las Perchas. Large wildlife such as deer, elk, and bear, and a large variety of smaller wildlife inhabit the area. During the winter and early spring roads to the trailheads may be closed by snow.

LENGTH: 3.8 miles
DIFFICULTY: easy

Penas Negras Trail (#32)

From the Vacas trailhead take Forest Road 70 for 10 miles to the Penas Negras trailhead.

The trail alternately may be used as a route *out* of the wilderness, after a hike in by the Vacas trail.

This scenic wilderness trail is recommended for experienced backpackers and horseback riders only. The elevation is high and the gradient reaches 10–15 percent for 2 miles. The scenic terrain traversed by the trail is sidehill for 1 mile, ridge for 1 mile, and rolling hills for 6 miles. Large wildlife, such as deer, elk, and bear, and a large variety of smaller wildlife are likely to be seen. Water may be scarce during the summer. During the winter and early spring roads to the trailheads may be closed by snow accumulation.

LENGTH: 8.0 miles
DIFFICULTY: moderate

San Jose Trail (#33)

Turn east from Highway 96 about 13 miles north of Cuba onto Forest Road 96. Follow Road 96 for 5 rough miles to the San Jose trailhead.

This is a wilderness trail recommended only for experienced backpackers and riders. The elevation is high and the gradient as great as 20–30 percent for the first 2 miles. This very beautiful route into San Pedro Parks Wilderness climbs sidehill for 2 miles and ridge for 3.8 miles.

Large wildlife such as deer, elk, and bear and a large variety of smaller wildlife inhabit the area. A fantastic route for fall aspen colors in late September and early October. Water is usually available in the first mile and in the high country.

LENGTH: 5.8 miles
DIFFICULTY: moderate to more difficult

Clear Creek Trail (#417)

A trail runs from north to south along Clear Creek's stream bed, connecting the Vacas and Anastacio trails. A gradient below 10 percent makes the trail suitable for family outings or backpacking training. Water can be obtained from Clear Creek but needs to be purified.

LENGTH: 2.8 miles
DIFFICULTY: easy

Perchas Trail (#418)

Another north-south trail joins the Penas Negras and Palomas trails. It follows the Rita de las Perchas, which rises gently at a gradient less than 10 percent, making the trail a recommended one for families and novices.

LENGTH: 2.3 miles
DIFFICULTY: easy

Anastacio Trail (#435)

Families and apprentice backpackers can further enjoy San Pedro Parks Wilderness by following this gentle, east-west oriented trail between the Vacas Trail and the Los Pinos Trail. Following the Rito de los Pinos and Rito Anastacio, the trail's gradient does not exceed 10 percent. The stream water should be purified before being used for drinking.

LENGTH: 3.3 miles
DIFFICULTY: easy

Jemez Ranger District

The southwestern part of the Jemez Mountains as far north as the northwest corner of the Baca Grant and the Rio Cebolla are included in the Jemez District. In this district are 14 established campgrounds.

East Fork Trail (#137)

Start at Battleship picnic area north of Jemez Springs on Highway 4. Leave a second car at Jemez Falls Campground on Forest Road 134, which turns off of the highway 7 miles east of the junction of Highways 4 and 126. Both trailheads have parking areas and restrooms, but no overnight parking is allowed at Battleship picnic area.

This is a very popular hiking trail, with heavy use in summer and fall. The gradient is steep in places, but the Forest Service plans to reduce the gradient to a maximum of 12 percent. Erosion is a problem in the first ½ mile, because hikers have not followed the switchbacks. Nudity is common at a warm spring halfway up the trail. The trail crosses private land for ¼ mile just east of the warm spring, but this land is not posted. Poison ivy is common. Due to the heavy traffic, camping is not recommended. The terrain includes 0.3 mile of valley, 2.3 miles of sidehill, 0.1 mile of stream bed, and 0.4 mile of plateau.

LENGTH: 3.1 miles
DIFFICULTY: easy to moderate

Cebolla Creek Trail (#68)

Take Forest Road 314 from the State Fish Hatchery to the end of the road, which is ½ mile past Seven Springs Campground. Park near Cebolla Creek. Leave a second vehicle at the bottom of Cebolla Canyon, which is reached by taking Highway 126 to Fenton Hill and a junction with Forest Road 144. Take Road 144 for 13½ miles to a junction with Pipeline Road and follow Pipeline Road west to the bottom of Cebolla Canyon.

The trail follows Cebolla Creek with no steep grades but

much scenery and many campsites. The route covers 4.1 miles of valley and 0.5 mile of stream bed. The fishing is fair. The canyon is a natural haven for deer, beaver, elk, wild turkey, and many other animals. This trail is excellent for photography. All water must be treated before use.

LENGTH: 4.6 miles
DIFFICULTY: easy to moderate

Calaveras Trail (#66)

This trail diverges from the Cebolla Creek Trail in Section 24, Township 20N, Range 2E, at the site of the old Lazy Ray Ranch. The Calaveras Trail then proceeds west to Penas Negras, which is located in the Cuba District. The elevation of the trail ranges from 8,200 feet at the start to a high point of 8,880 feet. There is a steep grade climbing out of Cebolla Canyon. The valley portion of the trail is 2.5 miles long, the sidehill portion 2.0 miles long, and the ridge portion 0.5 miles long. This trail offers day hiking, scenic and comfortable camping sites for backpackers and horseback travelers, and is good for cross-country skiing and snowshoeing. It also offers a challenge to map readers.

LENGTH: 5.0 miles
DIFFICULTY: easy to moderate

Las Vegas Ranger District

Located on the eastern edge of the national forest, the Las

Vegas District covers part of the Santa Fe Mountains and Pecos Wilderness. The wilderness is discussed under the Pecos District.

Two campgrounds are available—El Porvenir, located at the Pecos Wilderness trailhead, and Ev Long—and three picnic areas: Oak Flats, Baker Flat, and Big Pine.

Two main trails, the Hermit Peak Trail and the El Porvenir Canyon Trail, start from El Porvenir. The Hermit Peak route climbs 2,700 feet in 4 miles to the summit of Hermit Peak, then continues another 4½ miles to a junction with Trail #214. Hermit Peak offers a panoramic view of the eastern New Mexico plains stretching all the way to Texas.

El Porvenir Canyon Trail follows the canyon for 3 miles before entering Pecos Wilderness, then continues 3 more miles to a junction with the Beaver Creek and Hollinger trails. The Beaver Creek Trail, which is a section of Trail #247, joins Trail #251, which leads into the heart of Pecos Wilderness.

Pecos Ranger District

The Pecos District Ranger Station administers the Pecos Wilderness Area. Correspondence regarding hiking and camping should be directed to:

Supervisor
Pecos Ranger District
P.O. Drawer #3
Pecos, NM 87552

PECOS WILDERNESS

This huge wilderness area, comprising over 167,000 acres, is noted for its magnificent scenery. Included are 15 lakes, 8 major streams, and 21 tributaries. Elevations range from 8,400 feet up to 13,103 feet on the second highest mountain in New Mexico, Truchas Peak. Annual precipitation is 35 – 40 inches, half in summer, half in winter. Because of the elevation, summers are cool and winters cold. Temperatures can drop to 20 below zero in the winter.

Major tree species are ponderosa pine, Englemann spruce, limber pine, bristlecone pine, Douglas fir, white fir, and aspen. Wildlife includes elk, deer, bighorn sheep, black bear, blue grouse, and turkey. The lakes and streams are home for rainbow, brown, cutthroat, golden, and brook trout.

The following table lists entry routes into Pecos Wilderness with Forest Service trail numbers, road access, and trailhead information. Use the Santa Fe National Forest map along with the special Pecos Wilderness map to follow these trails. USGS topo maps are also useful.

Trail Name	Trail No.	Access Road No.	Trailhead Information
North Fork	223	FR 113	Parking
Middle Fork	266	FR 113/633	Parking
Gascon	251	NM 105	No parking, private land
Sparks	250	NM 105	No parking, private land
Lone Pine	214	NM 266	No parking, private land
Hermit Peak	223	NM 65	Parking, water, El Porvenir Campground
Porvenir	247–219	NM 65	Parking, water, El Porvenir Campground
Elk Mountain	199	NM 63	Parking
Rio Mora Loop	240	NM 63	Parking
Grass Mountain	241	NM 63	No parking
Iron Gate	249	NM 63	Parking, camping, water
Jack's Creek	245	NM 63	Parking, camping, water

(NM = State Highway, FR = Forest Road)

Dockwiler	259	NM 63	Parking, water, Panchuela Campground
Horsethief	253	NM 63	Parking, water, Panchuela Campground
Winsor Ridge	271	NM 63	Parking, Cowles Campground
Winsor Creek	254	NM 63	Parking, Winsor Campground
Spirit Lake	283	NM 63	Parking, Holy Ghost Campground
Lake Peak	non-system	FR 101	Parking at Santa Fe Ski Basin
Winsor	254	FR 101	Parking at Santa Fe Ski Basin
Rio Nambe	160	NM 4	Parking near Nambe Falls
Rio Capulin	158	NM 4	Parking near Nambe Falls
Rio Frijoles	154	NM 4	Parking at Forest Boundary
Agua Sarca	150	NM 4	Parking, Borrego Mesa Campground
Pajarito	227	NM 4	Parking, Borrego Mesa Campground
Toros (Sierra Mosca)	156	NM 4	Parking, Borrego Mesa Campground
Rio Medio	155	NM 4 or NM 76	Parking, Borrego Mesa Campground
Dome	153	NM 4 or NM 76	No parking, difficult to reach

Trail Name	Trail No.	Access Road No.	Trailhead Information
Quemado Ridge	151	NM 4 or NM 96	Parking, Borrego Mesa Campground
Quemado Creek	151	FR 400	No parking
San Leonardo	30	FR 154	Parking
Trampas Canyon	31	FR 207	Parking, Trampas Canyon Campground
Santa Barbara	24, 25, 26	FR 116	Parking, Santa Barbara Campground
Ripley Point	36	FR 116	Parking, Santa Barbara Campground
Angostura	18	NM 3	Parking, Angostura Campground
Agua Prieta		NM 3	

Tesuque Ranger District

The Tesuque District includes the southeast area of the Jemez Mountains, the Caja del Rio Plateau, and the southwest area of the Sangre de Cristo Mountains, east of Santa Fe. There are many camping and picnic areas in the various canyons. Surface water runs all year.

Dome Wilderness is located in this District, but is so new that little information has been published.

Alamos Trail (#113)

The west trailhead is reached by turning from Highway 4, west of Los Alamos, onto Forest Road 268, which leads in 5 rough miles to the trailhead. One east trailhead is the visitors center in Bandelier National Monument. An alternate east trailhead is at the boundary between Bandelier and the national forest.

This east-west trail crosses many of the north-south Forest Service roads in the Tesuque District. It connects with two trails in Bandelier National Monument: the Bland Frijoles Trail and the Frijoles Stone Lion Trail. It also traverses Medio Dia Canyon, Cochiti Canyon, and Capulin Canyon. Recreation possibilities include family outings and novice backpacking. Small wildlife abounds. The gradient generally is 0–10 percent with a 1-mile portion of 10–15 percent. The trail continues east from the forest boundary to the Bandelier National Monument visitors center. Logging units are on or near the trail on Cochiti Mesa, in Sections 19 and 20, R5E, T18N.

LENGTH: 7.8 miles
DIFFICULTY: easy to moderate

Alamo Springs Trail (#114)

From Los Alamos drive west on State Route 4 to Forest Road 289. Follow Road 289 south to Graduation Flats, then Forest Road 287 to the trailhead.

Road 287 is closed at Alamo Springs because of a 1978 forest fire. Until it is reopened, plan to walk from there.

This is a moderate trail proceeding into Bandelier National Monument. The gradient is 0–10 percent as far as the monument boundary. The trail traverses an area burned in 1978; at present the area is closed, as it is being logged for an indefinite time.

LENGTH: 1 mile
DIFFICULTY: moderate

Capulin Canyon Trail (#116)

From Los Alamos drive west on State Route 4 to Forest Road 289. Take Road 289 south to Forest Road 142 (St. Peter's Dome Road), then follow Road 142 to the trailhead.

This short Forest Service trail follows Capulin Canyon into Bandelier National Monument, where connecting trails cross the monument to the Rio Grande. The trail is primarily used in summer and fall, as the access roads become difficult during winter. The gradient is only 0–10 percent for 0.9 miles and 10–15 percent for 1 mile. The terrain is stream bed for 0.9 miles and sidehill for 1 mile. Backpacking is recommended for experienced families. Wildlife is present, and the route is very scenic. A fishing rod is recommended on the Rio Grande.

LENGTH: 1.9 miles
DIFFICULTY: moderate

Española Ranger District

The Española District includes land in both the western and eastern sections of Santa Fe National Forest. An area near Los Alamos contains the northeastern part of the Jemez Mountains; an eastern section, the southwestern part of the Sangre de Cristo Mountains.

There are no established campgrounds in this district, only a picnic area near the Los Alamos Reservoir. Most trails are short.

The first three trails described originate in the Española District but provide access to Pecos Wilderness.

Rio Capulin Trail (#158)

Take Highway 4 from Pojoaque (which is on U.S. 84) east to the Pojoaque Creek Road and Nambe Falls, where Trail #160 begins. Take Trail #160 east to its junction with the Rio Capulin Trail. Continue along the Rio Capulin and the Rio Frijoles to the junction of the Rio Medio Trail. The Rio

Capulin Trail enters the heart of Pecos Wilderness, providing access to the Capulin Meadows Trail, the Frijoles Trail, and the Upper Rio Medio.

This trail climbs from 8,600 feet to 10,000 feet in one 3½-mile stretch.

Rio Frijoles Trail (#154)

From Pojoaque drive east on Highway 4 to Cundiyo. Turn right just before Cundiyo and go 2 miles to the national forest boundary.

The trail follows the Rio Frijoles, ascending the canyon with many river crossings. In 5½ miles the trail reaches the Pecos Wilderness boundary and in another 2 miles the junction of the Rio Capulin Trail.

Rio Medio Trail (#155)

Drive north on Highway 4 just beyond the turn to Santa Cruz Lake, where a well-graded road diverges right (east) to Borrego Mesa Campground. Drive 9 miles to the campground. The trail starts south of the campground and follows the Rio Medio upstream to its source on the slopes of Pecos Baldy Mountain.

Vallecito de los Caballos Trail (#277)

Take Forest Road 442 from the northeast corner of Los Alamos to Guaje Canyon, then continue west along the canyon to the trailhead.

The trail climbs west-northwest from Guaje Canyon, to 9,800 feet. A 15–20 percent gradient along 1.7 miles of the trail could be difficult for the novice. A hiker should be experienced and in good physical condition before attempting this trail. The high desert terrain includes valley for 3.2 miles and sidehill for 1 mile. Heavy snow accumulation makes this trail inaccessible in winter and early spring.

LENGTH: 4.2 miles
DIFFICULTY: moderate

Agua Piedra Trail (#278)

Take Forest Road 442 from the northeast corner of Los Alamos to Guaje Canyon; follow the canyon west to the trailhead.

Leave Guaje Canyon and climb northwest; part of this trail crosses the Santa Clara Indian Reservation. Gradients are as steep as 30 percent in first and last miles, making the trail difficult for the novice. In addition, this area is at high elevation. Heavy snow accumulation in winter and early spring can make this trail inaccessible. The terrain is high desert.

LENGTH: 7.2 miles
DIFFICULTY: moderate

Rattlesnake Ridge Trail (#279)

This trail begins in Guaje Canyon as the Vallecito de los Caballos and Agua Piedra trails do.

With a very steep, 30–40 percent gradient the last ½

mile, it is recommended only for experienced hikers. Despite the desert-type terrain, the accumulation of snow in winter and early spring at this high elevation makes the trail impassable.

LENGTH: 2.4 miles
DIFFICULTY: moderate

Guaje Canyon Trail (#282)

Like the three preceding trails, this one begins in Guaje Canyon. A second access point is on the north side of the paved road just before the entrance to Camp May, west of Los Alamos.

This high-elevation trail is excellent for outdoor training or a family experience, despite several steep grades. The terrain consists of valley for 4.5 miles, sidehill for 2.5 miles, and ridge for 2 miles. There is some fire hazard in the area, despite the high, desert-type terrain. This is the most valuable recreational trail in the Los Alamos area, very scenic throughout and with excellent access at both ends.

LENGTH: 9.0 miles
DIFFICULTY: easy to moderate

Guaje Ridge Trail (#285)

The trailhead is reached by Pipeline Road west of Los Alamos.

This scenic ridge trail has steep gradients (15–20 percent for ½ mile). Terrain is sidehill for 2 miles and ridge for 2.3

miles. The high desert-type country is rendered inaccessible by winter and early spring snow.

LENGTH: 4.3 miles
DIFFICULTY: moderate

CIBOLA NATIONAL FOREST

A number of mountain ranges scattered throughout west-central New Mexico—the Datil, Gallinas, Magdalena, Bear, Manzano, Sandia, San Mateo, and Zuni Mountains—are included in 1,616,000-acre Cibola National Forest. With elevations ranging from about 5,000 feet to 11,301 feet, the vegetation varies from desert shrub to pinyon-juniper and forests of pine and spruce. Summer days are hot, with cool nights in the high country. Despite severe winters, the forest receives recreational use all year.

The forest is divided into four ranger districts: Sandia, Mountainair, Mt. Taylor, and Magdalena. Within the Sandia District are two wilderness areas—Sandia and Manzano—and in the Magdalena District are also two wilderness areas—Apache Kid and Withington.

Sandia Ranger District

SANDIA WILDERNESS

The Sandia Mountains are a north-south trending fault block that juts up just east of Albuquerque. Because of their proximity to the city, the range's 70 miles of trails are the most heavily used wilderness trails in New Mexico. The trails vary in length from ¼ mile to 28 miles and in elevation from 6,300 feet at the Three Gun Spring trailhead to 10,678 feet on the Sandia Crest. With the exception of the Piedra Liza Spring Trail, the trails described intersect the Crest Trail, which traverses the length of the Sandias.

Directions to trailheads in the Sandia District are given starting from the Sandia Ranger Station in Tijeras just south of I-40 on Highway 14.

Details on the many trails in the Sandias can be obtained by writing:

Sandia Ranger District
Star Rt. Box 174
Tijeras, NM 87059

La Luz Trail (#137)

Travel west on I-40 for 7 miles to Tramway Road (Exit 167), then drive north 4.2 miles to Montgomery Blvd. Go north another 4.2 miles to a 3-way stop. Proceed another mile to Forest Road 333, turn east, and drive 2.2 miles to Juan Tabo picnic ground. Continue east 1.7 miles to the parking lot. The La Luz Trail starts here. The trail starts at 7,000 feet and rises to about 10,000 feet through a series of switchbacks to the junction of the Crest Spur Trail (#34). The Crest Spur Trail climbs to 10,678 feet in a distance of 0.6 miles, while the La Luz Trail continues south 1.6 miles, where it ends at the upper tram terminal. The tram can be taken down to the lower tram terminal or the Tramway Trail descended to Juan Tabo picnic ground.

If you continue on the Crest Spur Trail, you can be met at the Crest parking lot or hike down to the tramway.

This difficult trail gains 3,600 feet in 7 miles.

Tramway Trail (#82)

Follow the La Luz Trail for 1 mile to the Tramway Trail junction. The Tramway Trail continues south 1.2 miles to a junction with the La Cueva Trail.

The Tramway Trail drops from 7,400 feet to 6,500 feet in an easy 3-mile walk.

La Cueva Trail (#83)

From Highway 46, go east on Highway 556 to Forest Road 333, then east 0.3 miles to La Cueva picnic ground. Turn right into La Cueva and go 1 mile to the last road. Follow the road about 250 feet to a turnout on the left side. The trail starts here and climbs through very steep terrain for ¼ mile to the Tramway Trail.

Piedra Liza Spring Trail (#135)

From the Juan Tabo picnic ground (see La Luz Trail), proceed north past the entrance 0.8 miles on a dirt road to the trailhead. The trail climbs from 7,000 feet to 8,400 feet, then crosses two canyons, descending to Piedra Liza Spring at 6,200 feet. This is a moderate hike.

Hikers can be met at the north end of the trail. Drive to

Forest Road 333, then go west on Highway 556 to I-25, which is taken north to Highway 44. Drive east on 44 for 8 miles, turn south on Forest Road 445, and go 2.75 miles to the spring.

Embudito Trail (#192)

From Montgomery Blvd. (see La Luz Trail) go east 0.7 miles to Glenwood Hills Drive, then north 0.4 miles to a stile and east 0.2 miles to the trailhead, near a water tank. The trail climbs southeast, from 6,200 feet to 8,400 feet in 4.1 miles, to a junction with the Three Gun Spring Trail (#195). It then climbs to 9,600 feet in another 1.6 miles to join the Crest Trail. The altitude gain and continual uphill climb make this a difficult trail.

Crest Trail (#130 North)

Drive west on I-40 to I-25, then north to Highway 44 and east to Forest Road 231. Go south on 231 for 2.1 miles to Tunnel Spring and the 6,000-foot trailhead. The trail climbs to 9,200 feet at its junction with the Osha Loop and 10K trails 8 miles south. Sandia Crest is reached by climbing for another 3.7 miles, to 10,673 feet. This trail gives exceptional views in all directions. On a clear day, you can see almost from Texas to Arizona.

Hikers can be picked up on the crest by driving north on Highway 14 to Highway 44, then up the back side of the Sandias to Highway 536 and the crest. Hikers who wish to descend by an alternate trail may go west on the Crest Spur Trail about 0.6 miles to the La Luz Trail, then 6.7 miles to the Juan Tabo picnic ground. Or you may hike 1.5 miles south to the tram terminal.

Crest Trail (#130 South)

Pass under I-40 and follow Highway 14 for 0.7 miles to the 1,500-foot trailhead. The Crest Trail goes north 1.0 miles to a junction with the Faulty Trail (#195), then southwest 1.1 miles to a junction with the Upper Faulty Trail. Continuing, the Crest Trail turns north and after 4.2 miles meets the Embudito Trail at an elevation of 9,600 feet. This route along the southern section of the crest continues north 3.4 miles to a junction with the Canoncito Trail at 9,200 feet. Another 1.3 miles north the Crest Trail crosses the Cienega Trail (#148) and continues north 1.8 miles along the crest to join the Tree Spring Trail (#147) and the 10K Trail at 9,400 feet. Finally, the trail swings northwest and goes on to Sandia Crest. This is a difficult trail because of the altitude gained.

   In a long, two-day trek you can hike the entire length of the crest, with the many intersecting trails allowing the option of descending.

Canoncita Trail (#150)

Go north on Highway 14 to Cole Springs Road and turn west to the trailhead, which is just inside the forest boundary. The trail climbs for 3 miles to join the Crest Trail at 9,300 feet.

Nature Trails

Two short nature trails enter the Sandias. One begins at the Crest observation deck and the other at the Summit House. Signs point out plant life and geologic features. Summer naturalist walks are scheduled.

A nature trail for the handicapped begins in the Cienega picnic area. This trail was designed for use by wheelchair hikers and the visually handicapped.

Its location just east of the largest city in New Mexico ensures that Sandia Wilderness receives heavy impact. It is certainly an interesting area to visit and hike, but other areas not far from Albuquerque invite the hiker and explorer to experience more remoteness and solitude. One of these, just a short distance south, is Manzano Mountain Wilderness in the Manzano Mountains.

MANZANO MOUNTAIN WILDERNESS

The Manzano Range is a long, narrow escarpment running north and south. Gentle terrain slopes down to the Estancia Valley on the east, but the west side drops dramatically into the Rio Grande Valley. The rugged country is cut by deep canyons.

Manzano Mountain Wilderness, established in 1978, protects 37,000 acres that vary from pinyon-juniper habitat at 5,000 feet to forests of ponderosa pine at 10,000 feet. Tajique and Torreon canyons contain one of the largest stands of big-tooth maple and Rocky Mountain maple in the Southwest. The fall contrast between red and yellow maples, oaks, and aspens and green conifers is spectacular.

The 64 miles of trail in the wilderness are used mostly for day hiking, which may be combined with photography, nature study, or wildlife viewing. Such birds of special interest as golden eagles and peregrine falcons are periodically seen. Hunters use parts of the wilderness. Nevertheless, despite being only an hour from Albuquerque, the wilderness is not heavily used, and a visitor seeking solitude may spend a day without meeting another person.

The Forest Service maintains several campgrounds, and the backcountry offers good camping, though you should always carry water. Forest Road 245 climbs from the town of Manzano to the crest of the range at Capilla Peak.

Albuquerque Trail (#78)

From the town of Tajique, take Forest Road 55 to the Fourth of July campground, then follow Road 55C ½ mile northeast to the trailhead. The trail climbs northwest for 1.7 miles to the Isleta Indian Reservation boundary.

Fourth of July Trail (#173)

From the Fourth of July Campground climb northwest for 1.3 miles to the Manzano Crest Trail (#170).

Manzano Crest Trail (#170)

From the end of the Fourth of July Trail, the backbone of the range may be followed south. The exhilarating Crest Trail takes you through wild, little-visited country before terminating at 10,098-foot Manzano Peak. Many side trails descend the eastern slope to forest roads, where a hiker can be met. Look for rock cairns and trail posts along the routes.

Bosque Trail (#174)

From the town of Torreon take Forest Road 55 for 7 miles west to the sign for Bosque Trail. The trail heads directly west for 2.2 miles to the Manzano Crest Trail. Bosque Peak can be climbed by traveling cross-country.

Trigo Canyon Trail (#185)

This trail starts at the John F. Kennedy Campground on the west side of the range, reached by Forest Road 33. The trail climbs 3½ miles to the Crest Trail.

Monte Largo Trail (#186)

Another route from the west begins at Monte Largo Spring, reached by Forest Road 33. The trail climbs for 5½ miles to meet the Crest Trail just below Manzano Peak. This trail is both primitive and steep.

Ojito Trail (#171)

Reach the trailhead by following dirt roads from Forest Road 33, then angling southeast ½ mile west of the Valencia-

Torrance county line. The steep, seldom-used route joins the Crest Trail after 5 miles.

Spruce Canyon Trail (#189)

The trail starts at Red Canyon Campground, which is found by driving south from Manzano on Forest Road 253 and following Road 253 west from the Manzano State Park turn-off for 3 miles to the campground. The Spruce Canyon Trail climbs to the Crest Trail in 3½ miles.

Red Canyon Trail (#89)

From Red Canyon Campground climb northwest to join the Crest Trail in 2.7 miles.

Contact the District Ranger at Tijeras for further information. The Ranger station at Mountainair also has information on Manzano Mountain Wilderness.

Mountainair Ranger District

GALLINAS MOUNTAINS

Located southeast of the Manzano Mountains are the Gallinas Mountains, a lesser range, the high point of which is 8,637-foot Gallinas Peak. The mountains support a herd of elk and mule deer, turkey, black bear, badgers, bobcats, and porcupines.

Forest Roads 99 and 102 take you to the summit of Gallinas Peak. The range is criss-crossed with unimproved dirt roads and jeep trails, but there are no maintained trails. Inquire at the Mountainair Ranger Station for the locations of trailheads. The address is:

Mountainair Ranger District
P.O. Box E
Mountainair, NM 87036

There are no topographic maps of this area yet.

Mt. Taylor Ranger District

The high point of the district and the San Mateo Mountains, Mt. Taylor, rises to 11,301 feet. Leading to this extinct volcano is one of the few maintained trails within the district (#77). The trailhead is reached by driving northeast on Highway 547 from Grants to Forest Road 193. Turn east on Road 193 and proceed to the junction of Forest Road 501. Turn back east on Road 501 for ¾ of a mile, where Trail #77 starts, on the north side of the road. This route leads to the summit of Mt. Taylor.

On the Forest Service map are a few unmaintained trails that lead from a dirt road into the southern canyons of the San Mateo Mountains. This dirt road leaves U.S. 66 14 miles east of Grants.

Another section of the Mt. Taylor District lies within the Zuni Mountains just east of the Zuni Indian Reservation. The proposed Continental Divide Trail will enter the district between Gonzales and Gonzales Lake off U.S. 66 and travels south along the Oso Ridge, the backbone of the Zunis. It leaves the district just north of Cerro Bandera near Highway 53.

The Zuni Mountains and the San Mateos are similar. The ascending hiker passes through pinyon and juniper at lower elevations, ponderosa pine and fir near 9,000 feet. An Englemann spruce forest covers the top of Mt. Taylor.

Magdalena Ranger District

The Magdalena District, located in western New Mexico, is divided into north, middle, and south sections. The northern section includes the Datil, Gallinas, and Bear mountains, the middle section the Magdalena Mountains, and the southern part the San Mateo Mountains (a different range from the San Mateos in the Mt. Taylor District). In the Datils, northwest of the town of Magdalena, grasses, pinyon, and juniper cover the lower areas and ponderosa pine the upper slopes, such as the northern edge on Madre Mountain. The Magdalenas, south of the town, rise abruptly from 6,000 feet to 10,787-foot South Baldy Peak. The San Mateos, paralleling the Rio Grande, reach 10,336 feet on West Blue Mountain.

Small stands of ocotillo are found in the eastern and southern portions of the range—perhaps the northernmost occurrence in New Mexico.

About 200 miles of trails provide access to the San Mateo and Magdalena mountains. They vary from easy walks to tough, steep challenges. Water is available in some areas but not all.

Weather is typical of the southwest mountains, with summer temperatures in the 100s at lower elevations and winters below freezing with snow and high winds. The newly formed Withington and Apache Kid wilderness areas are located in the Magdalena District.

MAGDALENA MOUNTAIN TRAILS

On the 92,000 acres of national forest in the Magdalenas are 63 miles of trails, mostly suited for day hikes. Loops can be planned, however, as most of the trails lead to South Baldy Peak.

South Baldy Trail (#11)

From Magdalena, drive 11 miles east on U.S. 60 to Forest Road 235. Follow Road 235 south; park 2 miles past Water Canyon Campground. These last few miles are rough, requiring either high clearance or slow, careful driving.

Road 235 continues to the summit of South Baldy, but the trail diverges, first ascending a tributary of Water Canyon for ½ mile, then climbing the ridge dividing Water and Copper canyons for ¾ mile. It circles the heads of a few drainages en route to a saddle and crosses a burned area. The trail rejoins Road 235 a mile east of the peak.

This short 3-mile trail is a quick way up 10,787 foot South Baldy, but climbing from the 7,520-foot trailhead can be strenuous if you are coming from the plains without acclimatizing. The trail can be hiked in summer or winter.

North Baldy Trail (#8)

This trail follows the main ridge of the Magdalena Mountains between South and North Baldy peaks. Views of such distant peaks as the Sierra Blanca, Mt. Taylor, the Sandias, and the Jemez Mountains are plentiful. Campsites are limited, and no water is available. Although this trail is nearly level, it is rated moderate in difficulty because of long stretches of primitive path. The round-trip distance of 10.2 miles makes a long hike. The best time of year is from mid-April to mid-November.

This trail leaves Forest Road 235 (see South Baldy Trail) on the east slopes of South Baldy Peak at a 10,320-foot trailhead 12 miles from U.S. 60. The first 0.1 mile is faint, and cairns must be followed to a small saddle. This is one of the steepest sections of the trail. The trail then contours on the north side of South Baldy through a dense stand of mixed conifers for ½ mile. The main ridge is reached in a small clearing. Here the trail turns north on the west side of the ridge, passing through aspen stands. After another 0.4 mile, the trail enters a clearing and meets the Copper Canyon trail. It continues another 0.9 mile and crosses a small clearing to a road. The trail continues, now on the east side of the ridge, just north of the road. After 0.8 mile, it enters a large grassy area, where Trail #25 is met.

A site suitable for camping is located near the junction. Beyond this junction the trail becomes rougher as it continues on the west side of the ridge. About 1½ miles past the junction, the trail climbs onto a sloping bench with scenic gray-white rock formations, then contours the south side of

North Baldy Peak through a dense stand of oak brush and ends on the North Baldy jeep road, at 9,720 feet.

LENGTH: 5.1 miles
DIFFICULTY: moderately difficult
MAPS: Magdalena and South Baldy quadrangles

Copper Canyon Trail (#10)

Drive to the entrance of Water Canyon Campground as for the Baldy trails, but turn right on Forest Road 406. Follow this road 1¼ miles to a parking area near a sign marked "Copper Canyon." The elevation here is 7,120 feet. Park and walk on the road to a gate. The trail starts left of the gate and is marked by a sign.

The trail begins where Forest Road 406 enters a parcel of private land in Copper Canyon, passing within 100 feet of a house. A sign advising hikers about large dogs is sometimes posted at the end of the road, and hikers should not take their own dogs on this trail. To avoid contact with the landowner's dogs, walk on the north side of the canyon until well away from the house. After passing the house, the trail continues along the canyon bottom on an old roadbed built about 80 years ago for wagon access. The canyon becomes narrower ¾ of a mile above the house, the roadbed disappears, and a trail becomes visible. Flowing water becomes more frequent, and cooler temperatures are evident as you travel farther up this canyon.

The ruins of an old prospector's cabin are found at the 3.2 mile mark. Just uphill from this is a junction where the trail splits into two legs, offering you a chance to reach the Magdalena Crest in two places. By using a mile of the North Baldy Trail between the legs of the Copper Canyon Trail, a loop of 9.3 miles can be made. Even in dry years, Copper Canyon has flowing water near the junction of the two legs, and a canyon-long flow in many years. This water nourishes a variety of interesting trees, such as walnut, box-elder, cottonwood, and alder, in the bottom of the canyon. There are a few places to camp in the canyon bottom near flowing water. The trail is rated "more difficult" because of the steep (25 percent grade) climb to the ridge beyond the junction.

The left, or southern, trail climbs continuously, with many switchbacks and a narrow path. It stays in mixed conifer most of the way. Fine views of South Baldy Peak and Copper Canyon appear in openings. The track disappears a few hundred feet from the top in a large grassy area, where the junction with the North Baldy Trail is found.

The right, or northern, leg is not as well maintained and climbs almost as steeply as the southern leg. Near the top, the trail crosses a parcel of private land on which mining and road building is evident. Just before the trail reaches the top of an east-west ridge, it intersects a road and follows it to the North Baldy Trail.

The best time of year for hiking the Copper Canyon Trail is from mid-April through mid-November. The southern leg climbs 3,000 feet, the northern leg 2,800 feet.

LENGTH: 4.3 miles (southern leg); 4.1 miles (northern leg)

DIFFICULTY: more difficult

MAPS: Magdalena and South Baldy quadrangles

Non-maintained trails in the Magdalena Mountains include:

Molino Peak Trail

This trail begins on Trail #14 at a point 0.6 miles west of the junction of Trails #14 and #12. An old sign marks the beginning of the Molino Peak Trail, which ends near Molino Spring after meandering through canyons and ridges east of Molino Peak. The trail ends on a jeep trail, which can be reached on the southeast side of the Magdalenas through an area extensively disturbed by mining activity.

LENGTH: 2½ miles

Italian Canyon Trail

This trail begins at the end of Trail #70 in a saddle just north of Italian Peak and descends into Italian Canyon. It follows the canyon bottom into Ryan Hill Canyon and joins Trail #17. No blazes have been found at the upper end, but blazes have been followed ½ mile up-canyon from Ryan Hill Canyon. Little tread exists on the overgrown trail.

By using this trail, a loop can be made of Trails #70, #17, and #14, with only a few hundred yards of road between Trails #70 and #14.

LENGTH: 1¾ miles

One of the loop-trip possibilities in the Magdalena Mountains is described here:

Trail #93–Trail #19

Start an overnight trip on Trail #19 in order to camp in the east fork of Sawmill Canyon, where water is abundant. A distance of 1.7 miles of road between the trailheads must be walked unless a car is left at each trailhead.

LENGTH: 10.0 miles

SOUTHERN SAN MATEO MOUNTAINS:
APACHE KID WILDERNESS

The San Mateo Mountains are similar to the Magdalena range in geography. Two new wilderness areas, Withington and Apache Kid, are located in this 32-mile-long range. Apache Kid is covered here, Withington in the next section with the northern San Mateos.

The 45,000-acre Apache Kid Wilderness includes the southern crest of the San Mateo Mountains. Rugged, narrow canyons, limited water, and few places to camp characterize the area, which is only a 3-hour drive from Albuquerque. The trail system consists of a 13-mile crest trail connected with 68 miles of side trails. Many loops and extended backpacks can be devised using the wilderness trail system. Travel off the trails is very difficult. Elevations range from 6,700 feet to 10,336 feet.

Visitor use is very light and is almost entirely by hunters, hikers, backpackers, and horseback travelers. The best hiking season is spring, when other areas are still snowed in and temperatures are moderate. A small developed campground at the Springtime trailhead can be reached by a well-graded and drained road and is the most popular access point. Hikers can use the Springtime Trail to reach various points between the campground and the trail's intersection with the Crest Trail. A developed spring generally provides water at the campground.

Apache Kid Trail (#43)

The Magdalena District's longest trail begins at Springtime Campground, follows the bottom of Nogal Canyon for a mile, and continues up and across the San Mateo Range for 13 miles. A total of 7,000 feet is gained and 4,480 feet lost in the course of this cross-country hike. Water is available at Twenty-Five Yard Spring, Blue Mountain, and Water Canyon. The trail passes the Apache Kid grave site, where the renegade Apache was reputedly killed by early ranchers. The trail ends at Grassy Lookout on Forest Road 138. Much of the route offers sweeping vistas west to Gila National Forest and east across the Rio Grande to faraway Lincoln National Forest.

Drift Fence Trail (#28)

On the west side of Magdalena turn south and follow Highway 107 for 26 miles to Forest Road 478. Turn right and proceed 1½ miles to a junction with Forest Road 86. Take Road 86 for 1½ miles to a junction with Forest Road 331. Proceed nearly 5 miles to the 6,360-foot trailhead, which is marked with a sign, in East Red Canyon. There is parking for 20 or more vehicles at the trailhead. This route is not recommended for passenger cars, especially Road 331.

This trail is poorly marked. Tread is evident rarely, and blazes on the sparse trees are few and far between, making navigation difficult. Nor is it particularly attractive, and water is lacking; Hartscrabble Spring, which is shown on the Forest Service visitors map, does not flow. However, the trail does offer solitude, as virtually the only users are ranchers hauling salt for cattle by horseback about once a year.

The trail begins where Drift Fence Canyon meets East Red Canyon and follows the bottom of the canyon, which is wide and gentle at this point. Vegetation is sparse, with a scattering of ponderosa pine in the canyon bottom and pinyon-juniper on the slopes. The canyon becomes narrower and deeper as you travel up it. About halfway up the canyon, the trail climbs up the canyon wall to bypass a narrow, rocky, and steep section, returning to the canyon bottom again after ¼ mile.

At 4.5 miles are the remains of Hardscrabble Spring, which consist of an old wooden box and pieces of pipe. From here the trail leaves the canyon bottom and climbs up onto the north and west side of the canyon. Look carefully for signs of the trail here: blazes, pruned trees, and cut downfall.

After a short climb, the trail enters a saddle on the ridge separating Drift Fence and Water Canyons. Then it passes through a gate and descends the west side of the ridge by several steep switchbacks. The trail ends at 8,000 feet at the bottom of the ridge in Water Canyon, where it joins the Apache Kid Trail.

LENGTH: 5.7 miles
DIFFICULTY: most difficult

SEASON: April 15–November 15
MAP: Blue Mountain quadrangle (7.5 minute)

East Red Trail (#31)

Reach Forest Road 331 as for the Drift Fence Trail, but proceed 2½ miles past the Drift Fence trailhead to the end of the road and the well-signed East Red trailhead. There is parking for 10 vehicles. This route is not recommended for passenger cars, especially Road 331.

The lightly used East Red Trail follows the bottom of East Red Canyon and climbs to the crest of the San Mateos. It begins in scattered pinyon and juniper, ascends into ponderosa pine, and finally enters mixed conifer on the crest. Sheer, 800-foot rock faces can be seen ⅔ of the way up the trail. There are no dependable water sources along this trail.

The first ¼ mile of the trail has a modern tread surface and is fairly easy to follow. The canyon then becomes wider and the trail fainter, with few trees for blazes. After 0.4 miles the Allen Spring Trail, which is not maintained or shown on the forest map, can be seen climbing the south side of the canyon. The East Red Trail continues in the bottom of the canyon, which narrows at 1.3 miles and passes two springs that usually flow only in the spring or in very wet years.

The vegetation begins to change, with more ponderosas and a few firs growing in the canyon bottom. The spectacular rock formations are located at 2.4 miles, where the trail begins to turn north and climb more steeply. Watch for bear droppings. Many nearby trees show evidence of bears tearing bark off with their claws. These marks and trail-sign damage indicate heavy use by bears in this portion of the canyon.

Where vegetation begins to change to mixed conifer with occasional stands of aspen, a small flow of water may be found, at New Lava Spring. At the spring the trail turns sharply and climbs to the crest of the San Mateos, where it joins the Apache Kid Trail ¾ miles from Grassy Lookout.

Beginning at 6,680 feet in East Red Canyon and ending at 8,920 feet at the Apache Kid Trail junction, the East Red Trail gains, 2,240 feet.

LENGTH: 4.9 miles
DIFFICULTY: more difficult
SEASON: April 15–November 15
MAPS: Grassy Lookout and Blue Mountain quadrangles (7.5 minute)

A number of loop or near-loop trips are possible in the Southern San Mateo Mountains. Other trips require car shuttles to put vehicles at each end of the hike. Only a few of the more attractive options are discussed here.

Apache Kid Trail–Trail #48

Between the Trail #48 trailhead and the Apache Kid trailhead at Springtime Campground are 4 miles of road that passes through pinyon-juniper country. As this road can be hot in the summer, the hike is best done by leaving a vehicle at each trailhead. If you start on the Apache Kid Trail, there is good camping at Twenty-Five Yard Spring, 5.3 miles up the trail. The Trail #48 junction is 0.2 mile beyond, and it is 7.9 miles down Trail #48 to the road. Starting the loop on the Apache Kid Trail means the climbing is done in a denser, cooler forest and on a better trail than if you begin on Trail #48.

LENGTH: 13.4 miles trail; 3 miles road

Trail #45–Trail #68

By going up Trail #45, the climbing is done on better trail than by climbing Trail #68. It is 8.2 miles up Trail #45 and the Apache Kid Trail to Blue Mountain Cabin, where camping and water are available. It is then 10.1 miles along the Apache Kid Trail and Trails #90 and #68 to return to the trailhead. Both Trail #45 and Trail #68 are rated "most difficult," and the lower ends of both can be hot in the summer. This loop is recommended only for experienced hikers.

LENGTH: 18.3 miles

Nonmaintained trails in the Southern San Mateo Mountains include:

Allen Spring Trail

This trail, shown on the USGS Blue Mountain and Grassy Lookout quadrangles, connects East Red Canyon with West

Red Canyon via Allen Spring. The trail that gently ascends out of East Red Canyon was well-constructed and is easily followed. The trail's west end, near West Red Canyon, also was well-constructed and has an easy grade, but is difficult to find.

LENGTH: 2¾ miles

Roberts Canyon Trail

From the Apache Kid Trail ½ mile south of its junction with Trail #61 blazes can be seen. These mark the old Roberts Canyon Trail, which was closed several years ago because rock slides and heavy brush made maintenance difficult. The trail eventually descends into Roberts Canyon and ends in Indian Spring Canyon.

LENGTH: 3½ miles

NORTHERN SAN MATEO MOUNTAINS:
WITHINGTON WILDERNESS

This section covers trails located in the San Mateo Mountains north of Grassy Lookout. The topography here is gentler than in the south and more accessible by road. Hikes are shorter and loop trips are generally not available. Water along the trails being scarcer, this area is best suited to day hikes.

Located on the northeast slope of the San Mateo Mountains, Withington Wilderness is a 3-hour drive from Albuquerque. It lies on a rugged east-facing slope below the San Mateo crest and above Big Rosa Canyon. Elevations range from 6,800 feet to 10,000 feet. The trail system, which totals 11 miles, includes two main trails running generally from a crest road to Big Rosa Canyon.

Travel off the trails is difficult. The north end of the wilderness is more or less inaccessible because of the lack of trails. Campsites are limited to a few places along the main trails where water is available intermittently.

Big Rosa Trail (#36)

From Magdalena take Highway 107 south for 23 miles to Forest Road 330. Turn right (west) and follow Road 330 for 8 miles. The sign marking the beginning of the little-used Big Rosa Trail can be easily missed, so watch for it to the right. Just uphill from the trailhead is parking for 3 cars. The trail ascends to the crest of the San Mateos, passing through scattered pinyon and juniper, ponderosa, aspen, and mixed conifers.

The trail has been relocated since the 1977 printing of the Forest Visitor's Map. Instead of beginning at the end of Forest Road 56 and following Big Rosa Canyon for most of its length, the trail now begins on Road 330 near where the now-closed Trail #92 is shown on the map. Climbing northwest, it joins an unnumbered trail that connects Trails #36 and #92, and follows this unnumbered trail northeast to the map's Trail #36; it then turns northwest with Trail #36.

The Trail #36 section begins in Rosedale Canyon and climbs over into Big Rosa Canyon on an old wagon road, which presumably connected the abandoned town of Rosedale with still-standing log cabins and prospects in Big Rosa Canyon. The trail climbs steeply on this road for ½ mile to a saddle, passes through a gate, and descends to Big Rosa Canyon. At 0.7 miles the trail joins an old logging road, and 0.1 miles farther it turns left up a side logging road. About 150 feet after making this turn, the trail turns left again and begins to climb up-canyon on still another logging road. About 320 feet after making this second turn, the trail diverges left from the logging road, then begins to climb parallel to a tributary of Big Rosa Canyon.

At 1.5 miles, the trail enters Withington Wilderness. Water sometimes runs here after a wet winter or following a rainy summer. At 2.0 miles the trail turns left and leaves both the canyon bottom and Withington Wilderness. It then climbs through a mixed conifer forest for the next 0.4 mile before entering a large clearing. Climb on the south edge of this clearing for a short distance to a logging road in a saddle. Turn left and follow this logging road for 0.1 mile before leaving it on the right. The trail is easy to follow through the dense forest for the next 0.3 mile. Within 350 feet of Forest Road 138 the trail enters a logging area, and blazes must be followed to the end of the trail.

The Road 330 trailhead is at 8,040 feet; the junction with Road 138, on the San Mateo crest, is at 9,880 feet.

LENGTH:	2.8 miles
DIFFICULTY:	more difficult
SEASON:	April 15–November 15
MAP:	Grassy Lookout quadrangle (7.5 minute)

Water Canyon Trail (#37)

This trail begins at 7,160 feet and ascends the length of Big Rosa Canyon and Water Canyon to a 9,400-foot elevation on the crest of the San Mateo Mountains.

From Magdalena drive south on Highway 107 for 17 miles. Turn right (west) on Forest Road 52. Proceed ¼ of a mile on Road 52 to Forest Road 56 and turn left (south). Follow Road 56 for 6½ miles to its end. The best place to park is on the unnumbered road that forks right beyond the trailhead (but before the end of Road 56), and enters a large meadow. The trail begins to the west, in a break in the trees where the road used to continue up the canyon. For travel off Highway 107, a high-clearance vehicle is recommended. There is parking for 10 vehicles at the trailhead.

Vegetation consists mainly of hardwoods in the lower areas and mixed conifer in the upper section. The steepest portion of the trail is the upper mile. There is undependable water in three places along the trail: 1 mile from the top, where the trail leaves the main canyon bottom, and in the two springs (Leke and Water) shown on the Forest Visitor's Map.

The first 1¼ miles of the trail follow an old logging road, which is passable to Water Spring. Since this road is included in Withington Wilderness, a barricade will be placed near the trailhead at the wilderness boundary. This first section passes through cottonwoods, walnuts, and box-elders. Blazes must be followed to stay on the trail, which offers the easiest route in the canyon bottom. About 0.3 miles past the last evidence of a road, the canyon narrows and a number of large side canyons meet the main canyon. Leke Spring, located in this area, is usually flowing.

Here the trail tread becomes more evident, and the trail has been classified semi-primitive for the remainder of the route. Fewer hardwoods are seen, and mixed conifer vegetation dominates. The grade increases. At 3.4 miles, the trail leaves the main canyon bottom, where a small area for camping and the undependable water flow are located.

The trail now ascends a south-facing slope, and ponderosa pines become more numerous. This open vegetation allows good views of the upper Water Canyon watershed to the south and the San Mateo crest. The climb ends at the head of a drainage in a saddle where Forest Road 138 is met.

LENGTH: 4.4 miles
DIFFICULTY: more difficult
SEASON: April 15–November 15
MAP: Grassy Lookout quadrangle (7.5 minute)

LINCOLN NATIONAL FOREST

It could be argued that Lincoln National Forest, which comprises 1,103,145 acres at elevations varying from less than 5,000 feet to nearly 12,000 feet, is the most diverse administrative unit in the Southwest. The lower elevations provide habitat for cactus, the upper elevations for blue spruce—and ski areas. Temperatures range from −15 to 40°F in winter, from 40 to over 100°F in summer. Spring is windy, drying tinder and increasing the fire danger.

Lincoln National Forest includes four mountain ranges. The Capitan and White Mountain ranges lie within the Forest's Smokey Bear Ranger District, the Sacramento Range in the Cloudcroft and Mayhill ranger districts, and the Guadalupe Mountains in the Guadalupe Ranger District. The Forest Service operates 18 campgrounds that are situated at elevations as high as 10,000 feet.

Smokey Bear Ranger District

In 1950, a bear cub was found clinging to a charred tree in the aftermath of a forest fire that ran through the Capitan Mountains, burning several thousand acres. In 1960, after the cub had been rescued, given a name, and made a national symbol for carefulness in the woods, the town of Capitan opened the Smokey Bear Museum, and the Mountain Gap and Forest Lookout Ranger Districts were combined as one district, the Smokey Bear.

The district now contains two wilderness areas—the White Mountain and the Capitan—in addition to six campgrounds that are open from May through September.

CAPITAN MOUNTAINS WILDERNESS

The 35,000-acre Capitan Mountains Wilderness was placed in the National Wilderness Preservation System in 1980. The wilderness is 12 miles long from east to west and ranges in width from 2 to 6 miles. The Capitan Mountains are one of the few ranges in the Southwest that run from east to west. The north side of the range consists of steep, rocky slopes with numerous canyons. On the main ridge are a number of meadows. The south face is less rocky but also has many large outcrops. Prominent summits are Capitan Peak, Chimney Rock, and Sunset Peak. Elevation ranges from 5,500 feet near the east end to 10,083 feet on Capitan Peak. Summit Peak, just outside the wilderness, is 10,179 feet high. The lower structures of the wilderness host pinyon-juniper communities. Mid-slopes are generally wooded with ponderosa pine and pinyon. The main ridge is covered with mixed conifers, including Douglas fir and ponderosa pine, and several large aspen groves.

The climate varies markedly with elevation. The lower areas can be very hot during summer, while the higher shaded areas are comfortable. During winter, the upper areas may be inaccessible due to snow. Spring brings moderate temperatures, as well as dry weather and high winds.

The most popular day hikes start from Pine Lodge and Mitt and Bar. Rock climbing is done at the east end of the wilderness. There is also opportunity for unique nature study in Capitan Mountains Wilderness.

The trail system in the wilderness includes the following trails:

Summit Trail (#58) follows the main ridge of the Capitan Mountains from the electronic site at the end of Forest Road 56 to the junction of the Pancho Canyon and Capitan Peak trails.

LENGTH: 10.1 miles

Mitt and Bar Trail (#60) originates south of the end of Forest Road 534 and reaches Forest Road 58 about 1 mile west of the electronic site. This trail passes through the wilderness for a short distance only.

LENGTH: 5.1 miles

Pierce Canyon Trail (#61) takes off on the south side of Forest Road 57 and connects with the Summit Trail.

LENGTH: 3.3 miles

Pancho Canyon Trail (#62) takes off to the south from the end of Forest Road 536 and ascends Pancho Canyon to the junction of the Summit and Capitan Peak trails.

LENGTH: 3.5 miles

Capitan Peak Trail (#64) originates near the Pine Lodge Summer Home area at the northeast base of the Capitan Range. The trail is very steep with many switchbacks.

LENGTH: 3.7 miles

North Base Trail (#65) crosses from Forest Road 130 near Pine Lodge to the end of Forest Road 256 in Seven Cabins and continues west for another ½ mile. Pinyon and juniper are the predominant vegetation in this foothill terrain.

LENGTH: 4.6 miles

Seven Cabins Trail (#66) begins at the termination of Forest Road 256 and ascends the range's north slope to the Summit and Pierce Canyon trails. This is a steep trail.

LENGTH: 3.8 miles

WHITE MOUNTAIN WILDERNESS

The 48,143-acre White Mountain Wilderness was established when the National Wilderness System was started in 1964.

The wilderness is 12½ miles long and ranges from 4 to 12 miles wide. The west boundary coincides with the national forest boundary; the south boundary borders the Mescalero Apache Reservation. Unlike many larger wilderness areas with numerous mountain ranges, this one consists of one long, north-trending ridge and its spurs. The west side of this ridge is steep and rugged with extensive rock outcrops, while the east side is gentler with broad, forested canyons and a few tiny streams.

Elevations range from a low of 6,500 feet at Three Rivers Campground on the west side to a high of 11,260 feet on Lookout Mountain near the south end of the wilderness. From Three Rivers to the crest are four different life zones, Upper Sonoran through Hudsonian. Abrupt changes in elevation—escarpments, rock outcrops, and avalanche chutes—make for striking contrasts in plant communities. Scattered along the crest are several mountain parks and grass-oak savannahs, which are the result of past fires.

The weather, too, is related to elevation. During the winter the higher elevations may be under 6 or more feet of snow while it is comfortably warm at 6,000 feet. In summer, while the desert is sweltering, you may wear a sweater or jacket in the high country. Spring is usually dry and windy throughout the wilderness. July and August are the rainy months, with frequent afternoon showers. Autumn is perhaps the most beautiful season, with oaks, maples, and aspens adding splashes of color to the hillsides. Snow usually begins to fall in the high country in November.

Of the many species of birds, five have critical habitats within the wilderness, mainly in the spruce-fir zone. They are the northern three-toed woodpecker, Clark's nutcracker, red-breasted nuthatch, Townsend's solitaire, and golden-crowned kinglet. The habitat is considered critical for these birds because of the scarcity of spruce-fir forests this far south.

White Mountain Wilderness includes two important watersheds: the Rio Bonito on the east and the west-side Sierra Blanca–Jicarilla system. These provide a major portion of the domestic water supply of Capitan, Carrizozo, Fort Stanton, Alamogordo, and Holloman Air Force Base.

More than 50 miles of developed trails wind through the wilderness, generally following either ridges or canyon bottoms. Crest Trail, extending north and south, ties together the trail system. Many old trails are not part of the maintained system yet continue to be used for hiking and prospecting.

Water, while not abundant, can usually be found in springs

and small streams scattered throughout the area; treating the water is always a good precaution. There are no visitor-convenience improvements of any kind within the wilderness.

Five access points to the White Mountain Wilderness are of interest to the hiker. They are, from north to south: Nogal Canyon, via Forest Road 108; Argentina Canyon, on the east side, via Forest Road 107; Three Rivers Canyon, on the west side; South Fork Campground, on the east side; and the Sierra Blanca Ski Area, on the southern boundary of the wilderness.

The range is traversed by the 21-mile Crest Trail, which runs southwest from Monjeau Lookout to the Sierra Blanca Ski Area, then north to Nogal Canyon. The trail passes through grass-oak savannahs, mixed conifer and aspen stands, and subalpine meadows and offers spectacular views of White Sands, the Malpais lava beds, and the Capitan Mountains.

A number of trails, most of which are easily negotiated by hikers, backpackers, and horses, connect the Crest Trail to east- and west-side trailheads. They are listed in the following table.

No.	Name	Length, miles	Trailhead	Remarks
19	South Fork	6.0	South Fork Campground	Streams, old beaver activity
33	Blue Front	5.2	South Fork Trail	Passes ruins of Great Western Gold Mine
35	Aspen	2.4	Bonito Creek	
36	Bonito	4.6	Argentina Canyon	Streams, old beaver activity
37	Little Bonito	1.4	Bonito Trail	Aspen stand
39	Argentina	2.5	Argentina Canyon	Large spring at top
50	Doherty Ridge	4.2	Private land on west side	Good deer country
53	Water Canyon	3.0	Private land on west side	
44	Three Rivers	5.6	Three Rivers Campground	Stream with rugged rock bluffs

Trails #50, #53, and #44 are difficult hiking with a pack.

If you are coming from lower altitudes, allow a day or two for acclimatization before attempting strenuous hikes with a pack. By late May, days are long and warm, but nights may be cold with temperatures in the 20s. Bring warm clothes and a good sleeping bag. Although the rainy season doesn't usually start until mid-July, showers are possible, so bring rain gear. Check at the Smokey Bear Ranger Station in Ruidoso to get information on fire and smoking restrictions.

Cloudcroft Ranger District

The Cloudcroft District contains the Sacramento Mountains, which occasionally do touch the clouds, and provides the setting for the most popular resort area in southern New Mexico. Cloudcroft offers wilderness sports opportunities throughout the year, including the state's southernmost ski area and one of the world's highest golf courses.

Developed trails include interpretive trails (one, La Posada Encantada is for the visually handicapped), national recreation trails, and wilderness trails. Views from the Sacramento Mountains extend east all the way to Texas, north to Santa Fe National Forest, west to Gila National Forest, and south into Mexico.

INTERPRETIVE TRAILS

La Posada Encantada (The Enchanted Path)

On this ¼-mile trail for the visually handicapped are 26 stations with both Braille messages and conventional signs. Foot traffic only is permitted. The trail is normally open from May 1 to October 31. There is a small parking lot for 10 vehicles adjacent to the south end of Sleepy Grass picnic area.

Silver Saddle and Apache Nature Trails

A trail circles each campground, with small metal signs identifying plants and other natural features. Trails vary in length for ½ to 1 mile. Foot traffic only is permitted. The normal season is from May 1 to October 31.

Nelson Vista Trail

On this ¼-mile trail 5 miles south of Cloudcroft, just off the Sunspot Road (Forest Road 64), are seven interpretive stations related to forest resource management. There is also a good view of Nelson Canyon and the Tularosa Basin. Foot traffic only is permitted. The normal season is from May 1 to October 31.

Cathey Vista Trail

This ¼-mile trail offers a spectacular view of the Tularosa Basin, San Andreas Mountains, White Sands, Alamogordo, and the west side of the Sacramento Mountains. At an elevation of 9,500 feet, it overlooks the basin, which is a full mile lower. There are two large interpretive signs, several smaller signs, and an undeveloped area suitable for picnicking adjacent to the large parking lot. The normal season of use is from May 1 to December 1.

NATIONAL RECREATION TRAILS

Rim Trail (#105)

From Slide Group Campground, 1 mile southwest of Cloud-croft, this trail meanders southwesterly 13½ miles to Atkinson Field, which is 1¼ miles west of Forest Road 64. Trail conditions are good, with a tread and a gentle grade that make for easy hiking. Signs are present at the trailhead and at appropriate locations along the trail. The trail is also open to trail-bike and horseback riders. Several points along the trail provide outstanding views of the Tularosa Basin, White Sands, and the San Andreas Mountains. The elevation along the trail is generally near 9,000 feet.

Carry drinking water as none is available along the trail. Undeveloped camping sites are available in Haynes Canyon, Karr Canyon, Atkinson Field, and adjacent to Forest Road 64D (Alamo Peak Road), but camping spots may be found all along the trail.

Trail #110 drops from Atkinson Field into Alamo Canyon and ends at Forest Road 90.

Douglas fir, white fir, southwestern white pine, ponderosa pine, Gambel oak, aspen, mountain maple, and forbs and grasses associated with Douglas fir habitat are found. The area provides habitat for mule deer, black bear, coyote, turkey, bobcat, squirrel, and numerous birds.

Portions of the trail will be closed occasionally between now and 1985 due to logging in progress. Information is available at the district office.

Dog Canyon Trail (#106)

From Oliver Lee State Park, 10 miles south of Alamogordo, the trail heads northeasterly 4½ miles to Forest Road 90B (Joplin Ridge Road). Trail conditions vary from good to poor for the first 2 miles, and the last 2½ miles are rocky and steep; this trail is for the hiker in good condition. The trail provides magnificent views of Dog Canyon, the Tularosa Basin, and the San Andreas Mountains.

This is an old Apache trail. It was one of their principal access routes to the Sacramento Mountains, because water is available all year. The "Eyebrow" portion of the trail was the scene of skirmishes between the Apaches and the U.S. Cavalry in the late 1800s. Frenchy, an immigrant from France and a noted personality in southern New Mexico history, lived in a small stone cabin near the mouth of Dog Canyon. An old stone line-cabin for cowboys is located 2½ miles from the trailhead and is often the destination of hikers.

Plans call for rebuilding the trail with a gentler grade when funds are available. The elevation ranges from 4,400 feet at the trailhead to 7,600 feet on Joplin Ridge—a 3,200-foot climb.

Water is available from Dog Canyon Creek near the canyon mouth and at the line-cabin but is not recommended for drinking. A spring-fed trough for wildlife is located a mile below the cabin. Summer daytime temperatures range from 90 to 110 degrees; winter daytime temperatures vary from 30 to 70 degrees. There are undeveloped campsites along the Joplin Ridge Road and limited camping spots along the trail. At Oliver Lee State Park are developed campsites.

The flora is typical of southern New Mexico desert country. The habitat is suitable for coyotes, deer, mountain lions, and numerous birds.

OTHER SYSTEM TRAILS

Osha Trail (#10)

This moderately difficult 2½-mile loop starts from U.S. 82 at the northwest edge of Cloudcroft, across from the old railroad trestle. It is well marked and signed, has a small parking area, and is recommended for foot traffic only. The normal season of use is from April to December.

Willie White Trail (#113)

From the junction of Willie White Canyon and the Rio Penasco, this 6-mile trail ascends Willie White Canyon and descends Telephone Canyon to Water Canyon. Several loops are possible. There are springs in Water Canyon and 2 miles up Willie White Canyon. The trail gets most of its use between April and December.

Alamo Peak Trail (#109)

This steep (15–20 percent grade), 3-mile trail connects Alamo Peak to the West Side Road at the Woods Ranch. From the trailhead on the south side of the road just before Alamo Peak Road (Forest Road 64D), the trail passes the Alamo Peak Military Compound fence, ½ mile west of the point where the Rim Trail crosses Alamo Peak Road. The Alamo

Peak Trail joins the Pipeline and Atkinson trails, which in turn connect with the Rim Trail at Atkinson Field, providing several loop possibilities. The trail receives heavy trail-bike use during summer and fall, especially on weekends.

Pipeline Trail (#110)

A 1-mile trail connects the Alamo Peak Trail and the south end of the Rim Trail. The trailhead of this very steep trail is at Atkinson Field. It provides possibilities for loops in combination with the Rim, Alamo Peak, and Atkinson trails. The lower ⅔ follows the City of Alamogordo pipeline. There is heavy motorcycle use during the summer and fall, especially on weekends.

Atkinson Trail (#111)

The very steep mile-long Atkinson Trail connects the Alamo Peak Trail and the south end of the Rim Trail, offering further loop possibilities. The trailhead is at Atkinson Field. Mostly in a canyon bottom, it receives little maintenance.

Additional system trails that receive no maintenance and may be difficult to find and follow are:

Deadman Trail (#107)
Escondido Trail (#108)
Domingo Trail (#112)
Table Trail (#115)
Apple Tree Trail (#116)
Burnt Trail (#117)

Beeman Trail (#118)
Indian Wells Trail (#119)
Bailey Trail (#121)
La Luz Trail (#122)

For more specific information, contact the District office.

Guadalupe Ranger District

The Guadalupe District adjoins Guadalupe Mountains National Park, which is across the Texas border, and Carlsbad Caverns National Park, which lies just to the east. Its 290,242 acres feature the Capitan limestone reef, a huge, exposed barrier reef deposited in ancient seas.

The combination of southern location and high topographic relief has resulted in a meeting in the Guadalupes of habitats characteristic of the Great Plains, the Rocky Mountains, and the Chihuahuan Desert. Cactus and columbine grow side by side. Texas madrone, Mexican buckeye, New Mexico alder, oaks, and junipers are found in this range. The district contains some of the finest deer range in New Mexico, inhabited by the Rocky Mountain mule deer and desert mule deer, as well as elk, a few bears, and over 200 bird species.

There are no developed campgrounds in this district, but camping is permitted in most of the area. Camping, hiking, and picnicking are year-round activities throughout most of the range.

Gasoline, groceries, and other supplies are available in Carlsbad or Artesia, both approximately 50 miles from the eastern boundary of the forest. There is no road directly from the national forest to Carlsbad Caverns. The National Park must be reached via the city of Carlsbad.

Daytime temperatures vary from 50 to 80 degrees, but nighttime temperatures may drop below freezing. March is the windiest month; the chilling effect of wind should be considered when choosing clothing and bedding.

Most of the district's trails are in its southern portion, close to the Texas border and Guadalupe Mountains National Park, but many jeep roads provide wilderness access throughout the district.

Two roads are suitable for any type of vehicle in all weather. Highway 137 is paved all the way across the district. Forest Road 540 is a good graveled road, which leaves 137 at a mailbox about 45 miles from U.S. 285 and heads south for 13 miles toward the southern boundary of the district. Other roads are suitable only for pickups and 4-wheel drive vehicles.

A Scenic Drive, the Rim Road, can be reached by going 12 miles north of Carlsbad on U.S. 285 to Hamilton Station and turning left onto Highway 137. Drive 48 miles to the intersection with Forest Road 67. Turn north on Road 67, which is the Rim Road, a dirt road that in 45 miles traverses ⅔ the length of the Guadalupe District. One segment of the road overlooks Little Dog-pup, a roadless, undeveloped RARE II area. Quite a variety of wildlife and plants may be seen on the drive. Take plenty of gasoline and water.

Sitting Bull Falls Trail (#68)

Go west from Hamilton Station on Highway 137 for 41 miles, where a sign marks the beginning of the trail. The main trail runs 3½ miles from Highway 137 to the Sitting Bull Falls picnic area. There is diverse vegetation and wildlife along the trail.

Sitting Bull Falls is a picnic ground for day use only. Available at the picnic ground are ramadas with picnic tables, fireplaces, garbage cans, restrooms, drinking water, and a trail to the waterfall.

Guadalupe Ridge Trail (#201)

From the south end of Forest Road 540, turn left on the Guadalupe Ridge Trail, which is a 4-wheel-drive road. Hike 8 miles to Dark Canyon Lookout, an ideal place for solitude, photography, and seeing wildlife. The vegetation includes pinyon, juniper, oak, Texas madrone (an endangered species), and ponderosa pine. Take your own water and please close gates.

Camp Wilderness Ridge Trail

From the south end of Forest Road 540, turn onto Forest Road 531 and proceed for ½ mile to an intersection with the Guadalupe Ridge Trail. Turn right. The Camp Wilderness Ridge Trail is a spur of the Guadalupe Ridge Trail. After 4 miles on national forest land, it passes into Guadalupe Mountains National Park and continues an additional 5 miles on park land, where it is called the Geology Trail. The walking is easy until you enter the national park, where it becomes more difficult. The trail overlooks North McKittrick Canyon and other scenic canyons; the hiker also encounters a variety of wildlife and vegetation.

Devil's Den Trail (#202)

Devil's Den Trail winds down the west slope of the Guadalupe Mountains. The beginning of this spectacular and challenging trail is marked by a sign on Forest Road 540, 13 miles from Highway 285. Diverse vegetation and wildlife are to be seen along the 4-mile trail, which also offers scenic vistas.

Lonesome Ridge Trail (#56)

Turn left from Forest Road 540 onto the Guadalupe Ridge Trail. Proceed for 2 miles to an intersection with the Lonesome Ridge Trail, which winds 3 miles through the south end of the Guadalupe District. It then runs for an additional mile on BLM land before ending on private land. This trail is difficult, especially in the Golden Staircase area, and is recommended for experienced hikers only. The country traversed includes scenic canyons and diverse vegetation and wildlife.

Pacific Slope Trail (#203)

The Pacific Slope Trail crosses the south end of the Guadalupe District for 3 miles, then wanders into Carlsbad Caverns National Park. This challenging trail is recommended for experienced hikers only. Hike on the Guadalupe Ridge Trail for 7 miles; the Pacific Slope Trail starts here at an intersection.

Mayhill Ranger District

The Mayhill District at present has no established hiking trails. The District has several church and scout camps and one developed picnic area—James Canyon, located off U.S. 82 between Mayhill and Cloudcroft. Camping is permitted in certain areas of the district.

The Mayhill topographic map can give an idea of the topography when you are planning a cross-country trip. Wildlife is abundant and includes mule deer and white-tailed deer, coyotes, bobcats, mountain lions, foxes, weasels, badgers, raccoons, squirrels, skunks, and porcupines.

For current information about the district, contact:

Supervisor
Mayhill Ranger District
P.O. Box 5
Mayhill, NM 88339

GILA NATIONAL FOREST

The 3½ million acres of this huge national forest consist of steep mountains, flat mesas, deep canyons, flood plains, and river channels. With elevations ranging from 4,200 feet to 11,000 feet, the terrain encompasses semi-desert shrub and grassland, pinyon-juniper and oak woodlands, and ponderosa pine, spruce, and fir forests. Riparian habitat is bordered by cottonwoods, alders, and sycamores. West of the Continental Divide the area is drained by the Gila and San

Francisco rivers and to the east by the Rio Grande and Mimbres River.

The Continental Divide Trail meanders through this deep canyon country for 170 miles, through such mountains as the Mogollon, Tularosa, Diablos, and the Black Range. In these mountain strongholds the Apache warrior Geronimo lived, and before him, generations of prehistoric cliff-dwelling tribes.

Gila National Forest contains two large wilderness areas and part of a third. Gila Wilderness and newly named Aldo Leopold Wilderness include vast areas of the forest, while a small portion of Blue Wilderness extends into New Mexico from Arizona.

There are nine ranger districts in this far-reaching forest and 28 campgrounds.

Paved roads in Gila National Forest are passable all year, except for short intervals when winter snows block canyon roads. Highway 15 between Silver City and the Gila Cliff Dwellings is narrow, winding, and steep in places. Do not take trailers higher than 18 feet between Pinos Altos and the junction with Highway 35. This section can be avoided by Highways 61 and 35.

Parts of the gravel or dirt roads may be muddy and chuck-holed during the summer rainy season, but they are usually passable unless washed by flash floods. Highway 61 north of its intersection with Highway 35 may be closed by snow or flash floods. Sedans are not recommended on this road. Highway 78 east of Mogollon is closed by snow most of the winter. Most of the road from Reserve to the Willow Creek–

Snow Lake area is used by logging trucks, requiring caution by other drivers. Passenger cars are not recommended on the road between Beaverhead and Snow Lake or the road to Turkey Creek beyond the pavement's end north of the town of Gila.

Most major trails are maintained and easy to follow, but those using river bottoms may be flooded by summer storms or runoff after a wet spring. Flooding frequently affects trails in the West Fork, Middle Fork, and main Gila River. Some trails shown on maps may be difficult to find. River bottom trails involve many stream crossings, so be prepared for wet feet. Most trails starting on the south and west side of Gila Wilderness or the Gila Cliff Dwellings area begin at lower elevations but climb to high country. In the Willow Creek–Snow Lake area trails start high, eliminating long climbs out of deep valleys.

Many water sources are not safe for drinking without boiling or purifying. Lower-elevation streams, watering tanks, stock tanks, and springs frequented by livestock are suspect. Natural springs and headwater streams are safer. Always, in the land of little water, carry plenty.

Winter nights are cold throughout the Gila. Lower elevations and south-facing slopes reach 20 degrees, but at 7,000 feet and higher, temperatures may drop to 0 degrees and lower. During the day, in sunlight, temperatures may get to 70 degrees and more in the mountains, into the 80s and 90s at lower elevations.

In the summer, temperatures can get into the high 90s at elevations up to 6,000 feet. Higher up, temperatures can reach the 70s and 80s during the day, dropping to 45 degrees at night.

July and August are the rainy months, and therefore the months when canyons can send flash floods on the unwary.

Over 1,200 miles of trails in the Gila can result in a lot of worn footwear and picture taking.

Black Range Ranger District

The Black Range District was formed in 1953 by combining the Kingston and Chloride districts. In 1979, the Beaverhead District was added to the Black Range District, which now totals 552,615 acres.

In 1980, Congress designated an area of 211,300 acres on the Black Range crest the Aldo Leopold Wilderness, in honor of the great conservationist. Much of Aldo Leopold Wilderness lies within the Black Range District.

The Black Range is a long uplift running from north to south, cut by deep canyons, flanked by escarpments and talus slopes. With the Continental Divide running along the crest, great diversity is found in the Black Range. Desert grasslands slope up to steep mountainsides covered with spruce, fir, and aspen forests. Elevations range from 4,200 feet to over 10,000 feet.

Within the district are 263 miles of trails.

South Diamond Trail (#68)

Part of this 17-mile trail follows South Diamond Creek, which is home to the rare, endangered Gila trout. From a trailhead at the end of a dirt road southeast of North Star Road, at the wilderness boundary, the trail follows old roadbeds. A homestead is passed 8 miles up the canyon. It is recommended that the Burnt Canyon Trail be used rather than the last 3½ miles of this trail to reach the Black Range crest.

Burnt Canyon Trail (#69)

Starting in South Diamond Creek as a spur trail to the Continental Divide, the Burnt Canyon Trail climbs over 1,000 feet in 3¾ miles to the crest, following a mountain stream through aspens and conifers.

MeOwn Trail (#707)

Another spur, this 4-mile trail goes from MeOwn Helitack Base near Highway 61 to South Diamond Creek. It follows an old road to MeOwn Hill, circles the hill to an open meadow, Rastus Flat, then descends to South Diamond Creek.

Black Canyon Trail (#72)

This trail travels 12½ miles along a permanent stream in Black Canyon, starting near the North Star Road and climbing to the Black Range crest, where it ends at Reeds Meadow. It is easily traveled, but heavy rains can make the creek crossings difficult. Most of the trail zig-zags through a wide canyon bottom along the stream bed.

Water Canyon Trail (#20)

From the junction of Trail #114 and Water Canyon, a half mile south of the Murphy Place, the Water Canyon Trail climbs west to the Crest Trail, which it meets 1.5 miles north of the McKnight fire cabin. Many unusual rock formations can be seen along Water Canyon. As you approach the head of the trail, it climbs steeply out of the canyon. The trail is in good shape but brushy in places. Water can be found year-round in the canyon bottom. Several nice camping sites can be found along the trail.

LENGTH: 5.0 miles
ELEVATION: 6,560 feet to 9,720 feet

Canyon Creek Trail (#31)

This major route into the Gila Wilderness heads south from the Hulse Ranch headquarters and follows Canyon Creek until the creek flows into the Gila River. Leading between high canyon walls and a flowing stream, this route is great for horseback travel. The trail starts on private land, so permission must be obtained from the owner. There are many good camping spots along the Gila River.

LENGTH: 4.2 miles
ELEVATION: 6,700 feet to 7,100 feet

Diamond Creek Trail (#40)

From Diamond Peak, this trail runs north and west; it is a

good trail with plentiful water. Douglas fir and stands of large aspen are abundant, furnishing good camping spots. The creek has been closed to fishing, because it is one of the few remaining natural habitats for the endangered Gila trout.

LENGTH: 8.6 miles
ELEVATION: 7,800 feet to 9,850 feet

Caledonia Trail (#42)

This trail, the primary route to Aldo Leopold Wilderness from the Lookout Mountain area, goes south from Forest Road 226 for ½ mile west of Monument Park Cabin. It is easy to follow and lies on a good grade, intersecting the Continental Divide Trail just over 3 miles from Road 226, and ending about 2 miles farther at Trail #40. Water is available at the Monument Park Cabin. Snow covers the trail almost all winter.

LENGTH: 5.4 miles
ELEVATION: 7,800 feet to 8,040 feet

Meadow Trail (#53)

This great trail begins at the Double Springs Ranch and leads south to the Gila River and Gila Wilderness, ending at a point known as the Meadows. The Meadows is a heavily used camping area, and visitors seeking solitude should camp elsewhere. Water is available year-round at the river. The trail begins on private land, so permission should be obtained.

The grade is good except for the last mile before the river, this span being moderate to steep.

LENGTH: 5.8 miles
ELEVATION: 6,300 feet to 7,300 feet

Crest Trail South (#79)

The trail begins at Emory Pass and leads south to Berenda Canyon, where it connects with Forest Road 888. Vegetation varies from firs and ponderosa pine to juniper, pinyon, and cacti. The trail passes several good vista points and camping areas. Very little water is available during summer. The trail generally follows the crest; the grade is not steep. Such wildlife as bear, mountain lion, and deer are common to the area.

LENGTH: 12.0 miles
ELEVATION: 6,400 feet to 9,410 feet

Crest Trail (#79)

One of the most scenic trails in the Black Range, the Crest Trail runs from Emory Pass to Reeds Peak, following the southern boundary of Aldo Leopold Wilderness from Hillsboro Peak to McKight Mountain. The trail is in good shape, with moderate slopes. Hillsboro Spring, Mimbres Lake, Willow Springs, and Squeaky Springs are intermittent water sources. With spectacular views, this is a "must" trail for photographers.

LENGTH: 10.0 miles
ELEVATION: 10,011 feet to 7,050 feet

Circle Seven Trail (#106)

The trail leaves Forest Road 157 3½ miles north of the old townsite of Hermosa and follows Forest Road 730 for about 2 miles to the trailhead at road's end. It follows the drainage of Circle Seven Creek to the Continental Divide. Water is usually present along the lower half of the trail. As you near the Divide, the trail, which is in good shape, climbs steeply out of the canyon. The point where the trail reaches the Divide makes a nice camping spot.

Rattlesnake Trail (#107)

From Reeds Meadow, this trail takes you through Rattlesnake Canyon and along Morgan Creek to Mud Springs. The trail is rough, steep, brushy, and sometimes hard to follow. Trail blazes are present, but you have to look for them. Good camping areas can be found, but no water is available along the trail.

LENGTH.   6.2 miles
ELEVATION: 6,480 feet to 8,920 feet

Lake Trail (#110)

Diverging east from the Crest Trail near Mimbres Lake, the Lake Trail follows North Seco Creek to Forest Road 891.

Between the Crest Trail and Trail #87, the Lake Trail is hard to follow, rough, and brushy. Inexperienced backpackers or riders should not use this trail. Water can be found in North Seco Creek. Campsites can be found along the trail.

LENGTH: 9.1 miles
ELEVATION: 6,400 feet to 9,620 feet

Spud Patch Trail (#111)

Leaving the Lake Trail 3 miles southeast of the old townsite of Hermosa, the Spud Patch Trail climbs through a mountainous area with large rock outcrops. Toward the top, the trail levels out in a stand of fir and spruce just south of Reeds Peak. Water is available all year along the lower portion of the trail and near the top, at Newman Spring to the north and Willow Spring to the south.

LENGTH: 5.9 miles
ELEVATION: 6,400 feet to 9,660 feet

Animas Trail (#114)

From the Crest Trail at Holden Saddle, the Animas Trail heads north down Holden Prong and Animas Creek. This is one of the most scenic trails in the Black Range, with ecological diversity, various geologic features, many camping spots, a good supply of water, and even a 50-foot waterfall. The trail is in good shape and is easily followed.

LENGTH: 13.3 miles

ELEVATION: 6,000 feet to 8,000 feet

East Curtis Canyon Trail (#116)

This short trail leaves the Animas Trail on Animas Creek, near the wilderness area boundary, and goes south to East Curtis Spring, climbing briskly past a 200-foot waterfall (when the creek is flowing). From the switchbacks, you can see slides that bears play in during the rain season. Beautiful views of Animas Canyon are offered from the trail. Water is seldom available before East Curtis Spring, and camping areas are scarce between Animas Creek and East Curtis Spring.

LENGTH: 2.7 miles
ELEVATION: 6,240 feet to 7,520 feet

Animas Divide Trail (#117)

This trail leaves Hillsboro Peak and follows the Animas Divide to Apache Peak, where it meets the Hermosa Trail. It offers some of the most scenic views anywhere in the Black Range. On a clear day, you can look east beyond the Rio Grande valley to Sierra Blanca Peak, which is east of Ruidoso. At night, from certain high points, you can see lights from several distant communities. The trail is easily followed despite brush in places. Water is rare along the trail, except at East Curtis Spring. Several good camping spots can be found along the trail.

LENGTH: 10.3 miles
ELEVATION: 7,360 feet to 10,011 feet

Sid's Prong Trail (#121)

The Sid's Prong Trail descends from Sid's Saddle to the bottom of Sid's Prong and crosses into Flower Canyon. Sid's Prong is one of the prettiest places in the Black Range, with open meadows and nice places to camp. The trail in Flower Canyon is rough and hard to follow, with new blow-down every year. Normally, a trickle of water flows year-round.

LENGTH: 5.9 miles
ELEVATION: 6,680 feet to 9,000 feet

Ladrone Trail (#127)

Leaving the Crest Trail 1¼ miles south of Hillsboro Peak, this trail descends east along Carbonate and Ladrone Creeks. The trail is steep, rough, and brushy, with annual washouts in the creek bottoms. After getting into the Middle Percha Creek drainage, the trail continues downstream to Forest Road 40E, which comes up from Kingston. In the spring and after rains, Mineral Creek and Ladrone Creek provide water. These creeks dry up during early summer, but there is water year-round in Middle Percha Creek. This trail passes Hillsboro Lake, where a small but beautiful camping area can be found ½ mile from the Crest Trail.

LENGTH: 3.5 miles
ELEVATION: 6,440 feet to 9,220 feet

Railroad Canyon Trail (#128)

One mile north of Railroad Canyon Campground, the Railroad Canyon Trail splits right from the Gallinas Trail, fol-

lowing the bottom of Railroad Canyon, then climbing out
into Holden Prong Saddle. The trail is in good shape and
easily followed. Water is present during the wet seasons, but
the canyon usually dries up between April and July. Several
nice camping areas are along the trail.

LENGTH: 3.1 miles
ELEVATION: 7,360 feet to 8,840 feet

Vicks Park Trail (#148)

Leaving the Animas Trail 1¾ miles east of the Murphy Place,
the Vicks Park Trail crosses Victoria Park, climbs Victoria
Canyon to Victoria Peak, and descends Long Canyon to
North Seco Creek. This trail is rough, brushy, and hard to
follow, especially in extremely steep Long Canyon, which
can be hazardous for horses or mules. Water is available in
Victoria Park Canyon.

LENGTH: 4.8 miles
ELEVATION: 6,400 feet to 7,000 feet

Hermosa Trail (#307)

From Cave Creek, the Hermosa Trail crosses Animas Creek,
goes up Hells Canyon and across South, Middle, and North
Seco creeks to Hermosa. The trail is in good shape, although
steep grades are encountered. The only source of water is
near Animas Creek. The better camping spots are close to
North Seco and Animas creeks.

LENGTH: 12.4 miles
ELEVATION: 6,320 feet to 7,000 feet

Hillsboro Bypass (#412)

This trail leaves the Crest Trail 1¼ miles south of Hillsboro Peak Lookout and circles the south side of Hillsboro Peak to Indian Saddle. It is easy to follow, although it is brushy, and blow-down may be encountered. No water is available. This trail offers spring access to the high country, when snow is still deep on the north side of Hillsboro Peak.

LENGTH: 1.5 miles
ELEVATION: 9,220 feet to 9,280 feet

Wolf Trail (#773)

The Wolf Trail heads south from Forest Road 141 for 6 miles west of Beaverhead and leads south to Black Mountain and Gila Wilderness. The Black Mountain Lookout provides a spectacular view in all directions of Gila National Forest. If the tower is staffed, for your safety ask permission before climbing up. There is no water available on the trail. Good camping spots can be found between Road 141 and Black Mountain.

LENGTH: 4.5 miles
ELEVATION: 7,700 feet to 9,300 feet

Murphy Trail (#794)

This short trail leaves Animas Creek at the Murphy Place and crosses to Victoria Peak Canyon, where it joins the Vicks Park Trail. The trail is in good condition, but there is a steep climb leaving the Animas. There is no water along the trail.

LENGTH: 1.1 miles
ELEVATION: 6,560 feet to 7,160 feet

Scenic Trail (#796)

From Emory Pass, the trail follows a ridge down to the Kingston Cemetery. The trail, which offers scenic views of the Black Range and of the Rio Grande valley, is in good condition, but the terrain is very steep if you leave the trail. There is no water and few camping areas.

LENGTH: 4.2 miles
ELEVATION: 6,300 feet to 8,228 feet

Byers Run Trail (#813)

Leaving the Divide Trail (#74), the Byers Run Trail extends east to Forest Road 895. The western 1½ miles is steep and in places not easily followed, but the trail then enters the creek bottom, where it stays in good shape. Some water is available. Halfway along the trail stands an old ponderosa snag with a carved cross evident in the wood.

LENGTH: 6.0 miles
ELEVATION: 6,400 feet to 8,900 feet

Luna Ranger District

The Luna District is actually part of Apache-Sitgreaves National Forest, which extends from Arizona into New Mexico, but it is administered by Gila National Forest. Most of the trails are not maintained. The maintained trails begin from Forest Roads near Luna.

For details, contact:

Luna Ranger District
P.O. Box 91
Luna, NM 87824

Glenwood Ranger District

The Glenwood District encompasses the western edge of Gila National Forest and Gila Wilderness. The San Francisco River flows through the district and into Arizona. U.S. 180 bisects the area from north to south. Highway 78 goes east along the border of the wilderness area.

The Mogollon Mountains rise here; a number of trails lead into the part of the range included in Gila Wilderness.

Crest Trail (#182)

The main trail begins at Sandy Point on Highway 78, 12 miles east of Mogollon, and climbs for 12.0 miles to Mogollon Baldy Lookout. Located on a 10,000-foot ridge, the trail is well used and easy to follow.

Year-round water is found at Bead Spring (1½ miles from

Sandy Point), Hummingbird Spring (4¾ miles), and Hobo
Spring (1½ miles). Bead and Hummingbird springs have
potable water, but water from Hobo, Little Hobo, and Black-
tail springs must be purified before drinking.

The Crest Trail is snowbound between December and
April but offers some of the most rewarding ski touring in
the Southwest.

SPUR TRAILS

The Crest Trail provides access to many different areas of
Gila Wilderness via spur trails.

Willow Creek Trail (#138) diverges at Bead Springs,
1½ miles from the trailhead.

Whitewater Canyon Trail (see below) diverges at Hummingbird Saddle, 4¾ miles from the trailhead.

Iron Creek Lake Trail (#172) diverges at Whitewater
Baldy 6¼ miles from the trailhead.

Holt-Apache Trail (see below) diverges south of Center
Baldy, 7¼ miles from the trailhead.

Turkey Feather Pass Trail (#102) diverges 8¼ miles
from the trailhead.

West Fork of Mogollon Creek Trail diverges at West
Fork Saddle, 10.5 miles from the trailhead.

White Creek Trail (#152) continues from the Mogollon
Baldy Lookout.

South Fork Trail (#212)

A trail follows the stream bed of the South Fork for 7 miles

from the old powerhouse site, 2¼ miles from the Catwalk,
to Camp Creek Saddle. The water in the creek is good all
year.

The trail is open year-round, except in heavy snow years,
though seasonal flooding may make many creek crossings
hazardous.

South Fork Creek offers good fishing, and the narrow,
rocky gorges offer exceptional scenic beauty.

SPUR TRAILS

East Fork Trail (#213) joins the South Fork Trail 5 miles
from the trailhead.

Glenwood Trail (#214) also joins the main trail 5 miles
from the trailhead.

Straight Up Trail (#215) joins the South Fork Trail 5½
miles from the trailhead.

Holt-Apache Trail (see below) joins the South Fork Trail
7 miles from the trailhead, at Camp Creek Saddle.

Holt-Apache Trail (#181)

The main trail begins ¼ mile east of Sheridan Corrals, 4¼
miles from U.S. 180. It climbs from Sheridan Gulch to Holt
Spring, then follows the ridge from Holt Mountain over
Grouse Mountain and Black Mountain to Center Baldy. From
trailhead to Center Baldy is 18½ miles.

The only good water near the trail is at Holt Spring, 5
miles from the trailhead; Nabours Spring, ¼ mile off the
main trail of the Spider Creek Trail, 10½ miles from the

trailhead; and Black Mountain Spring (formerly Stove Pipe Springs), 14½ miles from the trailhead. Other springs found along the trail require purification: Midnite Springs, 300 yards from the trail and 9 miles from the trailhead; Rock Springs, 9 miles from the trailhead; and Apache Springs, which is 25 yards from the Holt-Apache Trail on the Sacaton Trail, 15 miles from the trailhead. In the spring and in late August, Sheridan Gulch runs with good water.

The trail is often snowbound between December and April. In good years, the stretch from Holt Mountain to Sandy Point (see Crest Trail) offers excellent ski touring.

SPUR TRAILS

Side trails give access to Big Dry Creek, Whitewater Creek, and the South Fork of Whitewater.

Piney Basin Trail (#226) leaves the Holt-Apache Trail in Sheridan Gulch, 2 miles from the trailhead, for the North Fork of Big Dry and Johnson's Cabin.

Pleasanton Trail (#217) is reached at Holt Springs.

Straight Up Trail (#215) is reached on Holt Mountain, 5½ miles from the trailhead.

North Fork Big Dry Trail (#225) is reached 7¾ miles from the trailhead.

South Fork Trail (see above) is reached 8½ miles from the trailhead, on Camp Creek Saddle.

Camp Creek Trail (#218) is also reached on Camp Creek Saddle.

East Fork Whitewater Trail (#213) is reached 10 miles from the trailhead.

302 Hiking the Southwest

Deloche Trail (#179) is reached 10¼ miles from the trailhead.

Spider Creek Trail (#219) is reached 10½ miles from the trailhead.

Redstone Trail (#206) is reached 13½ miles from the trailhead.

Golden Link Trail (#218) is reached 15 miles from the trailhead, on Apache Saddle.

Sacaton Trail (#180) meets the Holt-Apache Trail at Apache Springs.

Whitewater Canyon Trail (#207)

The main trail goes from the parking lot in Whitewater picnic ground, situated at the end of Forest Road 95, for 16¾ miles to Hummingbird Saddle. The trail goes east up the Catwalk and stays by the creek for most of the distance.

Water is available from Whitewater Creek all year, except for a 2-mile trail section east of the old powerhouse site, where the trail climbs above the creek on its north slope, and where the trail leaves the creek above Redstone Park and climbs 3 miles to Hummingbird Saddle.

The trail is open year-round from the Catwalk to Redstone Park. From Redstone Park to Hummingbird Saddle may be snowbound between December and April.

Whitewater Creek has good year-round fishing.

SPUR TRAILS

Five trails give access to Whitewater Canyon from various roads:

Catwalk Trail (#207) begins at the Whitewater picnic grounds.

Gold Dust Trail (#41) begins on Whitewater Mesa just off Highway 78 and extends 2¼ miles to its junction with the Whitewater Trail 1 mile from the Catwalk.

Deloche Trail (#179) begins at Highway 78, 3 miles east of Mogollon. It meets the Whitewater Canyon Trail after 3¾ miles, 6¼ miles from the Catwalk.

Redstone Trail (#206) begins at Highway 78, 7 miles east of Mogollon and after 4¾ miles joins the Whitewater Canyon Trail 10¾ miles from the Catwalk.

Crest Trail (see above) crosses the Whitewater Canyon Trail 4¾ miles from Sandy Point at Hummingbird Saddle, 16¾ miles from the Catwalk.

Three trails connect with the Whitewater Canyon Trail from the south:

South Fork Trail (see above) intersects the Whitewater Canyon Trail 2¼ miles from the Catwalk.

Deloche Trail (#179) intersects it 6¾ miles from the Catwalk.

Redstone Trail (#206) intersects it 10½ miles from the Catwalk.

Windy Gap Trail (#180)

The main trail begins at the end of Forest Road 196 on Little Dry Creek.

The trail follows Little Dry Creek for 2½ miles, then climbs to Windy Gap and Simmons Saddle before traversing Sacaton Mountain to Apache Cabin, which is 9½ miles from the trailhead.

Little Dry Creek contains good water in spring and late summer. Good water holes can usually be found in the upper end of the canyon in midsummer. The only other good, year-round water source, Simmons Spring, is 500 yards from the trail at Simmons Saddle.

SPUR TRAILS

The only side trail is the Big Dry Trail (#220), which begins 3½ miles from the trailhead, at Windy Gap, and descends 2¼ miles into the Big Dry. It is a popular trail with fishermen interested in good fishing near the Golden Link Cabin on the Big Dry.

The trail up the Little Dry to Windy Gap and the Big Dry Trail are open all year. The trail between Windy Gap and Apache Cabin is snowbound from December through April and offers excellent ski tours during good snow years.

Mimbres Ranger District

The Mimbres District is quite spectacular and scenic. Most of its area is within either Gila Wilderness or Aldo Leopold Wilderness. The eastern boundary follows the crest of the Black Range; the Continental Divide Trail runs along this same ridge before crossing the district toward Silver City.

With Black Range peaks reaching above 10,000 feet, steep canyons and mountain weather characterize this district.

Campground and picnic facilities include:

Upper End Campground, located at Lake Roberts, 12

miles from Mimbres Ranger Station. Ten units are available, with grills, picnic tables, water, restrooms, and a nature trail. Across the road from Upper End Campground is an amphitheater, where programs are presented on Saturday evenings during the summer by the Forest Service.

Mesa Campground, also located at Lake Roberts and open from May 15 through the beginning of October. The 24 units include grills, picnic tables, and restrooms.

Lake Roberts Picnic Area, 13 miles from Mimbres Ranger Station. No overnight camping is allowed. Six picnic sites include grills, tables, water, and restrooms. There is a nature trail and a boat ramp at the lake.

Sapillo Group Campground, 2 miles southeast of Lake Roberts, furnished with 10 units with grills and toilets but no water.

Rocky Canyon Campground, located on Highway 61, 13 miles from Mimbres, has 2 picnic tables and toilets but no drinking water.

Upper and Lower Black Canyon Campground located on Highway 61, 25 miles from Mimbres. There are 2 picnic tables at the upper campground and 3 at the lower; each has restrooms but no drinking water.

Wright's Cabin, which is 13 miles east of San Lorenzo on Highway 90, with 3 picnic spots with grills and tables, a restroom, but no drinking water. Camping is not permitted.

Iron Creek Campground, located 10 miles east of San Lorenzo on Highway 90, offering 15 units with grills and tables, restrooms, and a nature trail. Water is sometimes available in the stream.

Emory Pass Vista, located 14 miles east of San Lorenzo on Highway 90, an observation point and picnic area with tables, grills, and a restroom.

Bear Camp Area, 10 miles east of San Lorenzo on Highway 90, equipped with 2 picnic tables, grills, and toilets. No drinking water is available unless the stream is running.

Gallinas Area, 8 miles east of San Lorenzo on Highway 90, with 5 tables, toilet facilities, and water when the stream is running.

Allie Canyon Trail (#100)

Beginning on Highway 61 at the national forest boundary near the Mimbres Ranger Station, the trail heads up Willa Wa Canyon and drops into Allie Canyon, then continues 9 miles to the head of the canyon and Forest Road 855. Allie Canyon has water most of the year. An old homestead is located where Hightower Canyon joins Allie Canyon.

Bear Canyon Trail (#104)

The trail extends 7 miles from Allie Canyon to the Fort Bayard Road (536), following old cavalry road that originated at Fort Bayard. Water can usually be found in Bear Canyon.

Deadman Trail (#104)

This trail connects the Bear Canyon Trail to Forest Road

855, following another old cavalry road for 3½ miles through the pine and chaparral foothills of the Pinos Altos Mountains.

Middle Mesa Trail (#716)

This 7¾-mile trail is often used by hikers in conjunction with the Tom Moore Trail to make a loop through the heart of Gila Wilderness. The trailhead is located at a sharp curve of the North Star Road north of Black Canyon. As it is dangerous to enter the North Star Road at this junction in a vehicle, park in a small clearing ¼ miles farther up the road. The trail traverses flat, prairie-like Middle Mesa for 5 miles, then drops into Corral Canyon. The trail continues through this canyon to the low, grassy hill country of the Community Pasture.

Black Canyon Trail (#94)

Often referred to as the Lower Black Canyon Trail, this 3-mile trail starts near the Lower Black Canyon Campground and continues down the canyon as far as the corral. There is no trail below the corral, except perhaps a cow trail that is not maintained. Due to the narrowing of Black Canyon, going upstream beyond the maintained trail is difficult on horseback and often difficult walking when the creek is high.

Military Trail (#709)

Part of the old military road that went north from Fort Bayard during cavalry days goes 6½ miles from Highway 15 to Lyon's Lodge on the East Fork of the Gila River. The trail offers fine views of Gila Wilderness and the Black Range.

Brannon Park Trail (#700)

This fairly heavily used trail connects Highway 25 to the Rocky Canyon Campground on Highway 61, an ascent of 11½ miles. Brannon Park, 3 miles from the campground, is the main attraction on this trail.

GILA WILDERNESS AND SOUTHWEST PART
OF MIMBRES DISTRICT

For details about any of the trails described below, or current conditions, contact the Mimbres District office, located on Highway 61, 4 miles south of Highway 35.

Link's Trail (#713)

This 4¼-mile trail, used mostly by cowboys, runs through rolling pinyon-juniper country between the Link's Ranch on Forest Road 609 and private land in Tom Moore Canyon. The trail starts just before the swinging wooden gate at the edge of the ranch.

Tom Moore Trail (#708)

This major trail crosses Gila Wilderness from the North Star Road at Tom Moore Canyon to Lyon's Lodge on the East

Fork of the Gila River, a distance of 15 miles. The trail through the wilderness is easy, as it follows an old roadbed to private land in Tom Moore Canyon. Here the trail turns south and passes through shallow, grassy hills before dropping sharply to the East Fork. Several river crossings in the last 2 miles can be difficult when the river is high. Check at the ranger station before hiking this part of the trail. An open meadow surrounded by large ponderosa pines was the site of a homestead. Around the edge of the park are the remains of an old split-rail fence that surrounded the park when it was cultivated 80 years ago.

Big Timber Trail (#95)

This trail from Brannon Park through Big Timber Canyon to Apache Creek is 4 miles long. The canyon is a wide-open, parklike area with tall trees and an understory of grass. Toward its mouth, Big Timber Canyon becomes narrow and rocky, but the trail is easy to follow. There are no system trails in Gila Wilderness beyond the junction of this trail with Apache Creek. Trees are blazed in parts of Apache Creek, but no trail is maintained.

Caves Trail (#803)

A ¾-mile trail leads down Rocky Canyon from the campground to an interesting area of steep cliffs, gorges, and caves. Use caution if you continue beyond the trail's end, as there are steep drops and slippery spots.

Turkey Cienega Trail (#740)

The first ½ mile of this trail follows an old jeep road to a barrier at the wilderness boundary. The trail ends 2 miles beyond, by a large stock pond at the end of a meadow called Turkey Cienega. The meadow was once cultivated and is rumored to be the original site of the GOS Ranch headquarters. Presently, the meadow is used as a wildlife study area by the Forest Service.

Railroad Canyon Trail (#96)

This trail begins at Highway 25 and ends 8¾ miles away at Apache Creek. In the first 5 miles it climbs out of the bottom of Sapillo Creek to a junction with the Gila Flat Trail at Lawrence (or "32") stock tank. The trail continues ½ mile along a divide and then drops gradually to Apache Creek.

Gila Flat Trail (#97)

From Highway 15 to this trail's junction with the Railroad Canyon Trail is 4¾ miles. The Highway 15 trailhead can be reached by continuing ¼ mile toward the Cliff Dwellings from Copperas Vista. The trail follows the wide divide between the Sapillo Creek watershed and Apache Creek.

Reserve Ranger District

The Reserve District includes over 500,000 acres with about

50 miles of trails, some well maintained, some primitive. Willow Creek area trails, the most used and best maintained, lead into the north end of Gila Wilderness. Four campgrounds near trailheads are good starting points for wilderness treks. Look on the national forest map for Trails #142, #705, #151, #138, and #762 through the Frisco Box, Trails #15 and #768 in the Eagle Peak Area, #157 from Gilita Campground down to Snow Lake, #761 up Cienega Canyon, the Mail Trail (#125), the Flying V Trail (#706), and Trail #74, which will be part of the Continental Divide Trail. Use topographic maps for details and for information, contact:

Reserve Ranger District
P.O. Box 117
Reserve, NM 87830

Silver City Ranger District

This District, which covers the southernmost part of Gila Wilderness, is split into north and south areas. The Burro Mountains constitute the southern area, while the Pinos Altos Range runs through the northern area. Highway 15 passes north from Silver City through the district to the Gila Cliff Dwellings.

Turkey Creek Trail (#155)

The Turkey Creek Trail begins at the end of Forest Road 155

north of the village of Gila, from a trailhead located where Turkey Creek enters the Gila River.

From the Gila River, the Turkey Creek Trail travels 16 miles before joining the Granite Peak Spur Trail (#150). The trail follows the creek bottom to Skeleton Canyon, where it leaves the bottom for 2 miles before returning and again following the bottom. The climb and ridge-crossing from Skeleton Canyon to Sycamore Canyon is on a south-facing mountainside that can be extremely hot during summer. This and the many creek crossings make hiking or horse travel moderately difficult.

Water will be found in Turkey Creek and Sycamore Canyon. During dry months, Turkey Creek becomes intermittent near the confluence of Miller Springs Canyon. During spring runoff or other periods of high water, backpackers should take extra tennis shoes for wading.

Trails connecting with the Turkey Trail are the Granite Peak Spur (#150), Little Creek Trail (#161), Diablo Range Trail (#177), Miller Springs Trail (#159), and Sycamore/Woodrow Trail (#158).

The most popular hike up Turkey Creek is to hot springs 4 miles from the trailhead, 1½ miles from where the trail swings up Skeleton Canyon. No maintained trail goes to the hot springs, and extensive wading and bouldering is necessary. The springs cannot be reached with horses. Because of the heavy use this area receives, hikers should be especially conscientious about packing out trash.

Near the trailhead is a small parcel of private land with buildings. Please respect the rights of the landowners.

Gila River Trail (#724)

The northern trailhead is located south of Gila Hot Springs at the Gila Bridge. The south entry is the mouth of Turkey Creek at the end of Forest Road 155. This 32-mile trail follows the Gila River, with various surfaces to walk on, including quicksand. Many crossings, combined with river fluctuations, erase the trail in many places in the canyon.

SPUR TRAILS

The Alum Camp Trail (#788) goes east from the river to reach Highway 15 about 1 mile below Grapevine Campground.

Spring Canyon Trail (#247) branches from the Gila River Trail 17 miles from the mouth of Turkey Creek and goes 6½ miles to Highway 15.

Granny Mountain Trail (#160) goes to Upper Turkey Creek, branching from the river trail 19 miles from Turkey Creek.

Packsaddle Trail (#732) goes to Goose Lake from the river in a distance of 4½ miles.

Sheep Corral Canyon Trail (#231) traverses 6 miles from a trailhead on Sapillo Creek ½ mile east of the Gila River to Sheep Corral and Forest Road 282.

Hikers and spring river floaters should note that going either downstream or upstream, it is at least 15 miles to the nearest trail leaving the wilderness—the Spring Canyon Trail or the Sheep Corral Canyon Trail. Therefore, be well prepared for any emergency. Also, portage paths circle the water-gap fences. Do not cut wire. Some cattle will be encountered along the river, and all gates you open should be closed. Further information for river floaters is available from local Forest Service offices.

Excellent fishing will be found in many places year-round. Because of its low elevations, this is a good cool-weather route.

Spring Canyon Trail (#247)

The trail begins ¼ mile west of Highway 15 on Sapillo Creek and reaches the Gila River in 6½ miles. The first section climbs from Sapillo Creek, which the trail parallels until it drops back into the canyon ½ mile from the Gila. The trail traverses rolling country above the creek, topography that makes for backpacking of moderate difficulty. This trail offers spectacular views of the Sapillo Box.

Water is available in Sapillo Creek at the trailhead, where the trail returns to the canyon bottom, and in the Gila River. Periodic springs may be found in canyon bottoms along the trail. Where the trail drops back to the creek it is rocky and steep for 100 yards. Saddle and pack stock should be led through this section. Most of the trail traverses south-facing hillsides with limited shade, making hiking very hot during summer. However, in cooler months this route to the Gila River is very pleasant.

If you stay in the creek bottom, you are faced with much wading and rock climbing; moreover, the bottom can be impassable during high water and flash-flood seasons.

Granny Mountain Trail (#160)

From the Gila River Trail, at 5,300 feet in Little Turkey Park, the Granny Mountain Trail climbs for 6½ miles to 7,100-foot Miller Springs Cabin. The trail's highest elevation is 7,650 feet. The hiking difficulty is moderate, because of the elevation gain and the southern, unshaded exposure of two-thirds of the trail.

Water is available from the Gila River and at Miller Springs. No other water is found along the trail, so carry water.

The Miller Springs Trail (#159) goes from Miller Springs to Upper Turkey Creek, while the Granny Mountain Trail continues from Miller Springs to Gila Center.

Exceptional views of river and canyons may be had from Granny Mountain. The trail is a convenient route from the Gila River to Turkey Creek and the Diablo Range, and elk, bear, and deer are found in vicinity of Miller Springs.

Sheep Corral Canyon Trail (#231)

The Sheep Corral, where this trail begins, is 7 miles west of Highway 15 on Forest Road 242. From the trailhead to Sapillo Creek is 6 miles and another ¼ miles to the Gila River. Follow Sheep Corral Creek 2 miles, then the Snow Creek Trail (#233) for ¼ mile. The Snow Creek Trail goes east to Farm Flat, then returns to Road 282.

The Sheep Corral Canyon Trail goes north through a gate and follows a road for 1 mile, then drops into Sapillo Creek Canyon.

Water is scarce, though it may be found in upper Sheep Corral Creek, in Sapillo Creek, and in the Gila River.

There is one of the most popular routes to the Gila River. Fishing is great for trout, bass, and catfish during certain times of the year on the Gila near the Sapillo's mouth.

Always close gates after passing through.

Rain Creek–Bud's Hole Trail (#189)

From the trailhead at Sacaton Airstrip above Rain Creek, adjacent to Forest Road 147, this trail goes 1 mile to Rain Creek and 5 miles from Rain Creek to the West Fork of Mogollon Creek. From there it is 2¼ miles to Bud's Hole on Mogollon Creek. Short sections of this trail—the beginning of the climb from Rain Creek, a point on the descent to the West Fork ½ mile from the creek, and a 100-yard rocky climb west of the creek—are very steep and may be difficult for some saddle and pack stock. These sections are moderate to difficult for backpackers.

The only water is found in Rain Creek, the West Fork, and Mogollon Creek, so water should be carried.

The Rain Creek–Bud's Hole Trail meets two other trails, both described below: the West Fork of Mogollon Creek Trail and the 74 Mountain Trail, which is joined on Mogollon Creek 1¼ miles from Bud's Hole.

Exceptional views are had midway between Rain Creek and the West Fork of Mogollon Creek of Rain Creek Canyon to the north and mesa country to the south. Fishing is good on the West Fork. Compared to other wilderness trails, this scenic, rugged route is lightly used.

Vehicles should be parked near the road signed as "Sacaton Trailhead," not on private land nearby. Do not use private facilities unless permission is obtained.

West Fork of Mogollon Creek Trail (#224)

From the Rain Creek–Bud's Hole Trail, this trail follows the West Fork of Mogollon Creek for 5½ miles to a junction with Trail #99. Of that distance, 3⅓ miles is in the canyon bottom, as the trail crosses the creek about 15 times before climbing from the creek, at 6,800 feet, to 8,300 feet in 2 miles. The trail is moderately difficult, except during high-water periods, when creek crossings may be difficult. Backpackers should be sure to pack extra shoes for the many creek crossings; during spring runoff, wet feet are unavoidable.

Water is available on the West Fork of Mogollon Creek and from an intermittent stream at the junction with Trail #99, except during dry periods.

From the junction with Trail #99, the West Fork Trail continues north 3 miles to West Fork Saddle, where it connects with trails providing access to Center Baldy, Whitewater Baldy, Mogollon Baldy, and others of the range's highest peaks. These trails are described under the Glenwood District.

Fishing is excellent for native brown trout at certain times of the year. The best fishing is in pools north of the point where the trail leaves the creek bottom. Scenic rock formations and caves abound in the upper parts of this creek.

Trail #99

From a junction with the West Fork of Mogollon Creek Trail above the creek, Trail #99 climbs steadily for 1½ miles to a saddle below Mogollon Baldy. The trail then crosses to the ridge just east of the peak, where it meets the Mogollon Baldy–Snow Park Trail (#152). In 3 miles Trail #99 has climbed from 8,300 feet to 10,050 feet, so be prepared for moderate to difficult hiking. The trail is often snow-covered late into the spring.

At the junction is an intermittent stream, but during dry periods do not rely on this water source. No other water will be found along the trail.

Turn east at the junction and hike 1 mile to Snow Park, or turn west and in 1 mile reach the Mogollon Baldy Lookout. One of the most reliable springs in this area is near the northeast end of Snow Park.

Spectacular views and pleasant high-country hiking characterize Trail #99. The trail, while passing below Mogollon Baldy, crosses old burned areas, with waist-high ferns in the summer and aspen stands. Practically the entire south half of the wilderness can be viewed from this trail. However, the trail is lightly used, making it attractive for those seeking high-country solitude.

74 Mountain Trail (#153)

The trailhead near Rice Ranch is reached from Cliff by Highway 293, Forest Road 147, and a road that forks right at a sign reading "L. Shelley 916 Ranch."

At a distance of 5½ miles from the trailhead, the 74 Mountain Trail crosses the Rain Creek-Bud's Hole Trail. From this point, it continues for 2 miles to Mogollon Creek. The trail follows flat mesa country for 1½ miles, then climbs and switchbacks toward Deadman Canyon. The trail then crosses pleasant, flat, pine-covered 74 Mountain before it drops to Mogollon Creek. This trail is easy to moderate for backpacking.

No water is available along the trail before Mogollon Creek. During wet seasons water may often be found off the trail, down Deadman Canyon, but this source should not be relied on. Water should be carried, especially during the hot months. About two-thirds of the trail to Mogollon Creek is exposed, with little or no shade.

The 74 Mountain Trail connects with the Gobbler Canyon Trail (#221), which leads to Snow Park, and to the Mogollon Creek Trail (#301), which leads to the Turbo Canyon and Woodrow-Sycamore Canyon trails (#158). The Mogollon Creek Trail leaves the Silver City District at Mogollon Creek, as it follows Trail and Rawmeat canyons to McKenna Park.

This wilderness entry is extremely popular during deer and elk hunting seasons. Also, this route is easier than others for backpackers for reaching adjoining areas of the wilderness. Fishing for native trout on Mogollon Creek is extremely good at certain times of the year.

The trailhead is located near private land. You are requested to park 100 yards east of the trailhead and away from stock water. Do not use private facilities unless permission is obtained.

Wilderness Ranger District

The major portion of Gila Wilderness lies within the aptly named Wilderness Ranger District, although many of the Gila Wilderness trails begin and end in districts already described. The following three trails lie within the Wilderness District. The accompanying table gives distances for 29 major trails within Gila Wilderness.

West Fork Trail (#151)

The 33½-mile West Fork Trail is one of the longer routes through the wilderness; it follows the West Fork Canyon, beginning in Gila Cliff Dwellings National Monument, for most of its length. The trail begins just to the right of TJ Corral on Highway 15. Horse travelers use a bypass that skirts Scorpion Campground and the Cliff Dwellings for 2 miles before joining the foot trail—Parking Lot Trail (#792)—at the west boundary of the monument. Remaining in the canyon bottom, the trail crosses the West Fork of the Gila River some 60 or 70 times before reaching the mouth of White Creek after 18½ miles. Numerous side canyons that empty into the West Fork can be used to measure your progress. Among these are: Grave Canyon (2¾ miles, on the right), White Rocks Canyon (3¾ miles, on the left), Nat Straw Canyon (6 miles, on the left), Ring Canyon (8½ miles, on the left), Hells Hole Canyon (12 miles, on the right), and White Creek (15½ miles, on the left).

The ¾-mile section approaching White Creek traverses

rockslides and yielding clay on a steep embankment. The West Fork here runs in a narrow gorge with falls and deep potholes in the rock.

From the mouth of White Creek, the trail continues up the West Fork bottom for ½ mile before it climbs 940 feet out the west flank to Cub Mesa. The trail crosses Cub Mesa, turns north to cross Packsaddle Canyon, and re-enters the West Fork Canyon. After 1¼ miles in the canyon, the trail again leaves the West Fork to turn up Turkeyfeather Creek, pass Turkeyfeather Spring, and continue to Turkeyfeather Pass. From the pass, the trail descends and follows Cooper Canyon to its junction with Iron Creek. Turning up Iron Creek, the trail follows a tributary of Iron Creek that leads down to Iron Creek Lake, passes the lake, and crosses the western end of Iron Creek Mesa. Finally, the trail drops to Willow Creek and ends at a loop of Forest Road 507.

Vegetation varies along this route with moisture and elevation changes. Ponderosa pine, Arizona sycamore, narrow-leaf cottonwood, and Arizona alder are found in the canyon bottom. Open stands of ponderosa cover Cub Mesa, Jack Ass Park, and Iron Creek Mesa. Douglas fir and spruce are found in Packsaddle Canyon and along Turkeyfeather, Iron, and Willow creeks.

Water is available for the length of the West Fork and at Turkeyfeather Spring, Iron Creek, and Iron Creek Lake.

The West Fork Trail intersects the Turkey Creek Trail (#155) just below the mouth of White Creek, the Trotter Trail (#30) ½ mile above the mouth of White Creek, the Mogollon Baldy Trail (#152) on Cub Mesa, the Lilley Park

Trail (#164) and Clayton Mesa Trail (#175) near Turkey-feather Pass, the Iron Creek Mesa Trail (#171) ¼ mile east of Iron Creek Lake, and the Whitewater Baldy Trail (#172) at Iron Creek Lake.

The first 5 miles of the West Fork above the Cliff Dwellings are some of the most frequently used trail in the entire wilderness. Those who seek solitude and prefer contact with fewer people may inquire at the monument visitor center for information on less-used areas.

Little Creek Trail (#160)

The 4-mile trail to Little Creek begins at a canyon entering the West Fork of the Gila River just south of the West Fork bridge, near TJ Corral on Highway 15. The trail climbs out of the river bottom for 3¼ miles before gradually descending a side canyon to Little Creek. From Little Creek, the trail continues south toward Little Turkey Park, Granny Mountain, and Brushy Mountain.

The adjacent terrain is vegetated with oak, juniper, pinyon, and ponderosa pine.

Water can be found in Little Creek near its mouth, except during the driest times of the year. Water is intermittent farther up Little Creek and 2 miles from a junction with the Turkey Creek Trail. The Little Creek Trail is not maintained but is preferable to the Ring Canyon Trail (#162) for reaching the McKenna Park area because of the availability of water.

This area is not heavily used and is suggested for hikers who seek solitude.

Little Bear Trail (#729)

Four-mile-long Little Bear Trail is one of the most popular trails. Beginning at the TJ Corral, the trail climbs gradually up an open pinyon-juniper slope and follows the crest of a ridge to a high point above Little Bear Canyon. Here it drops into a tributary of Little Bear Canyon, winding for 2¾ miles down to the main canyon bottom, which it follows to the Middle Fork of the Gila River and the Middle Fork Trail (#157). The last ½ mile of Little Bear Canyon (which contains a spring) is a deep, narrow gorge seldom wider than 45 feet.

Along the Middle Fork are two small springs, one 2 miles (and 14 river crossings) above the Little Bear Trail junction and the other little spring ½ mile up the Middle Fork from the Gila Visitor Center.

The Middle Fork Trail is not maintained. To hike up the river or down to the visitor center involves continual stream crossings, so be prepared for wet feet.

The most heavily used areas along the Middle Fork are near the small hot springs, at the Meadows, and 3 miles above and below the Little Bear Trail junction. Those who wish contact with fewer people may ask rangers for information about less-used trails.

Listed below are mileages for the most commonly traveled routes within Gila Wilderness. This table can be used as a quick reference for planning trips.

Gila Wilderness Mileage Chart

Route	Mileage
Gila Cliff Dwellings to Willow Creek via the West Fork	33½
Gila Cliff Dwellings to White Creek	17
Gila Cliff Dwellings to Hell's Hole	12¾
White Creek to Willow Creek	16¾
White Creek to Sandy Point via Turkeyfeather Pass	27¾
TJ Corral to White Creek via McKenna Park	22¼
TJ Corral to McKenna Park	17¼
TJ Corral to White Creek via Woodland Park	20½
TJ Corral to Woodland Park	10¾
Woodland Park to Lilly Park	6¾
White Creek to Mogollon Baldy	10¾
Mogollon Baldy to Hummingbird Saddle	7¼
Hummingbird Saddle to Redstone	5
Redstone to Whitewater Campground	11¾
White Creek to Trotter via Lilly Park	9¾
Gila Visitor Center to Little Bear via the Middle Fork	6½

Route	Mileage
Little Bear to the Meadows	8½
The Meadows to Trotter	14
Trotter to Snow Lake	7
Gila Cliff Dwellings to the Meadows via Big Bear	8¼
TJ Corral to the Meadows via Big Bear	9¾
TJ Corral to the Middle Fork via Little Bear	4¼
Upper Gila River Bridge to Turkey Creek via Gila River	31¾
Upper Gila River Bridge to Alum Camp	3¼
Alum Camp to Highway 15	1¾
Upper Gila River Bridge to Sapillo Creek	14¾
Sapillo Creek to Turkey Creek	17
Turkey Creek to White Creek via Sycamore and Turnbo Canyons	19¾
TJ Corral to White Creek via Little Creek and McKenna Park	21½

Quemado Ranger District

This District in the extreme northern part of Gila National Forest has few maintained trails, with the exception of a few branching out from the Jewett Campground. Trails #3, #4, #818, and unnumbered trails wander through the southern portion between Jewett Campground, Apache Creek, and Aragon. For information, contact:

Quemado Ranger District
P.O. Box 158
Quemado, NM 87829

BLUE RANGE WILDERNESS

The Blue Range Wilderness extends from Arizona into New Mexico. Although the wilderness actually is part of Apache-Sitgreaves National Forest, it is administered by Gila National Forest, and inquiries should be addressed to:

Gila National Forest
2610 N. Silver St.
Silver City, NM 88061

National Parks and Monuments

Carlsbad Caverns is the one national park in New Mexico. While the park is famous for its limestone cave system, within the park boundaries there is also a system of trails, including nature trails near the cavern entrance. In addition, off-trail hiking and backpacking is limited only by the imagination of the explorer and his ability to carry water. Elevations range from 3,600 feet at the base of the eastern escarpment of the Guadalupe Mountains to 6,300 feet atop Guadalupe Ridge on the Park's west boundary.

Topographic maps, available at the visitor center, should always be used because of poor trail conditions. A special 1:100,000-scale topo map of the area is sold by the Carlsbad Caverns Natural History Association, 3225 National Parks Highway, Carlsbad, NM 88220. Fire permits must be obtained at the center.

Most of the many national monuments in the Land of Enchantment preserve prehistoric archaeological sites. Most have short interpretive trails that explain the ruins and artifacts but have no established hiking trails. Backcountry hiking is permitted in some areas by permit only.

Following are the addresses of the national monuments in New Mexico. The superintendent of each monument should be contacted for further information, including restrictions on backcountry hiking.

Gila Cliff Dwellings National Monument
Route 11, Box 100
Silver City, NM 88061

El Morro National Monument
Ramah, NM 87321

Salinas National Monument
Mountainaire, NM 87036

Gran Quivira National Monument
Mountainaire, NM 87036

Fort Union National Monument
Watrous, NM 87753

White Sands National Monument
Box 458
Alamogordo, NM 88310

Chaco Canyon National Monument
Star Route 4, Box 6500
Bloomfield, NM 87413

Capulin National Monument
Capulin, NM 88414

Aztec Ruins National Monument
P.O. Box U
Aztec, NM 87410

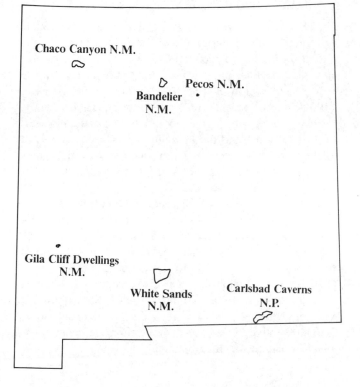

The national parks and monuments of New Mexico.

BANDELIER NATIONAL MONUMENT

Bandelier National Monument, situated in the canyonlands and mesas of the Pajarito Plateau and stretching into the foothills of the Jemez Mountains, has over 65 miles of hiking trails. Elevations range from 5,330 feet at the Rio Grande to over 8,600 feet in the upper sections of Frijoles Canyon.

While the area receives 16 inches of precipitation annually, it is dry country with high evaporation rates and quick run-off. Careful water and food planning is required, as well as a detailed study of topo maps to ascertain elevation gains and losses. Summers are hot with little shade in the back-country, but winters are mild.

In 1976, more than 23,000 acres of Bandelier was designated part of the wilderness system. Most of the remaining acres are also administered as wilderness.

The monument is reached by traveling 46 miles north from Sante Fe on U.S. 285 to Pojoaque, then driving west on Highway 4. An approach may also be made on mountain roads through the Jemez country from Albuquerque, but inquiries should be made beforehand as to road conditions. Two interpretive trails show the visitor the main archeological features of the monument.

Ruins Area Trail

Ranger-guided walks on this trail are conducted during the summer, or you can hike the trail alone using a guide booklet. This loop trail leads the hiker along a paved path from the visitor center at Frijoles Canyon through an impressive display of the architecture of prehistoric man. The Tyuonyi

Ruins, presumed to have been three stories high, and an excavated great kiva, largest on the Pajarito Plateau, are located here. The loop is about a mile long; the return route passes streamside vegetation.

Tsankawi Trail

This 2-mile self-guiding trail leads to the detached Tsankawi section of the monument and a large, unexcavated ruin. Part of the trail follows an ancient Indian path that has been worn into the soft volcanic rock as deeply as 18 inches in places. The start of the trail is reached by driving north from Frijoles Canyon for 11 miles on Highway 4. From the ruins, located on a high mesa, the views are spectacular, with the Rio Grande to the south, the Sangre de Cristo Mountains to the east, and the Jemez Mountains to the west.

Backcountry Trails

Lower Frijoles Canyon Trail

The most popular Bandelier trail starts at the southeast end of the headquarters parking lot and descends Frijoles Canyon, past two waterfalls, to the Rio Grande. The round-trip distance is 4 miles; the hike takes 3 hours. The trail crosses and recrosses the deciduous tree-lined stream bed until it quickly descends to the base of Upper Falls. Below Upper Falls, the trail becomes steeper, and Lower Falls comes into view. From Lower Falls, the route continues to the Rio Grande. The River Trail can be followed south, or you can turn back and complete the round trip.

Upper Frijoles Canyon Trail

A mile northwest of the headquarters, up Frijoles Canyon, is Ceremonial Cave, a prehistoric shelter 150 feet above the canyon floor. Farther upstream the canyon narrows, then opens into a wide stream bed with vertical walls as high as 500 feet. The trail continues, slowly ascending to pinyon-juniper woodland and Upper Frijoles Crossing junction. It is 6 miles from Ceremonial Cave to Upper Crossing, where the trail climbs 600 feet on steep switchbacks to the canyon rim. Continuing north, the route goes cross-country for 2 miles to Ponderosa Campground and to Back Gate, where Highway 4 heads back to the monument entrance. The total one-way distance is 8 miles.

Frijoles Rim Trail

This 4½-mile trail follows the south rim of Frijoles Canyon, passing many viewpoints overlooking the canyon. It climbs up out of the canyon near the visitor center, gaining 500 vertical feet, then skirts the rim to the "Y" junction, from which trails lead into the more remote backcountry. Vegetation changes from pinyon and juniper to ponderosa in the 650-foot gradual climb from the initial emergence on the rim to the "Y." You can return the same way or angle northwest to Upper Frijoles Crossing and follow the Canyon Trail back for 7 miles. There are many unexcavated ruin sites along the Rim Trail.

National Wildlife Refuges

National Wildlife Refuges are set aside for the preservation, study, and observation of wild creatures that live in a particular geographic area, or animals that just pass through, such as migrating birds. Each refuge has certain laws and regulations that pertain to hunting, fishing, picnicking, camping, and hiking. There are no established hiking or backpacking trails, with the exception of a few self-guided trails for wildlife interprctation. A listing of wildlife refuges follows. Write to the Refuge Manager for information on backcountry hiking.

Bitter Lake NWR
P.O. Box 7
Roswell, NM 88201

Las Vegas NWR
P.O. Box 1070
Las Vegas, NM 87701

Bosque del Apache NWR
P.O. Box 1246
Socorro, NM 87801

Maxwell NWR
Maxwell, NM 87728

Bureau of Land Management Areas

Thirteen million acres of BLM land in New Mexico are administered under the multiple-use concept of providing for and managing grazing, wildlife habitat, mineral development, historic resource protection, watershed use, timber, wilderness preservation, and outdoor recreation.

Most BLM land is undeveloped and provides opportunity for unlimited cross-country foot travel. Six developed recreation sites in New Mexico, described below, can be used as trailheads for the adventurous hiker who wants to plan his or her own trek into the wilderness reaches of the varied BLM terrain.

Aguirre Springs is located in the Organ Mountains on U.S. 70, 15 miles east of Las Cruces. The site is open all year and features camp units with shelters, tables and toilets. Firewood is sometimes provided, but it is best to bring your own. There are no trailer hook-ups and no water.

Aguirre Springs is part of the Organ Mountain Recreation Lands, a 35,000-acre BLM recreation area. Most of the surrounding mountainous terrain is accessible by hiking only. Two segments of the National Trails System depart from Aguirre Springs. They are Baylor Pass Trail, which crosses the mountains toward Las Cruces, and Pine Tree Trail, a mountain loop. For information contact:

BLM Supervisor
Las Cruces District Office

1705 N. 7th Street, P.O. Box 1420
Las Cruces, NM 88201

Three Rivers Petroglyph Site contains about 5,000 petroglyphs in a 50-acre area that is accessible by maintained
trails. Six picnic areas are furnished with tables, grills, shelters, and drinking water. There are toilets but no trailer hook-
ups. Vast stretches of BLM land extend north and south for
those who want solitude and quiet.

The site is located 30 miles south of Carrizozo on U.S.
54. For information, contact:

BLM Supervisor
Three Rivers Petroglyph Site
P.O. Box 1449
Santa Fe, NM 87501

Datil Well is on the old Magdalena Stock Driveway that
was used to drive cattle from Arizona and New Mexico to
the railroad at Magdalena in the 1880s. It is located just off
U.S. 60 one mile west of Datil. The site contains 22 camping
units with shelters, tables, water, and toilets but no trailer
hook-ups. A 3-mile trail goes through pinyon-juniper woodlands along the ridges west of the campground. BLM land
stretches southeast, and Cibola National Forest surrounds
the area to the north and west.

Santa Cruz Lake, located 20 miles north of Santa Fe on
Highway 4, is surrounded by national forest and BLM land.

There are 42 picnic shelters with fireplaces and tables near the lake. Water is provided, as well as toilets, but there are no trailer hook-ups. Boat-launching facilities are provided. A few short foot trails lead from the camping area into the surrounding foothills. For information, contact:

BLM Supervisor
Santa Cruz Lake
P.O. Box 1449
Santa Fe, NM 87501

Angel Peak, located about 40 miles southeast of Bloom-field off Highway 44, overlooks a vast badland area of eroded sandstone. There are shelters and toilets but no water or trailer hook-ups. Huge tracts of open BLM land surround this site and offer ample opportunities for badland hiking. For information, contact:

BLM Supervisor
Angel Peak
P.O. Box 1449
Santa Fe, NM 87501

Rio Grande Wild River, just west of the Questa District of Carson National Forest and 25 miles north of Taos, near Highway 3, was one of the first rivers to be protected by the National Wild and Scenic Rivers Act. There are developed campsites with shelters and tables, water at the visitor center, and interpretive exhibits. The area offers camping, hiking, backpacking, fishing, and river floating. Commercial float outfitters can be contacted through the Taos Chamber of Commerce. No hiking trails are established, but the topo map and local inquiries will provide information for cross-country travel. The site is surrounded by national forest and BLM land.

Recreational activities on BLM land include rockhounding, camping and picnicking, hiking and horseback riding, off-road vehicle use, and wilderness trekking.

BLM WILDERNESS AREAS

Decisions about many BLM wilderness areas are in limbo due to political maneuvering and lack of funds. One controversy concerns subterranean mineral rights in wilderness areas. The question has also been raised of whether any BLM land needs wilderness designation, since so much of the land is wild and remote. One could say that all BLM land is wilderness because of its potential for solitude in the vast, wild tracts. But recreational use of these lands and encouragement of others to so use them will generate support for their incorporation into the Wilderness System.

For more information and a BLM map price list, write:

BLM Office
P.O. Box 1449
Santa Fe, NM 87501

State Parks and Monuments

Most state parks do not maintain hiking trails, but interpretive trails, old jeep roads, animal trails, and horse trails provide backcountry access. Individual state park superintendents should be contacted for up-to-date information on hiking and backpacking. Following is a list of state park and recreational area addresses.

Belen Valley
1617 E. River Rd.
Belen, NM 87002

Bluewater Lake
P.O. Box 3419
Prewitt, NM 87045

Bottomless Lakes
Roswell, NM 88201

Caballo Lake
P.O. Box 32
Caballo, NM 87931

Chicosa Lake
Roy, NM 87743

Chilili State Park
(Not yet built)

Cimarron Canyon
P.O. Box 147
Ute Park, NM 87749

City of Rocks
P.O. Box 54
Faywood, NM 88034

Clayton Lake
Seneca, NM 88437

Conchas Lake
P.O. Box 35
Conchas Dam, NM 88416

Coronado State Park
P.O. Box 853
Bernalillo, NM 87004

Coyote Creek &
    Morphy Lake
P.O. Box 428
Guadalupita, NM 87722

Elephant Butte Lake
P.O. Box 13
Elephant Butte, NM 87935

El Vado Lake State Park
P.O. Box 29
Tierra Amarilla, NM 87575

Heron Lake State Park
P.O. Box 31
Rutheron, NM 87563

Hyde Memorial State Park
P.O. Box 1147
Santa Fe, NM 87503

Indian Petroglyph
(Maintained by City of
   Albuquerque)

Kit Carson State Park
P.O. Box 3197
Taos, NM 87571

Lea County
615 N. Marland, Space 14
Hobbs, NM 88240

Leasburg State Park
P.O. Box 61
Radium Springs, NM
   88054

Living Desert State Park
P.O. Box 100
Carlsbad, NM 88220

Manzano State Park
P.O. Box 224
Mountainair, NM 87036

Navajo Lake (Pine)
P.O. Box 6396
Navajo Dam, NM 87419

Navajo Lake (Sims)
P.O. Box 6367
Navajo Dam, NM 87419

Oasis State Park
P.O. Box 265
Portales, NM 88130

Oliver Lee State Park
P.O. Box 1845
Alamogordo, NM 88310

Pancho Villa State Park
Pancho Villa
Columbus, NM 88029

Percha Dam State Park
P.O. Box 32
Caballo, NM 87931

Rio Grande Gorge
P.O. Box 215
Penasco, NM 87553

Rockhound State Park
P.O. Box 414
Deming, NM 88030

San Gabriel State Park
(Maintained by City of
   Albuquerque)

Santa Fe River
P.O. Box 1147
Santa Fe, NM 87503

Santa Rosa Lake
P.O. Box 384
Santa Rosa, NM 88435

Smokey Bear Historical
P.O. Box 591
Capitan, NM 88316

Storrie Lake State Park
P.O. Box 3157
Las Vegas, NM 87701

Sumner Lake State Park
Alamo Route, Box 30
Fort Sumner, NM 88119

Ute Lake State Park
P.O. Box 52
Logan, NM 88426

Valley of Fires
P.O. Box 313
Carrizozo, NM 88301

Villanueva State Park
General Delivery
Villanueva, NM 87583

Area Supervisors

NE AREA

P.O. Box 1147
Santa Fe, NM 87503

NW AREA

P.O. Box 1147
Santa Fe, NM 87503

SW AREA

P.O. Box 273
Elephant Butte, NM 87935

SE AREA

Route 1, Box 49
Lake Arthur, NM 88253

In 1973, the New Mexico State Trails Study was completed by the State Planning Office of the Division of the Department of Recreation and Historic Preservation. This document provides historical perspective on trail concepts and primitive routes, a brief inventory of trails, legal considerations on acquiring and preserving trails, and recommendations. There has been no update on this study, and, due to lack of funds, further consideration for legislative action is not imminent. Inquiries about the study can be addressed to:

New Mexico State Planning Office
Division of Recreation and Historic Preservation
Santa Fe, NM 87501

Nine state monuments exhibit New Mexico's past:

Abo, ruins of a Spanish mission built about 1620 and abandoned in 1672 after years of drought and Apache raids.

Coronado, ruins of a prehistoric Indian pueblo where Francisco Vasquez de Coronado spent the winter of 1540–41 while searching for the Seven Cities of Cibola.

Dorsey Mansion, a 36-room Victorian estate built late in the 19th century by national Republican political figure Stephen W. Dorsey.

Fort Selden, site of U.S. Army fort established in 1865, boyhood home of Douglas MacArthur.

Fort Sumner, site of U.S. Army fort built in 1864 as a military reservation for Navajos and Apaches.

Jemez, remains of a 17th-century Franciscan mission.

Lincoln, frontier town, where Billy the Kid, Sheriff Pat Garrett, rancher John Chisum, and other pioneers engaged in range wars during the 1800s.

Mimbres, site of prehistoric Mimbres Indian culture.

Quarai, ruins of a Franciscan mission dating to the 1620s. For further information, contact:

Museum of New Mexico
P.O. Box 2087
Santa Fe, NM 87503

Indian Reservations, Museums, and Gardens

There are 23 Indian reservations and pueblos in New Mexico, each with its own governor and its own rules and regulations regarding outdoor recreation facilities and access. A variety of attitudes and regulations pertain to hunting, fishing, camping, and cross-country travel. Each tribal or pueblo governor should be contacted in writing for up-to-date information concerning tribal lands.

The Tourist Division of the Department of Development (113 Washington Ave., Santa Fe, NM 87503) can also be helpful in securing information and access to Indian lands. Further information may be obtained from:

U.S. Bureau of Indian Affairs
Albuquerque Area Office
P.O. Box 8327
Albuquerque, NM 87108

Tourists are welcome on all reservations on most days; the exceptions are certain ceremonial days. Special rules govern photography, sketching, painting, tape recording, and trespassing.

Write to the following addresses for information on the respective reservations.

RESERVATIONS

Ute Mountain

Northern Pueblo Agency
P.O. Box 849
Santa Fe, NM 87501

Jicarilla Apache

Northern Pueblo Agency
P.O. Box 849
Santa Fe, NM 87501

Navajo

BIA Navajo Area Office
Window Rock, AZ 86515

Mescalero Apache

Mescalero Agency
Mescalero, NM 88340

PUEBLOS

Zuni

Zuni Agency, BIA
P.O. Box 369
Zuni, NM 87327

Isleta

Governor, Isleta Pueblo
P.O. Box 317
Isleta, NM 87022

Acoma

Governor, Acoma Pueblo
P.O. Box 309
Acomita, NM 87034

Sandia

Governor, Sandia Pueblo
P.O. Box 608
Bernalillo, NM 87004

Laguna

Governor, Laguna Pueblo
P.O. Box 194
Laguna, NM 87026

Santa Ana

Governor, Santa Ana Pueblo
P.O. Box 37
Bernalillo, NM 87004

Zia

Governor, Zia Pueblo
General Delivery
San Usidro, NM 87053

San Felipe

Governor
P.O. Box "A"
San Felipe Pueblo, NM
  87001

Santo Domingo

Governor
General Delivery
Santo Domingo Pueblo,
  NM 87052

Jemez

Governor
P.O. Box 78
Jemez Pueblo, NM 87024

Cochiti

Governor, Cochiti Pueblo
P.O. Box 70
Cochiti, NM 87041

Tesuque

Governor, Tesuque Pueblo
Route 5, Box 1
Santa Fe, NM 87501

Pojoaque

Governor, Pojoaque Pueblo
Route 1, Box 71
Santa Fe, NM 87501

Nambe

Governor, Nambe Pueblo
Route 1, Box 117-BB
Santa Fe, NM 87501

San Ildefonso

Governor, San Ildefonso
  Pueblo
Route 5, Box 315-A
Santa Fe, NM 87501

Santa Clara

Governor, Santa Clara
  Pueblo
P.O. Box 580
Española, NM 87532

Picuris

Governor, Picuris Pueblo
P.O. Box 228
Penasco, NM 87553

Taos

Governor, Taos Pueblo
P.O. Box 1846
Taos, NM 87571

MUSEUMS AND GARDENS

Museums, gardens, zoos, and libraries are the best starting points for wilderness appreciation, for they contain concentrated information about the natural history and cultural history of the land. A short time spent learning the plant, animal, and cultural background of an area can intensify the outdoor recreational experience and allow the hiker to acquire both a greater appreciation for the natural world and a stronger motivation to help protect it. A brief summary of the New Mexico State Museum system is given here, along with a description of the Living Desert State Park in Carlsbad.

The Museum of New Mexico is a statewide system of four museums and nine state monuments that display various aspects of the art and history of the state. The Palace of the Governors in Santa Fe was the Museum's first home; today it is filled with historic exhibits of the multi-cultured development of New Mexico and the Southwest. The palace is the oldest continuously occupied building in the United States.

The Museum of Fine Arts is next door to the Palace of the Governors, with over 4,200 works of art, many by southwestern Indian artists. The Laboratory of Anthropology and the Museum of International Folk Art are located in the same area in Santa Fe.

The Living Desert Zoological and Botanical State Park

This park is a showplace for the Chihuahuan Desert and its natural history. Situated on the Ocotillo Hills overlooking Carlsbad, this zoo-garden covers 1,100 acres of sloping desert terrain, with more land reserved for future growth.

The zoo area contains over 50 species of Chihuahuan Desert birds, mammals, and reptiles. The park has tried to make animal enclosures naturalistic, as has the Sonoran Desert Museum in Tucson, Arizona. Animal exhibits include a nocturnal building, waterfowl area, reptile section, and elk, deer, javelina, pronghorn, bison, wolf, and coyote. Chihuahuan plant species are labeled along pathways leading to the zoo exhibits. Inside the entry building is an excellent selection of desert natural history books and pamphlets, a geological exhibit, and an information center.

A stop at this living museum makes an excellent preparation for the backcountry-bound hiker.

The Continental Divide Trail

An imaginary line, following the crest of the Rocky Mountains, divides watersheds that flow west to the Gulf of California and the Pacific Ocean from drainages that flow east to the Gulf of Mexico and the Atlantic Ocean. The Continental Divide reaches New Mexico from Colorado in the San Juan Mountains, runs southwest to the Zuni Mountains, south through the Black Range, and continues from the southwest corner of New Mexico into Mexico near the Sonoran-Chihuahuan boundary.

The proposed Continental Divide National Scenic Trail extends approximately 3,100 miles from the Canadian border in Montana to the Mexican border in the southwestern tip of New Mexico. The 1978 National Parks and Recreation Act established the Continental Divide Trail and directed the Forest Service, in cooperation with other government agencies and private land owners, to prepare a comprehensive plan for the trail.

Although the trail is still only a line on a map, various segments can be traveled. Contact the agencies and land owners that control the area crossed by the trail (see addresses below).

Almost 1,900 miles of the route use existing maintained and primitive trails. Elevation varies from 4,000 feet to 13,000 feet. The tentative route traverses terrain varying from high desert to forest land to alpine mountains and meadows. Considerable planning is necessary to travel along most parts of this route.

In New Mexico, the route curves through Sante Fe, Cibola, and Gila national forests, beginning west of Chama on the Colorado border and winding near the Divide to the Mexican border, which it reaches 25 miles south of Animas Peak after crossing Highway 79 west of Antelope Wells. It is shown as a black divided line on Forest Service maps. Another good map for an overview of the trail is the road map issued by the New Mexico State Highway Department and the New Mexico Department of Development. The entire route is shown as a dotted line.

Trip planning should include the use of USGS 7.5 minute topographic maps, BLM "surface quad" maps, and national forest maps. Agencies to contact for the New Mexico section of the trail, in addition to the national forests, whose addresses have been given, are:

New Mexico State Parks and Recreation Division
P.O. Box 1147
141 E. DeVargas
Santa Fe, NM 87503

Bureau of Land Management, State Office
Box 1149
Santa Fe, NM 87501

Jicarilla Apache Tribe
Tourism Director
P.O. Box 507
Dulce, NM 87528

Ramah Navajo Indian Reservation
Ramah, NM 87321

Information about the trail in general is available from:

Continental Divide Trail Society
P.O. Box 30002
Washington, DC 20014

U.S. Department of Agriculture
Forest Service
Rocky Mountain Region
11177 W. Eighth Avenue
Box 25127
Lakewood, CO 80225

West Texas:
The Trans-Pecos Region

The area of Texas included in this guidebook is bordered by the Rio Grande on the west and south, the Pecos River on the east, and New Mexico on the north. The rivers meet just above Amistad Reservoir near Del Rio. This area of West Texas is known as the Trans-Pecos. It is mainly Chihuahuan Desert lowlands, with vast expanses of desert grassland. The desert is interrupted by hills and mountain chains vegetated with oak woodlands and pine forests.

This small part of Texas includes two important hiking areas—Big Bend and Guadalupe Mountains national parks. Both contain unusual backcountry expanses that offer the explorer remote wilderness experiences, the best in Chihuahuan Desert hiking adventure.

The physiographic provinces of West Texas.

The Landscape

Among the deserts of North America, the Chihuahuan Desert is second in size only to the Great Basin. About 10 percent of its area is located in West Texas and southern New Mexico, while the rest extends south into Mexico, spreading into a vast intermountain plateau bordered by the Sierra Madre Occidental on the west and the Sierra Madre Oriental on the east. The two hiking areas described in this chapter lie within the Chihuahuan, although the desert terrain is interspersed with riparian habitat and montane vegetation.

Most of this desert lies above an elevation of 3,000 feet and consists of vast expanses of intermixed grasslands—"grass deserts"—used as cattle country. Annual rainfall ranges from 3 inches in the lowlands to 20 inches in the higher areas, most rain occurring between mid-June and mid-September. Summer temperatures are from 10 to 20 degrees cooler than in the Sonoran Desert, and winter temperatures can fall below freezing.

This combination of summer rain and winter cold results in a single growing and blossoming season—summer. Cacti are abundant, though less so than in the Sonoran Desert. There are many prickly pear types, hedgehogs, and a few barrel cacti. Many Sonoran Desert plant species overlap into the Chihuahuan Desert: yucca, agave, ocotillo, mesquite, and the creosote bush still dominating the desert landscape.

Agaves and yuccas are the characteristic Chihuahuan plants. The single most characteristic species is the *Agave le-*

cheguilla—called the "horse crippler" because it grows just high enough to jab hikers and horses. The agave was important to the Native American and is still used today. Industrial alcohol, mescal, tequila, soap, fiber, needles, and food are all derived from this plant genus. Agaves are sometimes confused with yuccas, but most yuccas have trunks that extend upward while the agave leaf-clusters grow at ground level.

The well-known, and misnamed, century plant is an agave and blooms as all agaves do: after a lifespan of several years (but not 100), the blooms appear on a fast-growing stalk, then the plant dies.

Two other characteristic Chihuahuan Desert plants are the candelilla, *Euphorbia antisyphillitica,* which produces a waxy leaf coating used in floor waxes and chewing gum, and the guayule, *Parthenium argentatum,* which yields rubber when processed.

The mixed landscape of desert lowland and mountain highland provides diverse habitats for the fauna, much of which is similar to the inhabitants of the Sonoran region. Cottontails, coyotes, kit and gray foxes, bobcats, peccaries, mule deer, and an occasional mountain lion are found. Bighorn sheep and pronghorn antelope roam the wilds, but in limited numbers.

This desert, being the least studied of the North American deserts, still holds secrets and surprises. One area that has been researched is Big Bend National Park. Its fascinating desert-mountain terrain covers 1,106 square miles in the southern tip of the Trans-Pecos region, bordered by the Rio Grande. Seventy-five mammal species have been reported, in addition to 55 reptile species, almost 400 bird species, and ten amphibian species.

Chihuahuan Desert Research Institute

Located on the campus of Sul Ross University in Alpine, Texas, the Chihuahuan Desert Research Institute conducts research and educational programs focused on the Chihuahuan Desert. CDRI also coordinates research projects with other universities and private organizations and acts as an international clearinghouse for information involving the Chihuahuan Desert. They are developing a computer listing of researchers, publications, and ongoing, completed, and planned projects. CDRI is guided by a Board of Scientists from the United States, Canada, Mexico, and Europe, who provide direction to the research efforts.

CDRI disseminates information about the desert to local schools and private organizations. They offer seminars and field excursions on the natural and cultural history of the Chihuahuan Desert. If hiking in Big Bend National Park is on your itinerary, stop in Alpine to visit the Institute. The library includes their research on the Chihuahuan Desert and information of general interest to the public about the region.

Big Bend National Park

Larger than Rhode Island, Big Bend resembles a wilderness museum of natural history—a museum detached from the rest of the United States, hovering on the border of Mexico with the nearest town, Marathon, 70 miles north and the next nearest, Alpine, 100 miles north. The nearest good-sized city is El Paso, 322 miles northwest. One gets a feeling for Texas just traveling to this desert outpost—the wide-open desert grasslands stretching for miles to the horizon. One starts wondering about things like spare tires, gas stations, and vultures when heading south on U.S. 90 from Van Horn to Alpine. The entrance to the park, 29 miles from the headquarters at Panther Junction, seems even more remote. Only when entering the visitor center at the headquarters does one become aware of the interconnecting communities of Big Bend. Panther Junction is the starting place for information about road conditions, interpretive programs, camping and supply facilities, and backcountry and float trips. The adventure continues from Panther Junction to three other ranger stations: Castolon, on the western boundary of the park; Rio Grande Village on the eastern boundary; and Chisos Mountains Basin, a woodland retreat 3,600 feet above the surrounding desert.

Castolon, which was a farming and ranching community in the early 1900s, is reached by a road called Camino Buena Vista—Road of Beautiful Views. Eight miles upstream is Santa Elena Canyon, one of the Rio Grande's deepest gorges

The national parks of West Texas.

Rio Grande Village is located in a grassy grove of cottonwood trees on the banks of the big river, 4 miles downstream from Boquillas Canyon, the longest of the river's three major gorges. Camping, fishing, winter naturalist programs, and self-guided nature trails are featured in this area.

Downstream and across the river in Mexico is the small community of Boquillas, the only legal point of entry from Mexico into the park. For a small fee one can be rowed across the river, rent a burro for the ¾-mile ride to town, and feast on tacos and tostadas. The Boquillas Canyon Trail is a short, 1.4-mile round trip from arid desert to junglelike flood plain and deep river canyon.

Chisos Basin is a woodland retreat nestled in a bowl-shaped depression in the midst of the Chisos Mountains. Chisos Basin offers camping, horseback riding, and the only food and lodging facilities in the park. A great variety of hikes and backpacks originate from the basin.

HIKING TRAILS

Incongruous overlapping life zones, cactus growing next to pine—the diversity of the Southwest is well displayed in Big Bend. From riparian habitat through desert grassland to mountain islands with patches of ponderosa pine, the hiker can traverse and climb through continuously changing scenery.

Temperatures range from more than 100 degrees along the river in the summer to an average of 36 degrees in the Chisos Mountains in the winter. Sunny skies predominate in the cold winter months, with brief periods of cloudy weather.

The rainy season extends from mid-July through early October, with thunderstorms resulting in locally heavy rain and flashflooding. Temperatures average 5 to 10 degrees lower in the higher elevations than in the desert and 5 to 10 degrees higher along the river.

We will describe trails near the river first, proceed to the cross-country desert trails, then ascend into the Chisos Mountains all the way to the top of Emory Peak at an elevation of 7,825 feet.

River Trails

Riparian habitat—the "ribbon oasis"—provides food, water, and shelter for the greatest concentration of life forms of any habitat. Within the river live channel catfish, blue and flathead catfish, shiners, mosquitofish, Mexican stonerollers, and killifish. Among the amphibians, which travel in both the aquatic and terrestrial worlds, we find the Big Bend slider and the spiny and softshell turtles. Leopard frogs croak along the river's edge. The warm-blooded beaver also lives along the banks, in burrows dug into the sides. Birds and insects abound. The endangered peregrin falcon has about five nesting sites in Big Bend, the heaviest concentration of successful aeries in the western United States outside Alaska.

Native and exotic species of plant life line the flowing oasis with reeds, grasses, tree tobacco, cane, trumpet flowers, tamarisk, honey mesquite, and willows. Holes used by Indians for grinding mesquite beans can be found along the banks.

River trails are a good place to start exploring the Big Bend and the Chihuahuan Desert. They put the drier country above into perspective. The Rio Grande, however, for all its life-giving virtues, is not potable, so carry drinking water.

Mesa de Anguila

This huge mesa slopes from the northwest down to the river's edge and provides a mixture of river and mesa trails. Begin either the River Trail or the Mesa Top Trail by asking a store owner in Lajitas (the nearest town) about access. Private property must be crossed to an old road, two gates passed, and cultivated fields traversed for a mile to a large, abandoned stone house, which is the trailhead.

The River Trail begins south of the stone house, crossing three passes before descending to the river's edge. The trail follows the river 7 miles to the west end of Santa Elena Canyon. Side trails lead from the river up to the mesa top. A 5-mile round trip can be made by turning left at the first junction with the Mesa Top Trail, 3 miles from the trailhead, going north to the mesa top and back west to the stone house. There are many side canyons to explore. This is the most heavily used trail in the vicinity.

The Mesa Top Trail heads east up the escarpment to a maze of trails, some easy to follow, others difficult. Permanent water is available at Tinaja Lujan, and seasonal water may be available at other tinajas but shouldn't be depended on.

Several days would be required to hike along the entire

River Trail and return along the Mesa Top Trail. Take plenty of water and talk with park rangers before venturing into this remote area.

MAPS: Lajitas and Mesa de Anguila (7.5 minute)

Santa Elena Canyon Trail

This 1.7-mile nature trail with interpretive markers begins at the parking area at the end of the Santa Elena Canyon Road. It crosses Terlingua Creek, climbs a flight of concrete steps, and descends to the river's banks within the canyon. The trail winds among boulders and ends where the river abuts the canyon walls. This trail is a good introduction to the Rio Grande riparian habitat.

Mariscal Canyon Rim Trail

The trailhead is reached by a long journey on unimproved dirt roads. Check with rangers about road conditions. The trail starts at the old Talley House, located at the end of the road to Talley. The first section of this 6.6-mile round trip uses 2 miles of an old burro trail. A steep hike then leads to the Mariscal Canyon Rim overlook, with a 1,000-foot drop to the river.

Downstream is the Cross Canyon Trail, which meets the river at the end of Cross Canyon. To reach this trail, travel cross-country to the east and pick up the trail in Cross Canyon.

WATER: none
MAPS: Mariscal Mountain (7.5 minute)

Cross Canyon Trail

This primitive trail connects Solis and Cross Canyon. From Solis, it follows the western edge of a grassy flat and runs west toward the cliffs of Mariscal Mountain. The trail climbs above the desert through a break in the cliffs, continues south along the base of the summit ridge, and descends Cross Canyon to the river. The 14-mile round trip can take a full day; the route is dry, so take plenty of water. The Mariscal Canyon Rim Trail can be found by crossing the summit ridge.

MAPS: Solis and Mariscal Mountain (7.5 minute)

Hot Springs Canyon Overlook Trail

About 3 miles west of Rio Grande Village on the paved road from Panther Junction is a turnoff onto a good dirt road. This road heads south 1½ miles to Hot Springs. The trail starts at the Hot Springs historic site at the mouth of Tornillo Creek. It parallels the river to a hill overlooking the entrance to Hot Springs Canyon. The 2-mile round trip features a spectacular view of the Sierra Carmen Mountains.

The Hot Springs resort was located a short distance up the trail. More than 200,000 gallons of water a day flowed in 1936, but the spring filled with silt in 1966 and today surfaces only in a few places at river level.

Boquillas Canyon Trail

Another introduction to the riverine environment is this short,

1.4-mile round-trip trail, which starts from a parking area at the end of the Boquillas Canyon spur road. It climbs a small hill and drops through huge reeds to the river, which it follows to the entrance to sheer-walled Boquillas Canyon. A high sand slide, formed by particles blown from the flood plain on the left, faces the canyon walls. Rangers regularly lead nature hikes on this trail, a must for those staying in Rio Grande Village.

Marufo Vega Trail

Just past the turn onto the paved road used to reach the crossing to Boquillas, Mexico, is the trailhead of this 6-mile trail to the Rio Grande. The trail follows a drainage north 1½ miles, then turns sharply right and follows a limestone ridge up to the east. The Strawhouse Trail intersects the Marufo Vega Trail here, before continuing north. At the top of the steep rise one can look south to Boquillas. The trail goes up the ridge and turns back north into a broad valley. About ½ mile along the valley, a rock cairn marks a short side trail that connects to the Strawhouse Trail. The main trail continues northeast and follows an arroyo and a drainage for a mile to a junction. One branch bends east, turns southeast, and drops into a drainage that turns north again before reaching the river. The other branch continues northeast over a broad pass, drops into a narrow canyon, and descends to the river, which it follows for a mile.

LENGTH: 12 miles round trip
DIFFICULTY: strenuous

WATER: none
MAP: Boquillas (7.5 minute)

Cross-Country Desert Trails

Desert flatlands, arroyos, ridges, hills, and canyons cover 98 percent of Big Bend. Most of the soils and gravels were eroded, carried, and deposited over the eons by water. Some were deposited by ancient volcanoes, and some in seas where the accumulated remains of marine life eventually formed layers of limestone.

Prehistoric Indians frequented the Big Bend area as long ago as 10,000 years. The Native Americans sustained themselves for thousands of years by hunting and gathering, following the animals and plants as season and opportunity dictated. Over 200 kinds of foods were utilized by these people: prickly pear pads and fruits, walnuts, persimmons, yucca blossoms and fruits, mesquite, palo verde, and ironwood beans. The *atlatl,* or throwing stick, was used to hunt rabbits and deer.

The desert is the toughest environment for plant and animal life to survive in because of the great variations in temperature and rainfall. The life forms that have adapted are many and varied, but man can change the desert to suit his needs and in changing it, destroy it. Part of an education toward finding a balance between man's needs and those of other species involves getting out and seeing the desert— taking the time to look closely at the environment and to reflect that building the system took millions of years, but that impatient man can upset the fragile balance quickly.

With these ideas in mind, let's describe the trails that wander through the landscape of Big Bend between river and mountain.

Chimneys Trail

From the paved road to Castolon, about 1½ miles south of the Burro Mesa Pouroff Road, a trail heads west to a series of high rock outcroppings—the Chimneys—visible to the left of the trail. The Chimneys served as landmarks to travelers for hundreds of years. There are Indian petroglyphs nearby, as well as the remains of shelters used by sheepherders. The Chimneys are passed 1½ miles along the trail, which is actually an old road. The route continues past Pena Spring to the Old Maverick Road, 7 miles from the trailhead. Another trail leads northwest from the Chimneys to a huge cottonwood tree that marks the site of Red Ass Springs. An old road leads from the springs to Maverick Road.

LENGTH: 4.8 miles round trip
DIFFICULTY: medium
WATER: none
MAPS: Cerro Castellan and Castolon (7.5 minute)

Mule Ear Spring Complex

This interesting, out-of-the-way area offers many possibilities to the adventurous hiker. A trail starts at the Mule Ear Overlook parking lot on the Castolon Road. This primitive route circles Trap Mountain to an old road that leads first to

Trap Spring and then to Mule Ear Spring. The old pipeline that can be seen carried water from Mule Ear Spring to the stock tank near the paved road. A rock corral and the remains of an old adobe house at Mule Ear Spring are evidence of early ranching in the area.

Several primitive trails begin at Mule Ear Spring. One goes north of Mule Ear Peaks to a five-way junction near the bed of a dry wash. The southern trail follows Smoky Creek all the way to the primitive dirt road that connects Buenos Aires and Black Dike. A branch of this trail turns back north to join the main trail a mile from the five-way junction. Another trail goes east from the junction for 1½ miles to Smoky Spring. A longer branch heads southeast to San Jacinto Spring and a primitive road near the river between Johnson Ranch and Loop Camp. Still another trail heads north from the junction to the Dodson Trail.

LENGTH: 3.8 miles round trip (to and from Mule Ear Spring)
DIFFICULTY: medium
WATER: usually available from springs
MAP: Cerro Castellan (7.5 minute)

Burro Spring Trail

A 2.2-mile hike leads through ocotillo, creosote bush, cactus, lechuguilla, and century plant to an overlook above Burro Spring. The trail begins from the road to the Burro Mesa Pouroff parking area. A return can be made by following the primitive trail that heads down the hillside on the left, down the wash, and back to the left along an old road.

Burro Mesa Pouroff Trail

A 1-mile round trip takes the hiker from the Burro Mesa Pouroff parking lot to the pouroff, which is at the head of a narrow box canyon. Another trail, indicated as "Top of Burro Mesa Pouroff," takes the hiker to the top of the cliff by the pouroff.

Ward Spring

Just over 2 miles south of the Old Ranch on the Castolon Road is the trailhead for this route to one of many springs along the western slope of the Chisos Mountains. The trail follows a pipeline that carried water from Ward Spring to a stock tank north of the parking area. The spring, visible from the parking area, runs year-round. Such springs and seeps provide water for the park's wildlife.

LENGTH: 3.6 miles round trip
DIFFICULTY: medium
WATER: usually available
MAP: Emory Peak (7.5 minute)

Dominguez Spring Trail

This remote, primitive route begins just east of the Jewel's Camp spur road, which leads to the river from the unimproved River Road in the southern area of the park. The trail goes 7¼ miles to Dominguez Spring, which is situated in a drainage of the Sierra Quemada (Burnt Mountains). The great escarpment of the Punta de la Sierra juts up to the left.

The first 4½ miles traverses open country; the trail then enters canyons of the Quemadas. The spring site is marked by a rock dam and a well-preserved rock house.

Farther up the drainage are more springs; the main drainage can be followed to the Dodson Trail.

LENGTH:	14½ miles round trip
DIFFICULTY:	strenuous
WATER:	some
MAPS:	Reed Camp and Emory Peak (7.5 minute)

Elephant Tusk–Fresno Creek Trail

This very primitive trail starts from the Black Gap Road 5 miles south of Glenn Spring. A metal stake by the road marks the trailhead. The trail leads to the northeast side of Elephant Tusk, then continues in the same drainage to a low pass that leads to Fresno Creek at the base of Tortuga Mountain. Fresno Creek can be followed back to the road to complete a 16-mile loop, or the trail's continuation can be taken to the Dodson Trail. There is year-round water in Fresno Creek.

LENGTH:	16 miles round trip
DIFFICULTY:	strenuous backpack
WATER:	some
MAPS:	Glenn Spring and Emory Peak (7.5 minute)

Ore Terminal Trail

A primitive 4-mile trail begins in the wash just below the

entrance to the Canyon Overlook near Boquillas Canyon and leads over open limestone hills to the Ore Terminal. The trailhead is the same as the Marufo Vega Trail's. Look for two wood towers a mile up the wash on the east bank. Follow the cables up the hillside to an old trail marked by cairns. The route turns west, climbs a hillside, and crosses a pass north to a better-marked section. The trail climbs another hillside, circles the head of a deep canyon, then emerges onto the flat area where the Ore Terminal is located. This terminal was used to service the tramway of the Corte Madera Mine from 1909 to 1919. The 6-mile tramway carried 7½ tons of zinc, silver, and lead ore per hour.

Two other cross-country routes to the terminal start from the unimproved Old Ore Road. One starts from the turnoff into Ernst Canyon, crosses the ridge, and meets the old road in Ernst Basin. It then turns south-southeast and in 4 miles reaches the Ore Terminal. From the junction in Ernst Basin, another primitive route heads directly north for 8 miles to the Telephone Canyon Trail.

Another route to the terminal from the south starts a mile east, on the paved road from the Rio Grande Village turnoff to Boquillas. Another primitive route, this trail travels through a rough canyon for 3 miles to join the main Ore Terminal Trail.

DIFFICULTY: strenuous
WATER: none
MAPS: Boquillas, Ernst Valley, and Roys Peak (7.5 minute)

Strawhouse and Telephone Canyon Trails

Starting at the end of a turnoff from the Old Ore Road, the 20-mile, primitive Telephone Canyon Trail crosses desert mountains, the Sierra del Carmen, and the Dead Horse sub-range, from west to east. The route is marked by cairns for the first 3 miles, to a junction with the trail coming north from Ernst Tinaja. The Telephone Canyon Trail continues north and east for 6 more miles, where it meets the Strawhouse Trail coming from the south. The trail then crosses the Dead Horse Mountains for another 16 miles to a primitive road that leads to the Adams Ranch, which is at Still-well Crossing on the Rio Grande.

The Strawhouse Trail runs for 14 miles between the junction with the Telephone Canyon Trail and the Marufo Vega Trail just north of the Ore Terminal trailhead. The trail generally follows the Ernst Valley.

No water is available along either of these isolated routes, which are for backpackers with a knowledge of map and compass and previous Big Bend experience. Take plenty of water and then some more.

DIFFICULTY: strenuous
WATER: none
MAPS: Roys Peak, Boquillas, Ernst Valley, and
Sue Peaks (7.5 minute)

Dog Canyon and Devil's Den Trails

These two trails are located in the northern "panhandle" of

Big Bend, 5 miles south of the entrance at Persimmon Gap. The Dog Canyon Trail starts at the interpretive sign near the bridge over Bone Springs Draw and follows the level canyon floor, eventually skirting the boundary between the park and an adjoining ranch 200 yards beyond the canyon. This 5-mile round trip should not be attempted in rainy weather because of the possibility of flashflooding. Massive displays of layered limestone line the canyon.

The Devil's Den Trail starts at the same trailhead. Follow Bone Spring Draw toward Dog Canyon as far as Nine Point Draw, then follow a wash that enters from the south to Devil's Den. This deep wash is a mile long and contains potholes that fill after a rain. The spectacular den is cut deep into the limestone bedrock, and provides photographic possibilities.

DIFFICULTY: medium
WATER: some in Devil's Den
MAPS: Dagger Flat and Bone Spring (7.5 minute)

Grapevine Hills Trail

This great 2.2-mile round-trip trail leads into the heart of the Grapevine Hills and the rock formations that make the hike a delight. The Hills are a laccolith—a mushroom-shaped underground lava flow that pushed up the rocks above and was later exposed by erosion. The trail follows a sandy wash and starts at a parking area near the end of the Grapevine Hills dirt road.

DIFFICULTY: easy
MAPS: Terlingua and Chisos Mountain (7.5 minute)

Banta Shut-In

This primitive 15-minute round-trip route through flat desert terrain starts from a parking area, just south of the K-Bar Research Station, 4 miles southeast of Panther Junction. It follows a series of old roads, the first going south for 100 yards, then east for a mile to an old north-south road. The trail turns south on the road for ¼ mile to another road, which turns east. This road goes to Estufa Spring, now dry. The Estufa drainage continues east into Tornillo Creek, just south of the Banta Shut-In. The "shut-in" is a narrow, jagged canyon cut by erosional forces through the laccolith to form the wash.

An alternate return route, requiring a car shuttle, involves following the bed of Tornillo Creek north for 9 miles to the Fossil Bone Exhibit on Highway 385 at the Tornillo Creek Bridge.

DIFFICULTY: strenuous day hike or backpack
WATER: sometimes available
MAPS: Roys Peak and Panther Junction (7.5 minute)

Slickrock Canyon

A primitive route through Slickrock Canyon begins halfway between the Croton Spring Road and the Castolon Road junction. It follows Oak Creek northwest, then turns north into the deep, colorful canyon that drains Onion Flat to the north and passes the east side of Slickrock Mountain. An alternate return route is an old road that starts on the south side of Onion Flat, goes between Slickrock Mountain and Croton Peak, and heads south back to the highway.

LENGTH: 10 miles round trip
DIFFICULTY: strenuous day hike
WATER: none
MAPS: The Basin and Tule Mountain (7.5 minute)

Chisos Mountains Trails

The Chisos Mountains—the heart of Big Bend—were formed over 60 million years ago from successive eruptions of volcanic rock and now cover about 40 square miles. The island supports characteristic desert-mountain plant and animal communities. Once home to a band of Mescalero Apaches and later used for grazing, the southernmost mountain range in the United States is now home for an overlap of diverse flora and fauna communities. Cactus and maple, century plant and fern, pine tree and prickly pear are neighbors. Certain tree species grow farther south here than anywhere else—ponderosa, Arizona cypress, Douglas fir, quaking aspens, oaks, and maples. The drive from Panther Junction up to Chisos Basin should be done slowly to savor the quick succession of life zones.

Lost Mine Trail

The trailhead is a parking area at 5,800-foot Panther Pass. This self-guiding nature trail makes an excellent introduction to the Chisos Mountains and their mysteries. From the parking lot it crosses the northern slope of Casa Grande Peak to a point high on the west ridge of Lost Mine Peak; 32 sign-posts describe the natural history of the Chisos. The average time for the 5-mile round trip is 4 hours, and the view is worth the time. A guide pamphlet, available at Panther Junction and the trailhead, is a good source of information for the rest of the Chisos Basin hikes.

Boulder Meadow Trail

Starting at the Basin, this 3-mile round trip takes one through the Chisos' pinyon-juniper woodland to a grassy meadow covered with boulders. For a longer trek, continue beyond Boulder Meadow to Pinnacle Pass, located between Toll Mountain and Emory Peak. The 7,100-foot pass offers an excellent view of the Basin.

Emory Peak Trail

From Pinnacle Pass, the Emory Peak Trail climbs to the right, following a ridge to the summit of the 7,825-foot high point of Big Bend. The view is great in all directions. Boot Canyon lies along the southeast side of the peak, and Laguna Meadow lies at the base of the west-facing talus slope.

Boot Springs

Continuing from Pinnacle Pass for another mile, a trail reaches Boot Springs, in the center of Boot Canyon, 4.5 miles from the Basin trailhead. A cabin used by the Park Service sits above the spring. The volcanic formation shaped like an upside-down cowboy boot is located at the pouroff of Boot Canyon, 0.4 miles south of Pinnacle Pass.

Boot Canyon is famous among ornithologists for providing habitat for the Colima warbler. This small gray and yellow songbird, seen in the area from April through September, is found nowhere else in the United States. A great variety of trees grow in the canyon bottom, including ponderosa pine, Douglas fir, and Arizona cypress.

Juniper Canyon Trail

About 0.2 miles beyond Boot Springs is a trail junction. The trail that turns left (east) from the Boot Canyon Trail climbs over a pass and descends to the end of the Juniper Canyon Primitive Road. The trail passes Upper Juniper Spring, where an old cement tank marks the former use of the area for cattle grazing.

East Rim Trail

The trail that continues south from the Boot Springs Trail beyond the Juniper Canyon Trail junction passes a small dam built by Homer Wilson, who ranched the western side of the Chisos prior to 1944. Continue to the East Rim Trail junction. The trail bears left and follows a side canyon to the East Rim, which overlooks Juniper Canyon. The trail then runs south and west along the edge of the Chisos Rim to the South Rim.

South Rim Trail

The South Rim is the high point of a 13-mile loop that circles Emory Peak via Boot Springs and the South Rim Trail, which skirts Emory Peak to the west through Laguna Meadow. The South Rim escarpment drops 2,500 feet to the desert floor, where the 33-mile Outer Mountain Loop, a primitive back-packing route, lies. To the south, the mountains of Mexico are visible more than 80 miles away. Looking east, the Sierra del Caballo Muerto, or Dead Horse Mountains, rise, extending into Mexico as part of the Sierra del Carmen. The 9,000-foot Fronterizas Range, at the southern end of the Sierra Carmen, is 50 miles distant.

Laguna Meadow was frequented by prehistoric Indians, as evidenced by the mescal pit found near the north end. The pit was used as an oven for cooking sotol hearts and maguey or tips of young century plant stalks. A log cabin, built by an early sheepherder, can also be seen. The meadow lies halfway between the Basin and the South Rim on the 7-mile South Rim Trail.

The Window Trail

This 2.6-mile route follows the Chisos Basin drainage from the Basin trailhead and ends at the pouroff, or window, that opens northwest into the desert below. This trail passes through open chaparral and drops to Oak Creek, following the canyon to where it narrows to 20 feet at the base of the window. Such interesting birds as the black-chinned sparrow, crissal thrasher, and varied bunting can be seen in summer. Maples and oaks provide shelter. This is one of the most popular trails in the Basin, and horseback trips are offered to the window through the Chisos Remuda in the lower Basin.

Pine Canyon Trail

This trail starts at the end of the primitive Pine Canyon Road and follows an old road past the remains of the Wade ranch well and watering tank. Sometimes referred to as Wade Canyon, this drainage continues winding up through a section of junipers, pinyons, and oaks. Higher, ponderosa pine, Texas madrone, and Emory and Grave's oaks appear. This, one of Big Bend's most beautiful trails, ends at the base of a 200-foot cliff where a waterfall comes alive after a heavy rain. A round trip covers 4.5 miles.

Outer Mountain Loop

This 33-mile circuit is the most varied of the long Big Bend backpack treks. Much elevation is gained and lost, and a tremendous mixture of plant and animal life passed. The first and last sections of the route are the Boulder Meadow and South Rim trails, respectively. Starting at the Basin trailhead, the route goes to Boot Spring, then down the Juniper Canyon Trail to the Juniper Canyon Road, down the road to the Dodson Trail, west on the Dodson Trail to Blue Creek, up Blue Creek Canyon to the South Rim Trail, and back to the Basin trailhead via Laguna Meadow.

The Dodson Trail section is 11.5 miles long. The first part, between Juniper Canyon Road and the Dodson Place—the site of an old ranch—is easy to follow because cairns mark the way. The trail goes west around the south slope of the hillside below the ranch site. Spring water is found in the drainage 1 mile west of the Dodson Place.

LENGTH: 33 miles
DIFFICULTY: strenuous
WATER: available
MAPS: Emory Peak, Glenn Spring, The Basin (7.5 minute)

Optional Routes for Experienced Hikers

Big Bend contains a lifetime's worth of canyons, ridgelines, peaks, arroyos, flats, hills, and river banks. For the experienced desert hiker and backpacker, there are countless geologic, botanical, and animal-spotting adventures waiting in the wilderness. To leave the trails and head cross-country, however, requires a certain level of experience and knowledge in order to safely negotiate this rugged, dry topography. With the opportunities goes the responsibility of checking with the rangers and finding out as much as possible about the proposed route. Things change, sometimes overnight, and the Park Service personnel are there to help and to interpret the environment. Use their knowledge and keep them informed of your intentions.

Two rugged, off-trail routes are described here.

Sue Peaks Climb

The Sue Peaks are the highest of the Sierra del Caballo Muerto—Dead Horse Mountains—on the eastern border of the park. One route to these desert summits involves a 15-mile round-trip hike over terrain tough and steep enough to challenge even an experienced and conditioned hiker. Take the Old Ore Road south from Dagger Flat Road for 4 miles. Follow an open drainage east to where one can climb to the ridge that leads to the summit of the peaks. The climbing is on limestone, with desert vegetation blending with giant dagger yuccas above 5,000 feet. Pinyons and junipers are found west of the summit.

This type of hike requires good planning and preparation and plenty of water. None is available along the route, and over 3,500 feet of elevation is gained from the road to the 5,854-foot summit of Sue Peaks.

Cross-the-Park Hike

The ultimate in Big Bend backcountry experience is a Cross-the-Park hike, combining various existing trails and cross-country trekking. One route mentioned in the *Hiker's Guide to Trails of Big Bend National Park, Texas* is the following:

Starting at Stillwell Crossing, travel from Adam's Ranch to Roys Peak via the Telephone Canyon Trail on the first day. Cross to Dugout Wells on the second day. Climb to Upper Juniper Spring on the third day and cross the Chisos Mountains by the Boot Canyon and South Rim scenic loop to Blue Creek (or follow the Outer Mountain Loop, either stopping at the spring just west of the Dodson Place or continuing to Blue Creek). On the next day hike to Luna's via the Chimney Trail. The last day is a cross-country walk to Lajitas. Water and food can be cached along the way, possibly at Roys Peak, Blue Creek Ranch, and Luna's. This excursion in desert topography takes one through all the splendor of Big Bend and poses all the challenges a hiker could desire.

GENERAL INFORMATION

Big Bend visitation is fairly evenly distributed over the year, with the heavy seasons from May 1 through June 30 and September 1 through December 30. The park is crowded during the Easter, Thanksgiving, and Christmas holidays.

The park is a nature preserve; plants and animals are protected. Collecting rocks and artifacts and the use of mineral or metal detectors is prohibited. Hunting or the use of firearms is also prohibited. Pets must be kept under physical restraint and are not permitted on trails or in public buildings. Motorized vehicles can be used only on park roadways. No off-road vehicle travel is allowed. Ground fires are prohibited.

Fees and Campground Information

ENTRANCE FEES

None

CAMPGROUNDS

Chisos Basin. Elevation: 5,400 feet. Tables, grills, overhead shelters, water, and comfort stations, but no hook-ups. 65 sites. $3.00 per site per night.

Rio Grande Village. Elevation: 1,850 feet. Tables, grills, overhead shelters, water, and comfort stations, but no hook-ups. (Hook-ups are available at the nearby trailer park; inquire at grocery store.) 100 sites. $3.00 per site per night.

Cottonwood. Elevation: 1,900 feet. Tables, grills, water, and pit toilets. 35 sites. $2.00 per site per night.

Primitive campgrounds. Numerous roadside campsites are located throughout the park. No services or facilities are provided, and backcountry permits are required.

CAMPING LIMITATIONS

Occupancy of developed campsites, including the Rio Grande Village trailer park, is limited to 14 days. Occupancy beyond 14 days may be authorized on a daily basis if sites are available for new arrivals.

Services

Gasoline and groceries are available near all campgrounds. Showers and laundry facilities are available only at Rio Grande Village. Prepared food and lodging are available only in Chisos Basin. Call (915) 477-2291 for reservations.

Tours and Naturalist Programs

Guided horseback trips are available at the Chisos Remuda, (915) 477-2374. No guided auto or bus tours are available. Nature walks, workshops, and evening slide programs are given by park naturalists. Bulletin boards at ranger stations have schedules.

Transportation and Roads

No public transportation is available to or within the park. Bus and rail connections are available to Alpine. Nearest commercial airport is Midland/Odessa, 250 miles northeast.

Three paved roads lead to the park: 1) U.S. 385 from Marathon to north entrance; 2) Highway 118 from Alpine to west entrance; 3) Marfa to Presidio on U.S. 67, Presidio to Study Butte on Ranch Road 170, Highway 118 to west entrance.

All principal roads in the park are paved. Improved dirt roads are usually in good condition and accessible to normal passenger cars, except following storms. Unimproved back-country roads generally require high-clearance vehicles and/ or four-wheel-drive. Current road conditions should be checked at nearest ranger station.

RECREATIONAL VEHICLES

Steep grades and sharp curves to Chisos Basin; not advised for autos towing trailers over 20 feet long.

Activities

SWIMMING

Swimming in the Rio Grande is neither prohibited nor encouraged. It can be dangerous due to undercurrents, step-offs, and quicksand.

FISHING

Fishing is allowed in the Rio Grande. No fishing license is required. Catfish are commonly taken.

HIKING IN GENERAL

Big Bend is wild and unusual, remote and mystical. Desert springs are unreliable. Plan a backpack in advance of arriving, but allow leeway for changes after checking with the rangers.

RIVER TRIPS

Three options are available: 1) Bring your own gear; 2) Rent gear in Study Butte or Lajitas; 3) Hire a guide service that provides permits, food, equipment, and shuttles. For river conditions call (915) 477-2251, ext. 210.

Vegetation and Wildlife

About 1,000 plant species have been identified. Various plants bloom through the year, depending on the weather. Most blooms occur March–May and June–October.

Seventy-five species of mammals, about 400 species of birds, and 65 species of reptiles and amphibians have been recorded in the park.

For more information, write to:

U.S. Department of the Interior
National Park Service
Big Bend National Park, TX 79834

or

Big Bend Natural History Association, Inc.
Big Bend National Park, TX 79834

Guadalupe Mountains National Park

Added to the National Park System in 1972, Guadalupe Mountains National Park was established to protect a little-known, remote, dry, hard, imposing fortress of limestone layers deposited beneath Permian seas between 380 and 225 million years ago. Innumerable lime-secreting algae and other organisms formed the beds of the ancient seas, beds that were eventually lifted far above sea level during the last 10 to 12 million years.

This limestone reef—the world's largest fossil reef—extends some 350 miles across western Texas and south-eastern New Mexico, though most is buried beneath arid plains and desert. The reef is exposed along the 40-mile eastern Guadalupe escarpment as far as Carlsbad Caverns National Park and again to the south in the Apache Mountains and Glass Mountains near Van Horn and Alpine, Texas.

The national park includes a huge wedge where the limestone is exposed as a mountain range. The tip of this wedge is looming, ominous El Capitan, an imposing fortress with cliffs rising 2,000 feet. The park contains 76,293 acres, which cover the most scenic and rugged portions of the range, its northern boundary being the New Mexico-Texas border.

The Guadalupes contain the four highest peaks in Texas, the highest being 8,751-foot Guadalupe Peak, which shoots up 5,000 feet from the 3,650-foot Chihuahuan Desert floor at the foot of the western escarpment. This abrupt elevation change, combined with Guadalupe's southern location, creates a unique climate and results in great varieties of plant and animal life through the park.

The biological communities in the Guadalupes are limited by the water supply. Air masses rise up the sheer limestone walls, creating moisture-laden clouds that drop over 20 inches of precipitation per year in the mountains, while the surrounding lowlands receive about 10 inches. The vegetation in the canyons and on the ridges produces shade that reduces evaporation at the higher elevations. Temperatures can be 10 to 15 degrees lower in the mountains than on the desert below, with cooler ground temperatures and cooling winds. Summers are hot and winters cool in the lowlands.

The mountains create their own weather, and sudden storms and flashfloods can surprise the unwary backcountry trekker. Spring and autumn winds and electrical storms are common. Late-summer convectional storms create spectacular desert downpours accompanied by lightning and thunder. Temperatures can drop quickly at the higher elevations, and snow is common in the mountains in winter.

The mixing of plant communities in the Guadalupes occurs because the southern and eastern limits of some Rocky Mountain species overlap the northern limits of Mexican species. Ponderosa pine and bigtooth maple, found on north-facing slopes and canyon washes, are at the eastern end of their ranges, as they are in Big Bend National Park. Rocky Mountain juniper is at its southern limit, and chinquapin oak is at the western edge of its range. Texas madrone, a common tree in Mexico's Sierra Madre, is at its northern limit.

It is thought that during recent geologic time, the lowlands have become drier, while the mountains have retained a relatively higher proportion of water, this disparity leading to the unusual diversity of microclimates and biological communities in the Guadalupes.

At the edge of a plant community's range, especially in small, isolated patches, the plants are exposed to greater environmental stress. Certain species are stressed enough in the Guadalupes to be locally endangered: bigtooth maple, serviceberry, Texas madrone, Arizona starleaf, New Mexican forestiera, Rocky Mountain juniper, Texas mulberry, bullgrass, finestem needlegrass, and Mexican buckeye.

There are rare and endangered animal species within the park also: Davis Mountains cottontail, Texas antelope, ground squirrel, peregrine falcon, Guadalupe Mountain ude, gray-footed chipmunk, and western Botta's pocket gopher.

The lowlands surrounding the Guadalupes are typical Chihuahuan Desert, with the characteristic creosote bushes, ocotillo, sotol, prickly pears, cholla, and the ever-present agaves. Sloping upward, the desert vegetation merges with shrubs and trees like junipers, pinyons, oaks, and Texas madrone. The upper slopes and ridges of the range contain stands of Douglas fir, ponderosa pine, and limber pine. Especially in the upper bowls, with a heterogeneous environment in terms of precipitation, shade, and temperature, conifers mix with woodland species of oaks, ashes, walnuts, and maples.

Human history starts with the many Indian tribes that frequented the still remote area as long as 12,000 years ago. The most recent Indians, the Mescalero Apaches, fought bitterly to protect their homeland from exploitation but were gradually subdued by ranchers and the U.S. Cavalry. Ranching spread after the Civil War and continues in the surrounding lowlands today.

Two men in particular contributed to the effort to make the Guadalupes a national park. In the early 1920s, Wallace E. Pratt, former president of Humble Oil (Exxon), acquired lands to the south and north that extended into McKittrick Canyon. J. C. Hunter, Jr., also an oilman and rancher, owned 72,000 acres that included most of the high country of the Guadalupes. Both men recognized this area as scenically unique and biologically important, and donated large parcels of land to the National Park System. Mineral rights and ownership of large land tracts were donated by Texaco and the State of Texas. The Park Service continued to acquire land and is today developing the area to its full park potential.

HIKING TRAILS

Over 80 miles of backcountry trails provide access to the Guadalupes. Topographic maps, information about trail conditions, weather information, and permits are available at Frijole and Dog Canyon ranger stations. Dog Canyon, located at the north end of the park, can be reached from Carlsbad. Drive 12 miles north from Carlsbad on U.S. 285 and turn left on Highway 137. Highway 137 is paved for the first 47 miles but becomes a gravel road for the remaining 10 miles into Dog Canyon. The drive takes about 2 hours.

Dog Canyon Area

Trails from Dog Canyon give access to the northern high country of the park. They intersect and loop, so that a variety of hikes of different lengths are possible.

Dog Canyon Campground is in a remote, beautiful area filled with colors in autumn. The campground is still being developed, and water can be scarce; bring plenty in your vehicle. The latest information on campground facilities, water availability, trail conditions, and road access to the campground can be obtained from park rangers.

Marcus Trail

This 6-mile round-trip hike is an introduction to the Guadalupes. The trail heads west along a ridge after following a drainage for ¾ mile from the Dog Canyon trailhead. It then descends steeply into West Dog Canyon, where it meets the Tejas and Cox Tank trails. The Marcus Campsite is near the junction. Cairns mark part of the route but may be difficult to follow in places.

Cox Tank Trail

Beginning from the junction of the Tejas Trail with the Marcus Trail, the Cox Tank Trail takes the hiker southwest for 1.5 miles past an earthen dam and a water tank. The trail gradually ascends to a ridge, turns southeast, and climbs to the junction of the Bush Mountain Trail at the crest of Blue

Ridge; from Cox Tank to the junction is 2.2 miles. This section of the trail—from West Dog Canyon to the junction with the Bush Mountain Trail—gains almost 2,000 feet of elevation and provides western vistas toward Cutoff Mountain, Dell City, and the salt flats. Look for cairns marking the seldom-used trail. A short distance east of the Bush Mountain Trail junction is the Blue Ridge Campsite, situated along the 1.3-mile section of the Bush Mountain Trail that descends to the junction of the Tejas Trail, which comes in from the north, and the Lost Peak-Mescalero Trail.

Lost Peak-Mescalero Trail

A loop can be made using the Marcus, Cox Tank, Bush Mountain, and Lost Peak-Mescalero trails. The Lost Peak-Mescalero Trail descends 5.5 miles from the junction of the Tejas Trail. (The Tejas Trail then coincides with the Lost Peak-Mescalero Trail for 0.3 miles, then heads south again.) The Lost Peak-Mescalero Trail continues 1 mile to the Mescalero Campsite, where the remains of an old Mescalero Apache camp area, including mescal pits, are found. The trail continues another ½ mile to the junction of the McKittrick Trail, which comes in from the east. In another ½ mile one reaches the summit of Lost Peak (7,830 feet), from which there are good views of the reef gradually sloping down into the flat country of New Mexico. After dropping off the Lost Peak ridge, the trail descends 2½ miles through Upper Dog Canyon and follows an old wagon road through a beautiful wooded section to the Dog Canyon Ranger Station.

McKittrick Canyon Area

McKittrick Canyon combines the plant and animal life of a riparian habitat with Chihuahuan Desert biota; and further up the canyon are ponderosa pines—legacies of cooler climates of the past. This shady, watered canyon provides an environment little affected by the dry, hot, bare desert surrounding it. This biological oasis and the geologic history exposed in the walls of limestone make McKittrick Canyon an outdoor laboratory. It should be seen, heard, felt, and smelled during a slow exploration. A brochure available at the trailhead describes the natural and human history of the canyon and is intended to enrich the hike to Pratt Lodge.

Felix McKittrick was an early settler who lived in a dugout in the canyon. Wallace Pratt, mentioned as a donor of land to the Park Service, built his first cabin near the junction of North McKittrick Canyon with the main canyon. Constructed of native limestone, Pratt Lodge now serves as the McKittrick Canyon Ranger Station. Pratt and his wife lived in the canyon almost 30 years, buying up land for ranching. When he was 80, Pratt decided to donate 5,632 acres to the National Park Service. He thought of the canyon as a museum of natural history and dedicated it to the people of the world.

McKittrick Canyon Trail

The trail ascends the canyon for 2¾ miles to Pratt Lodge. Continuing beyond the ranger station, the trail crosses the North McKittrick Canyon Trail, which connects the park trails with the Lincoln National Forest trail system. The

North McKittrick Canyon Trail is more wash than trail as it winds back and forth across the Texas/New Mexico border before crossing the national forest.

The main trail continues 1 mile to a cool grotto that features ferns, stalactite and stalagmite formations, and a picnic area with a few stone tables. From the trailhead to the grotto is 4½ miles—an excellent day hike in the confines of a secluded canyon. A half mile farther is the junction of the South McKittrick Canyon Trail. The South Canyon Trail is not recommended because of the difficulty of the canyon floor for hiking and the fragility of the environment.

The main trail ascends the ridge to the Lost Peak-Mescalero Trail, passing Turtle Rock on its way to the high country. It climbs to McKittrick Campsite, located 7 miles from the parking lot and clearly marked about 100 yards north of the trail. This site is the first place on the trail where camping is allowed, camping being prohibited within McKittrick Canyon.

From the campsite, the trail ascends to a high point of 7,916 feet before descending to the Lost Peak-Mescalero Trail.

The 20-mile round-trip hike up and down McKittrick Canyon is one of the most rewarding in the park, considering the variety of terrain, natural history, and views. A relaxed, observation-oriented hike can teach the explorer many things about the millions of years of evolution and adaptation that have resulted in the natural beauty of this landscape.

Contact the ranger station at Pratt Lodge if you plan to camp. The gate across the road is closed at night, and it is best to check with the rangers for daily hours of opening and closing.

Pine Spring Area

The Pine Spring Campground is the main access point to the high country of the Guadalupes. It is located ½ mile from U.S. 62/180 on a short road that branches northwest at Pine Springs. There is space for parking but at present no facilities for recreation vehicles. Picnic tables and grills are available, but no ground fires or wood gathering is permitted, only charcoal fires and stoves. Water is not available at the campground but can be obtained from a faucet at the Frijole Information Center.

Pine Springs was an important water source on an early stagecoach route that passed around the Guadalupes and headed west to California. The Pinery was a stagecoach station on the old Butterfield Mail Route. Earlier, Indian tribes used the area for water and camping; mescal pits are still to be seen. The U.S. Cavalry used this oasis in its wars against the Mescalero Apaches. In 1931, an earthquake caused the lower spring to stop flowing.

Guadalupe Peak Trail

This trail climbs more than 2,400 feet from Pine Spring Campground to the highest spot in Texas. A direct route from Pine Spring Campground heads west for 100 yards, then angles up and southwest to a junction with a trail coming in from the north. Just beyond this junction, the Guadalupe Mountain Trail cuts back northwest for ½ mile to a set of switchbacks, then ascends to the Guadalupe Peak Campsite, located ¼ mile from the summit. The distance from the campground to the 8,749-foot summit is 4 miles. To get up Guadalupe Peak and back in one day you should be in good shape, start early in the morning, and take plenty of water, as none is available on the route. Strong winds are encountered at times, and winter storms can make this high country as intimidating as snowstorms make mountains farther north. In a way they can be more intimidating here, because they are unexpected in the normally dry desert.

On the summit are a register and a monument put up by American Airlines in 1958, commemorating the first transcontinental mail route, which crossed Guadalupe Pass. The views encompass both Texas and New Mexico. Northwest is Shumard Peak, which at 8,615 feet is the third highest point in Texas; farther in the same direction is Bush Mountain (8,631 feet), the second highest point. Northeast is 8,368-foot Hunter Peak. The Chihuahuan Desert extends to the south, west, and east; the Delaware Mountains are to the southeast and the Sierra Diablo to the south. West and southwest are the salt flats and the Dell City farming region.

The trail described is relatively new, constructed by the Park Service. It will allow vegetation to rejuvenate along the older trail—which follows the Pine Canyon floor for 2 miles before angling up a shoulder to the summit—and slow down erosion on the old trail from too many hiking boots.

Devil's Hall Trail

The first 2 miles of the trail along the Pine Canyon stream

bed coincide with the original route to the summit of Guadalupe Peak. But where the original Peak Trail turns south and climbs a shoulder to the summit, the Devil's Hall Trail continues upstream to a narrow, well-shaded, and usually watered area. It is a good trail for observing the stratified limestone layers of the reef and studying the riparian plant life.

Pine Top Trail

This trail, re-routed by the Park Service, now covers more distance than the old trail but with a more gradual climb. The old trail ascended Pine Spring Canyon, then followed a steep drainage that branched to the north from Pine Canyon, ending in a very steep series of switchbacks that led to the junction of the Hunter Peak Trail.

The newer route follows the original trail to a turnoff from Pine Spring Canyon that heads north of the original trail and gradually climbs north and west. It crosses the old trail and continues west to 6,600 feet, where it turns back north again and climbs to the junction of the Hunter Peak, Tejas, and Bush Mountain trails. This 3-mile trail gains over 2,000 feet of elevation, ending in the high country. The Pine Top Campsite is located ¼ mile northwest on the Bush Mountain Trail.

Bear Canyon Trail

The Bear Canyon Trail coincides with the Pine Top Trail for a short distance, then cuts back east toward Lower Pine Spring. A newer, re-graded route turns north at Lower Pine

Spring and angles up to meet the original trail above Upper Pine Spring and generally follows it to the crest and the Hunter Peak Trail. The Bear Canyon Trail gains 2,000 feet in 2 miles.

The trail follows a pipeline built by the Hunter Ranch in the 1930s. Water was pumped from Pine Spring all the way to the top of the canyon, where it was fed by gravity to other tanks in the Bowl area, providing water for stock and wildlife in the high country.

Hunter Peak Trail

The high-country Hunter Peak Trail connects the Pine Top Trail with the Bear Canyon Trail by following the south-facing rim of the Guadalupes; it also joins the Tejas, Bowl, Bush Mountain, and Juniper trails.

A side trail takes one to the summit of 8,368-foot Hunter Peak, which provides magnificent views in all directions. The heavily forested Bowl area is to the north; to the northeast stretches the reef, sloping down toward Carlsbad; Guadalupe, Shumard, Bartlett, and Bush Peaks loom to the west and southwest. The distance between the Pine Top Trail junction and the Bear Canyon Trail junction is 1½ miles. In a long day, one could hike up either the Bear Mountain Trail or Pine Top Trail, cross the Hunter Peak Trail, and descend the other of the two trails.

The Bowl Trail

Starting just west of Hunter Peak, the Bowl Trail drops into the thick pine and fir forest of the Bowl. A remnant of past geologic times, when forests covered much of west Texas, the Bowl is a delightful, isolated environment with a great variety of wildlife and coniferous-forest plant life. In the more recent past wildlife shared the Bowl's vegetation with horses, sheep, goats, and cattle.

The trail joins the Tejas Trail in the middle of the Bowl, which is about a mile across.

Juniper Trail

This route links the Pine Top Trail to the Tejas Trail by traversing along a ridge south of the Bowl and dropping into the Bowl, where it meets the Tejas Trail. The Juniper Trail is 1½ miles long.

The Tejas Trail

The Tejas Trail, the longest trail in the high Guadalupes, is the north-south artery of the high country. It generally follows an old jeep road that once brought people up to the high areas. The trail, which generally descends from south to north, starts at the end of the Bear Canyon Trail on the rim, crossing the Bowl and continuing to a junction with the Lost Peak-Mescalero Trail in a distance of 4 miles. It diverges from the Lost Peak-Mescalero Trail about 100 yards west and heads north, slowly descending for another 4 miles to the junction of the Marcus and Cox Tank trails. A 1½-mile side trail takes the hiker to the New Mexico-Texas border. Cairns are the best guidelines for following the more indistinct parts of the trail, and topo maps are useful.

Bush Mountain Trail

From the Pine Top Trail, this scenic route follows Pine Spring Canyon west and climbs to the 8,676-foot summit of Bush Mountain. The Bush Mountain Campsite is passed 2.6 miles along the rim from the Pine Top Trail. In the next 2 miles, the trail heads north along the Blue Ridge and offers views west to the salt flats and desert lowlands. The third leg of this trail turns back east beyond the Cox Tank Trail junction, passes the Blue Ridge Campsite, and goes another mile to join the Tejas Trail.

Other Trails

Many short trails leading to springs and unmaintained trails cross remote lowland areas of the park; most are reminders of bygone ranching days. Unmaintained trails also cross the high country—trails that hikers make, often following wildlife paths, as shortcuts. Use of these seldom-marked trails is discouraged by the Park Service. At least check with rangers and discuss other possible routes that are shown on maps.

GENERAL INFORMATION

Remember that the Guadalupe Mountains are remote, dry, and undeveloped. Once you leave the trailhead, you are on your own. Little water is available in the summer. Trails are often not maintained and hard to follow. The Guadalupe Peak quadrangles (15 minute and 7.5 minute), with shaded relief and trails overlaid, are essential for hiking. A compass and the knowledge of how to use it are also vital, and one must keep aware of terrain features and their relation to the map. Plan hikes considering time, distance, and elevation gains and losses. Many trails are steep, requiring good cardiovascular conditioning. The remoteness and slow development of this park is one of its attractions; let's hope it stays that way.

Guadalupe Mountains National Park is located 55 miles southwest of Carlsbad, New Mexico, and Carlsbad Caverns National Park; 110 miles east of El Paso; and 65 miles north of Van Horn. The park is open year-round.

The closest overnight accommodations to the Guadalupes are in White's City, 40 miles northeast of the park. Accommodations are also available in Van Horn. Limited camping facilities are available in the park at Pine Canyon Campground. Since the park is still being developed, check with the information center at Frijole Ranger Station or by writing:

Superintendent
Guadalupe Mountains National Park
3225 National Parks Highway
Carlsbad, NM 88220
Phone: (915) 828-3385

Backcountry Regulations

It is prohibited to disturb, harm, or remove rocks, plants, wildlife, or historic objects.

Camping is permitted only at Pine Canyon Campground

and designated backcountry sites. Reserve these sites at the ranger station at Frijole. A free permit is required for backcountry hiking.

No wood fires are allowed in the backcountry. Carry a camping stove. No picnicking is permitted near water sources, nor is washing or bathing in water sources permitted. These rules are necessary for the protection of wildlife.

Pets are not permitted in public buildings or on trails.

Written permission from the Park Superintendent is necessary before entering a cave.

The use of firearms is prohibited.

It is necessary to sign in and out for hikes at the trailheads for safety and courtesy. Cross-country hiking is discouraged because of both environmental impact and safety considerations in this remote area.

Human waste should be disposed of by digging a hole 4 to 6 inches deep, burning the paper, and covering the hole.

Campgrounds will accommodate 20 persons per site on a first-come, first-serve basis. No trenching is allowed around tents.

Technical mountain climbing is discouraged, because of the poor quality of the rock.

Bibliography

Arizona Office of Economic Planning and Development. *Explore Arizona*. Phoenix.

Arizona Office of Tourism. *Arizona Campground Directory*. Phoenix.

Arizona Office of Tourism. *Arizona Indian Country*. Phoenix, 1978.

Barnett, John. *Guadalupe Mountains National Park*. Carlsbad, N.M.: Carlsbad Caverns Natural History Association.

Big Bend Natural History Association in cooperation with the National Park Service. *Hiker's Guide to Trails of Big Bend National Park*. Big Bend National Park, Texas, 1978.

Comeaux, Malcolm L. *Arizona: A Geography*. Boulder, Colorado: Westview Press, 1981.

Cowgill, Pete and Glendening, Eber. *Trail Guide to the Santa Catalinas*. Tucson: Rainbow Expeditions, 1975.

Deckert, Frank. *Big Bend, Three Steps to the Sky*. Big Bend National Park, Texas: Big Bend Natural History Association, 1981.

Evans, Harry. *50 Hikes in Texas* (revised edition). Pico Rivera, Calif.: Gem Guides Book Co., 1978.

Ganci, Dave. *Hiking the Desert*. Chicago: Contemporary Books, 1979.

Hill, Mike. *Hiker's and Climber's Guide to the Sandia Mountains*. Albuquerque: Adobe Press, 1977.

Hoard, Dorothy. *Los Alamos Outdoors*. Los Alamos, N.M.: Los Alamos Historical Society, 1981.

Kurtz, Don and Goran, William D. *Trails of the Guadalupes*. Champaign, Ill.: Environmental Associates, 1978.

Little, Mildred J. *Camper's Guide to Texas Parks, Lakes, and Forests*. Houston: Pacesetter Press, 1978.

Overhage, Carl. *Six One-Day Walks in the Pecos Wilderness*. Santa Fe, N.M.: The Sunstone Press, 1980.

Richter, Fred. *A Guide to the Trails of the Magdalena Ranger District: Rough Draft*. Albuquerque: U.S. Forest Service District Office, 1981.

Santa Fe Group of the Sierra Club. *Day Hikes in the Santa Fe Area*. Santa Fe, N.M.: The National Education Association Press, 1981.

Shelton, Napier (based on an earlier work by Natt Dodge). *Saguaro National Monument, Arizona*. Washington, D.C.: National Park Service, 1972.

Sheridan, Michael F. *Superstition Wilderness Guidebook*. Phoenix: Publisher's Press, 1975.

Snyder, Ernest. *Arizona Field Guide*. Tempe, Arizona: The Lamont Company, 1978.

Sutherland, Patrick K. and Montgomery, Arthur. *Trail Guide to Geology of the Upper Pecos*. Albuquerque: University of New Mexico Press, 1975.

Taylor, Cachor. *Hiking Trails and Wilderness Routes, Chiricahua Mountains of Arizona*. Tucson: Rainbow Expeditions, 1977.

U.S.D.A. Forest Service. *Backpacking*. Washington, D.C.

U.S.D.A. Forest Service, R. Max Peterson, Chief. *The Continental Divide National Scenic Trail*, Comprehensive Plan, Environmental Assessment. Denver: Forest Service Recreation and Lands.

U.S.D.A. Forest Service. *Forest Conservation*. Washington, D.C., 1976.

U.S.D.A. Forest Service, Office of Information. *The Forest Service Roles in Outdoor Recreation*. Washington, D.C., 1978.

U.S.D.A. Forest Service. *Recreation Sites in Southwestern National Forests*. Albuquerque, N.M., 1980.

U.S.D.A. Forest Service, Office of Information. *Wildlife for Tomorrow*. Washington, D.C., 1976.

U.S. Dept. of the Interior. *New Mexico Wilderness Study Area Decisions.* Santa Fe, N.M.: Bureau of Land Management, New Mexico State Office, 1980.

U.S. Dept. of the Interior, Heritage Conservation and Recreation Service. *National Recreation Trails.* Washington, D.C., 1978.

Wagoner, John J. *This is Painted Desert.* Holbrook, Arizona: Petrified Forest Museum Association, 1971.

White, John E., Jr. *Recreation Opportunity Guide Pilot Project, Santa Fe National Forest, U.S. Forest Service.* Albuquerque: University of New Mexico Press, 1980.

Index